Praise for

The Longevity Imperative

"Finally, a manifesto to guide the longevity revolution. Should be required reading for every physician and politician. A revelation on every page."

—David Sinclair, author of *New York Times*–bestseller *Lifespan*

"Wide-ranging yet personal, *The Longevity Imperative* definitively places population aging on the very short list of megatrends that will transform how we live tomorrow."

—Joe Coughlin, author of *The Longevity Economy*

"As improvements in medical science and living standards ensure that most of us now live to be old, how do we make sure that we age well—that we are 'evergreen'? That is the question at the heart of Andrew J. Scott's striking new book, which argues persuasively that aging is as big a challenge for humanity as climate change or artificial intelligence. Scott has some wise suggestions as to how exactly we can do it." —Niall Ferguson, author of *The Ascent of Money*

"An aging society has long been seen as a grave future economic threat, but what if longer lives could be turned into a source of economic growth? In this striking book, Scott outlines why changing how we age is so important, what needs to be done to succeed, and just how large the potential gains are to both individuals and nations." —Nouriel Roubini, author of *Megathreats*

"The world is undergoing an unparalleled demographic change. We are witnessing not just aging, but a longevity revolution as billions around the world are set to live longer, healthier lives. This engaging book does not just draw attention to this underappreciated transformation. It also outlines how we need to change our economy, with an 'evergreening' strategy that allows people to flourish many times during their lives and remake our norms and institutions. This is a must-read book with an important message and many lessons."

—Daron Acemoglu, coauthor of *Power and Progress*

"The good news is that, globally, we're living longer, healthier lives than ever before—the even better news is that Scott has written the perfect guidebook to this brave new, older world. Look through Scott's longevity lens and, aided by deft analogies and so many surprising statistics I nearly wore out my highlighter, it will change the way you think about getting older. The traditional 'aging society' narrative is a depressing one about too many old people. *The Longevity Imperative* shows us how we should reshape our thinking and create a more optimistic, happier, healthier, and wealthier future together. Whether you're a government planning for the future of education, healthcare, and public finances or an individual wondering what extended lives might hold for your family and your pension, you can't afford not to read this book."

—Andrew Steele, author of *Ageless*

"Scott is uniquely positioned to explore the opportunities and challenges of longer lives in the twenty-first century. Whereas most predictions about future trends are grounded on the tacit assumption that we will live in the future as we do today, the only thing we truly can count on is that change will continue. Scott paints a picture of a range of possibilities that will emerge from scientific discoveries and technological advances. He also argues that if we change the way we live, longer lives can greatly improve the quality of life at all ages. Scott's lessons will not only educate readers but introduce them to a consummate storyteller and remarkable man."

—Laura Carstensen, Stanford University

"Inspiring, enlightening, and uplifting, *The Longevity Imperative* demands a radical rethink of aging by putting forward a blueprint for how to live well today, tomorrow, and in the future. A wake-up call for business leaders and politicians and a must-read for anyone who wants a life well lived."

—Noreena Hertz, author of *The Lonely Century*

"In every sense, longevity is the opportunity of our lifetime. The 'evergreen agenda,' brilliantly and compellingly set out in this book, provides the key to unlocking this opportunity for the benefit of individuals, economies and societies alike."

—Andy Haldane, CEO, Royal Society of Arts, and former chief economist, Bank of England

"Once in a while, a book comes along that resets our thinking—this certainly does that! It is an important work will stimulate you to rethink your own, and our collective future."

—Linda Yueh, Oxford University

"This is an extremely important book addressing one of the most important phenomena the human race has ever encountered: the ability to live longer and healthier lives. Despite recent setbacks in COVID, this trend to increasing longevity can only continue and will be a dominant theme in the lives of future generations. Medical science is already making progress to prevent and treat diseases early, and the recognition of what makes a healthy lifestyle is advancing. Scott picks up these opportunities and places them in the context of how society will manage these changes. The key underpinning arguments are economic, and these are carefully discussed and articulated. The world has been slow to think of the effects longevity will ultimately have on all aspects of life, but many of the key issues are discussed here. Putting a man on the moon may seem like an impressive achievement, but increasing life expectancy so that many of those born today will reach one hundred years of age is much more impressive and impactful. That is why you must read this book."

—John Bell, Regius Professor of Medicine, Oxford University

"Scott has written a book that is a must-read for anyone concerned about the world. There are issues we should all be advocates for, and the longevity imperative is right up there with climate change and geopolitics. It is equally important, and without someone of Scott's ability writing about it, we would be none the wiser. Please read and please talk about this."

—Jim Mellon, chairman, Burnbrae Holdings

The Longevity Imperative

Also by Andrew J. Scott (and Lynda Gratton)

The 100-Year Life: Living and Working in an
Age of Longevity

The New Long Life:
A Framework for Flourishing in a Changing World

The Longevity Imperative

*How to Build a Healthier and More Productive Society
to Support Our Longer Lives*

ANDREW J. SCOTT

BASIC BOOKS

New York

Basic Books
Hachette Book Group
1290 Avenue of the Americas, New York, NY 10104
www.basicbooks.com

Printed in the United States of America

Originally published in 2024 by Basic Books UK in Great Britain
First U.S. Edition: April 2024

Published by Basic Books, an imprint of Hachette Book Group, Inc. The Basic Books name and logo is a registered trademark of the Hachette Book Group.

The Hachette Speakers Bureau provides a wide range of authors for speaking events. To find out more, go to hachettespeakersbureau.com or email HachetteSpeakers@hbgusa.com.

Basic books may be purchased in bulk for business, educational, or promotional use. For more information, please contact your local bookseller or the Hachette Book Group Special Markets Department at special.markets@hbgusa.com.

The publisher is not responsible for websites (or their content) that are not owned by the publisher.

Typeset in Janson Text LT Std by Manipal Technologies Limited

Library of Congress Control Number: 2023948367

ISBNs: 9781541604506 (hardcover), 9781541604513 (ebook)

LSC-C

Printing 1, 2024

To my parents—Ray and John
and
My children—Helena, Louis and Kit.
My links in the chain of life

Contents

If youth but knew; if old age but could

Henri Estienne

Introduction

Would you like more time?

How about if I gave you an extra hour today? Sixty minutes to do with as you wish. You could catch up on sleep or finally get ahead with that work project. Perhaps you would choose to spend it with family or friends. Alternatively, you might just delight in enjoying some quiet time of your own.

If that sounds appealing, what about if I could make the week last for eight not seven days? A whole extra day for you to do whatever you wanted. Now I am getting the hang of time transformation, how about if I stretch the year out to last thirteen months? An extra four weeks! Does that sound appealing?

I of course can't give you this gift of time but I can let you in on a secret. Actually, it isn't really a secret but something we all know yet fail to act on. You already have been given more time. And not just an hour here, an extra day there or a whole month but years and years of additional time.

This is because of increases in life expectancy. Over the last hundred years life expectancy has increased by around two to three years every decade. That's more time than any of my thought experiments above. No matter where you live or how old you are, you can expect to live longer than past generations.

Does this additional time feel as appealing as the extra time I initially offered? Do you get the same sense of excitement, of pressure taken off you and new alternatives opening up? Or do you feel ambivalent? Uncertain about the benefit of living longer? That is how a lot of people feel. They see those extra years coming at the end of their life whereas they want the time now. And they fear that instead of being able to make use of that extra time they will become ill and frail and run out of money.

But what if those later years weren't characterized by illness, frailty and a lack of resources? What if they were healthy and engaged? That would bring enormous benefits. The longer we maintain our health, our productivity and our sense of engagement the more options we have when we get older and the more we value longer lives. And it is not just our later lives that get better. With the prospect of more years ahead, we can do things differently today. We can rethink the way we live our whole life.

Right now though we are not set to reap the benefits of these longer lives. That is because we haven't adapted to one very profound change in the human condition: that each of us is now likely to become very old. The problem is that doesn't sound like a very profound change. After all, there have always been old people and old people were always previously young. But what is currently revolutionary is the fact that now more young and middle-aged people can expect to become the very old. Throughout human history, only a minority lived long enough to become the old. Now it is the majority who will have that experience. That really does change everything. It means we need to invest a lot more in our future years in order to achieve better outcomes. If we don't then we run the risk of experiencing what we most fear. Longer lives therefore create a new longevity imperative—to age well.

The dramatic implications of this shift and the resulting emergence of a longevity imperative are what this book is about. Individually and collectively we need to pursue what I call an "evergreen" agenda. According to *Merriam-Webster's Collegiate Dictionary*, an evergreen plant is one that "remains green and functional through more than one growing season." In a wider sense, the word means remaining "universally and continually relevant." That is what we need to achieve over our longer lives. We need to make sure that our health and all the other things that matter to us extend to match our now longer lifespan. Past progress created longer lives. Future progress is about how we make the most of this additional time by changing the way we age.

In this book, I want to explain why this longevity imperative is so important, both to you as an individual but also to wider humanity. I outline in detail the innovations an evergreen agenda demands: the substantial changes to how you plan your life and career; in the way our health system, economy and financial sectors operate as well as the necessary seismic shifts in cultural and philosophical views of what it is to be old and how we age.

I also want to correct the problem that longevity receives far too little attention given its importance. Worse, when it does get attention it is misrepresented as being only about an "aging society" and a rising number of older people. Correcting this lack of attention and misunderstanding is a major motivation for writing this book. We need to talk about and build a longevity society not an aging society.

At London Business School I teach a course on the world economy. In the first class, I ask my students to tell me about the major trends they think will shape their lives and careers in the decades to come. I stand at the front of the classroom with my pen in hand poised and ready to write their suggestions on the board. In reality, I don't need to wait. I know what the first two topics are that they will mention— artificial intelligence and climate change. When it comes to forces that are set to change our world, those are the two that governments, business and individuals currently agree will dominate.

After these two topics have been discussed the students roam far and wide with other suggestions. As the energy in the class starts to subside and the number of issues mentioned slows someone will put their hand up and say "Demographic change." At that point, I push them a little further and ask what they mean and they invariably say "an aging population and more old people." The tone of voice is flat and the implication always negative. If AI and sustainability spark involved, enthusiastic debate about how we urgently need to improve our future, the reference to an "aging society" triggers nothing. Discussion ends with the phrase "more old people." It is as if it is obvious that more old people is a bad news story and there is little that can be done. Debate about an aging society rarely goes beyond mention of spiraling health costs, a pensions crisis, dementia and care homes. It is never seen as exciting, challenging or interesting.

There is a sense of acceptance and acquiescence rather than reform and adaptation. Above all it is seen as being about old people and not relevant to the student who raises the point.

I want this book to help you realize, both from the perspective of your own life as well as the viewpoint of society, that longevity is just as critical for our future as AI and sustainability. That it is equally as fascinating and demands the same level of radical change if we are to avoid future bad outcomes.

But there is also something distinctive about longevity as an aggregate trend. While it is a force that will change the world around us it is also a reality that affects each of us individually in a profound way. It is above all about your life and how you respond to the prospect of more time. That is why this book features both the personal and the societal viewpoint. It is impossible to think about how you live your own longer life without thinking about how society will need to adapt. Understanding this aspect of the longevity imperative is crucial if we are to realize an evergreen agenda and jettison the "aging society" narrative.

The aging society narrative encourages seeing longer lives as a problem and not an opportunity. It leads to the damaging idea that there are too many old people and we are living too long; to a focus on the end of life rather than taking action across all of life. It demands resources to meet the needs of older people, rather than also supporting the young to prepare for longer lives. That creates a growing generational conflict pitching young and old against each other.

It also turns one of humanity's greatest achievements into a prospective nightmare. Instead of celebrating the reduction of grief over lost children, of fewer parents snatched away in midlife and more grandparents and even great-grandparents meeting their grandchildren, it sees greater longevity as a burden. Not only is that a perverse way of seeing a triumph of human development, it darkens unnecessarily our view of our future lives.

The challenge we really face is to adapt to a radical change in the human condition—that the young can now expect to become the very old. That is why we need to seize the longevity imperative and become "evergreen." We need to focus on constructing a society that prepares us for longer lives and ensuring that the quality of life matches its newly found quantity. That is how we seize the opportunities that more time can offer us. This book shows what must change both for individuals and for society in order to do so.

Part I outlines the evergreen agenda and explains why it matters by answering the following questions:

- What has happened to life expectancy, what is likely to happen and what constitutes the longevity imperative?
- How do we age and what can we do to age better?
- Why is the evergreen agenda so important *now* and why does it signal a new era for humanity?

Part II addresses the major changes required to deliver the evergreen agenda. It does so by exploring the following questions:

- How do we change our health system and our own behaviors to ensure longer lives are healthy ones?
- How do we pay for longer lives and deliver an economic longevity dividend, and what does that mean for our careers?
- What changes are required in the financial sector and your own financial behavior in order to remove the risk of running out of money?

Part III focuses on the required shifts in our beliefs, culture and psychology of aging and old age. It examines questions such as:

- How do we find purpose in this longer life and how do we adapt our psychology and culture around aging and drop agist assumptions?
- How do we achieve intergenerational fairness if the young are faced with norms and institutions that don't support their longevity in a society with a rising proportion of older people?
- What are the major roadblocks to a successful evergreen society and how do we overcome them? What steps should you take to further your own evergreen future?

For decades, governments and policymakers have been aware that a major demographic transition is underway. But the aging society has diverted attention from the most pressing problem. The challenge is not about how we deal with more old people in the future, it is about how we adjust to living for longer now. Our past inaction means we need to make significant changes and make them soon.

It is time to embrace the evergreen agenda.

PART I

A New Imperative

I

A New Age

You have to prove that you know what you're doing. You have to have longevity. You have to stay around.

Venus Williams

In a book about longevity, I should probably begin by discussing my own. I was born in London in May 1965. It was the year that saw the first NASA spacewalk, the funeral of Sir Winston Churchill, the assassination of Malcolm X and the release of *Rubber Soul* by the Beatles. I knew nothing of all that, of course. Nor were my parents paying much attention to the events of the day. Their joy at my arrival was mixed with grief. I was born one of a pair of identical twins and my brother David was only a few days old when he died. As Elvis Presley knew only too well, a missing twin never really leaves you.

My parents were not unusual in having to mourn the loss of a newborn. In the UK in 1965, the most common age of death was the first year—babies and infants aged under one.[1] Today the most common age to die is eighty-seven years old. Of the many historical changes that have transformed how we live this surely is the most fundamental change of all. If David and I were born today, I suspect we would both survive. My alternative life with a twin brother—a life I have often imagined and dreamed of—would have become a reality.

That is what this book is about—the way changes in longevity are making alternative lives possible. Based on past achievements let alone whatever the future might bring, people of all ages now need

9

to plan for a longer life. I will show that this goes much further than just preparing for an extended retirement. It represents nothing less than a new era for humanity.

In Samuel Beckett's play *Waiting for Godot*, one of the characters bleakly declares that humans "give birth astride a grave, the light gleams an instant, then it's night once more." It's a twentieth-century theatrical echo of the much-quoted Thomas Hobbes description of seventeenth-century life as "nasty, brutish and short." The gloomy outlook of both playwright and philosopher reflects the reality that for most of history humans faced a significant risk of imminent death, however young or old they were. Perhaps that is why traditionally so much of the day was devoted to preparation for an afterlife.

But due to improvements in mortality the light is gleaming longer and the eternal night has been postponed. Over my lifetime, life expectancy in the UK has risen by nine years—from seventy-one to over eighty—and in the United States by seven years—from seventy to over seventy-seven. That is a substantial increase especially given that the United States and UK aren't even particularly good at supporting high life expectancy. Countries such as Japan and Spain have seen even larger increases and have significantly higher life expectancy. Further, it isn't just rich countries that now experience long lives—global life expectancy is currently over seventy-one years.[2] But these averages hide the true extent of how long the lives are that we need to prepare for. According to the American Academy of Actuaries a child born today in the United States has a more than 50 percent chance of living to ninety-five.[3] That single statistic expresses the essence of the drama now affecting us all. For the first time in several thousand years of human development, the young can expect to become the very old. That is a remarkable achievement.

History is no stranger to old people, of course. The elders of the past are more numerous than you might imagine, given that only a century and a half ago life expectancy at birth was below forty years—a somber outlook reflecting tragically high infant mortality rates. But if you could survive those dangerous early years then you had a reasonable chance of living into your forties and fifties, with a further significant minority surviving into their seventies or eighties. That is why more than two thousand years ago the Roman philosopher Cicero was extolling the virtues of growing old in his famous essay "On Old Age," written when he was sixty-four years old.

The difference though between Roman times and now might best be expressed by adapting some words by Winston Churchill. Never in human history have so many lived for so long as they do today. What used to be a rare outcome for a minority is now a commonplace for the majority, at least in high-income countries. How long we might live for is also changing. The fastest-growing demographic in the world is people aged a hundred or more.

All this requires major changes in how we live our lives. To understand why, let's consider for a moment my present life as a Londoner. London is a great city, but the risk of rain is a near constant. I often find myself checking the weather forecast. If there is only an 11 percent chance of rain, I won't bother with a raincoat. If there is a 36 percent chance, then I may take an umbrella but not a raincoat. If rain is 70 percent likely, then it's raincoat on and umbrella packed. The point here is a simple one. The actions we take now depend on the likelihood of future events. When the chance of future rain is small I do nothing, when it is high I take action in order to produce better outcomes.

I chose those particular percentages for a reason. They accurately describe my reactions to weather forecasts, but I borrowed the figures from Swedish longevity data.[4] In 1851 a fifteen-year-old in Sweden had only an 11 percent chance of reaching the age of eighty. By 1951 that chance had grown to 36 percent. Today, based on conservative assumptions, it's up to 70 percent. My point is this: just as we need to think about raincoats and umbrellas if there's a 70 percent chance of rain, we also need to discover a longevity equivalent of protective gear when there's a 70 percent chance that we're going to live to be eighty years old. Everything changes when the young can for the first time in human history expect to become the very old.

Throughout human history our lives were too short to give much thought to the challenges facing us in later life. Yet today our lives are extending to lengths our ancestors would never have imagined. That creates a twofold challenge—how should we live those additional years and how should we behave in the decades before them? When living into your eighties and nineties becomes the most likely outcome, different priorities apply. I call these a challenge but they are also an enormous opportunity.

But when I ask people how they feel about living to be a hundred, they invariably reply that they would want to do so only if they remained in good health and they raise fears about being lonely, bored and irrelevant. These are the deep-seated anxieties we all share about the prospect of a longer life. Will we run out of money? Will we become trapped in misery in bodies that have betrayed us? Will we be pushed to the side and become an irrelevance?

If a young American now has a 50 percent chance of living to ninety-five, these problems become sharply more relevant for us all. A new longevity imperative has been created—to age well. We need to become evergreen in the sense of surviving and thriving over time and across our now longer lives.

Aging well is obviously tied to maintaining decent health but that is not all. It also obliges you to manage your career and finances differently. It involves thinking about where you find pleasure and purpose at different periods of your life. It means finding and investing in good relationships. All of this is required if you are to avoid the risk of outliving your health, money, purpose and relationships.

Currently our approaches to these issues fail to place enough emphasis on the length of life we can expect. They were understandable when there was a minority chance of the young becoming old but not any longer. If we are going to live to our tenth or even eleventh decade, we cannot simply cross our fingers and hope that all ends well. If our biggest fear is about living too long in bad health, isolation and financial insecurity, we need to change now to avoid that fate. The common mistake though is to assume that you don't need to think about old age until you are old. By then it is probably too late. That's why the evergreen agenda requires reshaping what we do at all ages.

Entering a New Era

The argument of this book is that we have already achieved one longevity revolution whereby the majority can now expect to become
the very old. That propels us toward a second longevity revolution
where we respond to those long lives by changing how we age.
That is what defines the newly minted longevity imperative.

The implications of this second longevity revolution are enormous for us as individuals and societies, but they go even deeper in
terms of what it means for humanity as a whole. Society naturally
tends to focus on the most pressing health problems that affect the
largest proportion of the population. When 30 percent of children
died in the first five years of life, it was not surprising that reducing
infant mortality was the top priority. As progress was achieved against
infant diseases, the focus turned to middle age and reducing what
the World Health Organization terms "premature" deaths—dying
before the age of seventy. Today around half of all deaths globally
(and more than 80 percent in countries such as Japan) occur over
seventy years of age. Humanity's fight against disease has entered a
new era. It is now targeting the illnesses that strike later in life.

This requires a shift in our definition of what constitutes a "premature" death, but much else besides. It means thinking of aging
not as inevitable but as something malleable which can be slowed
and even postponed. It demands that we stop underestimating the
capacity of older people. If the likelihood is that most of us will reach
these later years then we need to act and age differently from past
generations.

That is the opportunity that beckons us toward a second
longevity revolution and ushers in a radical new era for humanity.
Age-related diseases differ in a significant way from other illnesses.
In the past, when progress was made in treating or curing a particular disease, medicine could move on to a different challenge. That
dynamic doesn't work with aging. The better we get at growing
old, the more we will want to live for even longer in better health.
If the average person is doomed to spending their eighties in

poor health, it is not much of an advertisement for longevity. But if we can make our eighties healthier, the next challenge will be prolonging those benefits into our nineties. Once our ninety-year-olds are thriving, next on the way will be sporty centenarians. In short, we are poised at a breakout moment for humanity that will see profound change in how we age and how long we live.

A Longevity Society Not an Aging Society

None of this is to suggest that we are on the verge of achieving eternal life or that change will necessarily be rapid. There are clearly limits to what current medical genius can achieve and what human biology will allow. There are also many ethical and social issues that need to be thrashed out and which are discussed later in this book. It does mean, though, that even more resources will be directed toward ensuring we live healthier for longer.

We have already seen these forces in action: in 2021 the American and Israeli billionaires Jeff Bezos and Yuri Milner ploughed $3 billion into Altos Labs, a biotechnology research company specializing in rejuvenation treatments. The California-based company has recruited a number of high-profile scientists to investigate cellular restoration programs that might delay or even reverse the aging process.

While it's easy to scoff at billionaires seeking the elixir of life, the value of healthier, longer lives matters to us all. Offered the prospect of healthier longevity, billions of people are likely to turn to products and services that help them age well. That goes beyond radical new drug treatments to include what we eat and drink, how we manage our finances and our education, and how we spend our leisure time. It will be these decisions of billions of ordinary people and not just elixir-chasing billionaires that will form an evergreen economy.

But for this to happen we need to recognize the importance of the longevity imperative, realize how malleable aging is and stop underestimating the capacity of our later years. If we don't do this then we face the very real prospect of creating a self-fulfilling prophecy of later years spent lacking resources, purpose and health rather than enjoying the benefits of longer, healthier and more engaged lives.

Unfortunately, it is the former unsustainable path that we are currently embarked upon. The main narrative about longer lives is invariably about an aging society—that is, a rise in the proportion of older people and a change in the age structure of the population. This narrative is couched in the gloomy tones of a weakening economy, rising pensions, surging health care costs and a "tsunami" of age-related diseases.

We need instead to focus not on changes in the age mix of the population but on changes in how we age. It's not that an aging society isn't important or that it doesn't raise pressing issues. The fact that more people are getting old and may require increasing amounts of care is a practical issue confronting governments and families everywhere. But the aging society narrative conceals the more positive agenda—the urgent need to adapt to the fundamental change of the longevity imperative. An aging society raises important questions about how to support a rising number of older people, a longevity society, by contrast, is about all of us, and is about how we support the greater number of years we now face.

Getting the Facts Straight

To explain the demographic and longevity trends of past centuries I could refer to my own family history. After all, demographic change is the most personal of aggregate forces. My great-great-grandfather John Scott was born in Kent in the south-east of England in 1825 and moved to London in his twenties. Last year I found online a copy of his wedding certificate, which listed him as a laborer with a signature of a simple "X." The certificate revealed that he was married in a church in Paddington just a few minutes from where I now live and which I must have walked past hundreds of times oblivious to the connection. He died in 1876, aged fifty-one. His son, George, was born in Notting Hill in 1859 and died (in a railway carriage, according to records) at the age of sixty-three. George's son, my grandfather Jack, was born in 1889 and died at seventy-five in 1964. My father, another John, was born in Wood Green, London, in 1925 and lived until he was seventy-seven. Exactly a hundred years separate the births of the two Johns—my great-great-grandfather and my father. Each generation of Scott men lived longer than their father, and over that century of lengthening lives their age at death increased by twenty-six years.

Uncannily, that increase is an exact match for broader demographic trends. In an influential paper two leading demographers, Jim Oeppen and James Vaupel, introduced the concept of "best practice life expectancy."[5] It is defined as the highest level of life expectancy in any country in a particular year. Over time the country which defines best practice has changed. Back in 1840 it was Sweden, but since then the baton has been passed back and forth between Norway, Australia, New Zealand, Iceland and Switzerland. Right now best practice life expectancy is in Japan, where women in 2021 have a life expectancy of nearly eighty-eight (compared to seventy-nine in the United States and eighty in the UK).

Oeppen and Vaupel showed that since the 1880s best practice life expectancy has increased on average by two to three years every decade. So the Scott family experience of an extension of twenty-six years over a hundred years is bang on trend. This sustained increase in life expectancy is one of humanity's most impressive achievements. While major events such as world wars or the great influenza pandemic of 1918 inevitably decreased life expectancy, the effect was always temporary. The underlying trend reasserted itself pretty quickly.

My family tree also reflects another major trend—a falling birth rate. My grandfather Jack was one of seven children raised by my great-grandparents, George and Ellen. My mother was one of five children and my father one of three. Had my brother David survived my parents would have had three children, but they were left with two: my sister and me.

Today in the US and UK, the total fertility rate has fallen to an average of only 1.65 births per female lifetime.[6] What that means is that in the absence of immigration the US and UK population would decline. The same holds true for France, Germany and Italy where the overall fertility rates are currently 1.8, 1.5 and 1.2 respectively. In South Korea it is as low as 0.8. It's a sufficiently widespread phenomenon that according to the United Nations a quarter of all countries will experience a declining population between now and 2050.

This combination of longer lives and falling fertility rates is leading to a significant change in family dynamics. My three children (I am bucking the historical trend) were lucky enough to meet all four of their grandparents. By comparison, I met three of mine; my father met two of his and my grandfather met only one. Indeed, in many families there will soon be more grandparents than grandchildren. In China and Japan, it is common for parents to have just one child. If each parent was also an only child, then a family would consist of four living grandparents, two parents and one grandchild. There would be no uncles, aunts or cousins to invite to weddings or funerals, fewer presents on festive occasions and no surprise bequests from distant family members. This is the family version of an aging society.

Population structures worldwide have historically been defined by a pyramid, with many young at the bottom and relatively few old at the top. Today those pyramids are becoming inverted. They now resemble the shape of mass-market cruise ships with multiple levels climbing ever higher from alarmingly skinny hulls. Consider the admittedly extreme case of China where for every person over sixty-five in 1950 there were 7.5 children aged under fifteen. Today there are 1.5 children per adult aged sixty-five plus and by 2050 that figure will have dropped to 0.5.

These four components—longer lives, fewer children, declining populations and the old outnumbering the young—are the building blocks of an aging society narrative. Like the Four Horsemen of the Apocalypse from the Book of Revelation, they seem to forecast decline and a loss of vitality. Rather than a dramatic apocalypse, the aging society narrative is better summed up by T. S. Eliot's warning that the world will end "not with a bang but a whimper"—and presumably a wheezing, mumbling one at that. Yet all this gloom may prove misplaced. As we shall see, the reality of aging is far more nuanced. There is reason to look forward with optimism. But to do so requires a new mindset, and so we turn from a discussion of an aging society and its focus on changes in the age structure of the population to the issue of longevity and longer lives.

How Long Will I Live?

When I talk about the growing chance of each of us living a hundred-year life, one of the first responses I hear is a denial that life expectancy is increasing. This was the case even before the Covid-19 pandemic. The argument was frequently expressed in a tone that suggested declining life expectancy was almost welcome as it would solve the problems of an aging society. If people are worried about living too long, then perhaps it isn't surprising that they're not too concerned when their prospects for longevity appear to diminish.

So is life expectancy falling or not? The short answer is no—for most people and in most countries life expectancy continues to rise and can be expected to do so for many years to come. You can in other words expect to live a long life, one longer than your parents and the younger you are the longer you can expect your life to be. To understand why this is the case it is necessary to clear up some misunderstandings.

What Impact Did Covid-19 Have on Life Expectancy?

As I write this, the latest data from the World Health Organization shows that globally the Covid-19 pandemic has led to nearly 7 million deaths,[7] although that is widely considered an underestimate and between 20 and 30 million is a more likely figure.[8] That's a terrible loss of life which has inevitably exerted a negative effect on life expectancy. In 2020, in twenty-seven out of twenty-nine high-income countries, Covid-19 caused a measurable decline in life expectancy.[9] The biggest fall was in the United States, where life expectancy decreased by more than two years. That collectively represents the biggest fall in life expectancy since the Second World

War. Five years of previous gains in life expectancy were wiped out in just under half of the countries. The big question is whether these declines are likely to prove permanent. Already in 2021 most of the affected countries (with the exception of the United States) saw a recovery in life expectancy as vaccinations kicked in and the severity of the pandemic abated.[10] In Scandinavia the recovery in 2021 was sufficiently large for life expectancy to be almost unchanged on its pre-pandemic level. In Norway it was even higher.

The same phenomenon occurred after the First World War, the great influenza pandemic and the Second World War. In each case, there were sharp declines in life expectancy that later proved temporary. That is because headline numbers focus on what is known as *period* life expectancy, a measure calculated using the mortality rates from a particular year. It is clearly no surprise when using this approach that when mortality rates are unusually high, life expectancy falls. When the cause of those mortality rates is removed—the war ends or the pandemic passes—these period-based calculations bounce back. That is why major destructive events of the past didn't permanently affect life expectancy trends and why life expectancy measures are likely to recover as Covid-19 recedes.

How rapid this bounce back will be remains unclear. The 767 million cases of Covid-19 globally will leave many people suffering from continuing health problems. There is also evidence in some countries that health systems are struggling with backlogs of other diseases for which pandemic restrictions delayed treatment. But based on past experiences, Covid-19 itself is unlikely to prove a long-term brake on life expectancy trends, however worrying its short- and medium-term effects.

Are We Living Longer?

But what were the life expectancy trends that Covid disrupted? Had life expectancy started to decline or level off anyway? The good news is that in most countries life expectancy was rising and is widely expected to continue to do so in the years ahead. For instance, in the ten years before Covid, according to the World Bank, 202 out of 210 countries saw life expectancy increase (the eight exceptions were Brunei, Mexico, Seychelles, Saint Vincent, Syria, Turks and Caicos, Venezuela and Yemen).

Even "best practice life expectancy"—defined as the country with the highest life expectancy at any point in time—rose over this period (by just over one year), showing that we have yet to reach a limit on how long we can live for. Further, given most countries lag behind best practice, there is plenty of scope for catch-up. As a result, life expectancy grew even faster than best practice in 171 countries in the ten years before Covid.

Slowing Not Falling

Given these global trends, why is there such widespread resistance to the notion that life expectancy is increasing? One reason is a common statistical confusion between levels and growth rates. While life expectancy continues to rise in many countries, its rate of improvement has been slowing. In the fifty years before 2010, high-income countries saw life expectancy rise by an average of around three months every year, but between 2010 and 2019 that rate of progress halved.

To understand why this slowdown is happening, conjure up the image of a collapsible telescope with five different segments. When the telescope is completely collapsed, it is at its shortest and its length is that of one segment. You can make the telescope longer by pulling out each segment. However, once you have fully extended the first three segments, you can only make the telescope longer by extending the fourth and fifth segment.

Life expectancy is the same. It can increase by improving the chances of a one-year-old reaching age twenty (first segment becomes extended), a twenty-one-year-old reaching forty (second segment), etc. However, when a newborn has a 100 percent chance of living to sixty, further gains in life expectancy at birth can only happen through increases to life expectancy at sixty. That is effectively what is happening now in high-income countries. Based on 2020 data a newborn girl in Japan has a 99.6 percent chance of living to twenty, a 99 percent chance of reaching forty and a 96 percent chance of making it to sixty.[11] It is as if the first three segments of the telescope are already fully extended. Previously life expectancy gains were being driven by expanding all the segments of the telescope. Now they can only be driven by expanding the fourth and fifth segments. That is why life expectancy gains are slowing.

It would, however, be a big mistake to think that slower gains in life expectancy mean you need to think *less* about longevity. From a longevity perspective, life expectancy gains aren't slowing down— they have always been slower at the most advanced ages. In fact there is evidence to suggest that the rate of improvement at the oldest ages may even be rising.[12] In other words, it is as if the fourth and fifth segments of the telescope are being pulled out faster than before.

That is why preparing for greater longevity remains even more important for all of us. Don't be fooled by news of slowing life expectancy growth into thinking that adjusting to longer lives is no longer a problem. The opposite is the case given that most of the gains to life expectancy are now concentrated at older ages.

Problems in the US and UK

There is, though, another reason why many people dismiss the relevance of longer lives. In three consecutive years—2015, 2016 and 2017—US life expectancy declined (albeit marginally)—from 79.05 years to 78.88. Larger declines occurred in the Covid-affected years of 2020 and 2021, as life expectancy fell to 76.1 years.[13] The data is incontrovertible, and it raises a crucial question. Was this pre-Covid drop due to peculiarly American factors? Or was it, like so much else exported from America, a nascent global trend?

On average, as in other high-income countries, Americans can still expect to live longer lives than past generations. But American life expectancy isn't as high as in other rich nations, and the gap is widening and shows worrying trends. The longevity imperative has a twofold importance for the US. As elsewhere, there is a requirement to make the most of longer lives but in addition there is the need to raise American life expectancy up to the level of other countries.

The gap between top longevity performers and the US has widened in recent decades and now stands at eight years. That's the inevitable consequence of continual increases in best practice but stalling life expectancy in the US. It isn't just against best practice that the US falls short. American GDP per capita is six times higher than China's, but China has now overtaken America in life expectancy league tables.

This relative decline is not due to a lack of money being spent on health. According to the World Bank the US spends nearly $11,000 per person a year on health care.[14] That's around twice the average among high-income countries. But having the world's best hospitals and spending the most money on medicines isn't the same thing as having the best health care system or the best health.

Delving deeper into the numbers provides insights into why American life expectancy lags behind. Although life expectancy *at birth* declined slightly between 2015 and 2017, life expectancy at age sixty-five and eighty actually increased during those years. The same happened again in 2021. In other words, the fall in life expectancy was not driven by increases in mortality at older ages but in earlier years.

A further insight comes from realizing how life expectancy in America depends a great deal on where exactly you lie on a frighteningly broad spectrum of social status. The gap in life expectancy between the richest 1 percent and the poorest 1 percent is fifteen years for men and ten years for women.[15]

These two factors come together in what Princeton economists Anne Case and Angus Deaton term "deaths of despair."[16] This is a reference to the rising number of deaths from alcohol, drugs or suicide, predominantly of white non-Hispanics without a college education. In 2017 alone, there were 158,000 deaths in this category. By 2020 that number had increased to 187,000—around 5 percent of all deaths even as the pandemic was raging. These deaths of despair, by increasing midlife mortality, have played a significant role in America's poor record on life expectancy. But it isn't the only factor. Americans are also more likely to die from obesity, homicides, road accidents and infant deaths.

Sadly my own country, the UK, is now also showing signs of stalling life expectancy, with inequality, deaths of despair and strains on the health system all contributing. The result has been a downward revision in future life expectancy. Life expectancy is still expected to increase, just not by as much as previously projected.

It is a mistake though to interpret these trends as showing a longevity imperative is no longer needed. Life expectancy continues to rise in most countries. Even in the US and UK the norm is still for long lives and especially for those with higher levels of education and income those lives continue to get longer.

Instead the lesson to learn from these stalling trends in the US and UK is that life expectancy is malleable and shaped by our actions, our environment and the effectiveness of our health care systems. Life expectancy can go down as well as up. That is why we need to understand the social and economic policy choices that will not only support our longer lives but make them possible in the first place, and ensure they are a possibility for all and not just the wealthiest.

For a country as rich as the United States to see infant and midlife mortality rising and life expectancy lag behind China and best practice by so much is a major problem. When the US economy enters a recession and GDP declines there is always a major policy response; interest rates are cut and fiscal policy is loosened. The same proactive government approach needs to happen in response to declines in US life expectancy. Americans are currently missing out.

Is There a Limit to How Long I Will Live?

If life expectancy is still increasing in most countries an obvious question is how far can it rise? To understand the potential limits to human lifespan we need to turn to that rare thing—a famous actuary. In particular our focus is on Benjamin Gompertz, born in eighteenth-century London. Because of his Jewish faith Gompertz was prevented from attending university, so educated himself. He turned out to be a gifted mathematician, giving much credit for this to his membership of the Spitalfields Mathematical Society. The society operated a commendable rule whereby "if a member asked for information and applied to one who could give it; [that member] was obliged to give it, or be fined one penny."

Living when he did, Gompertz was more than aware of the risk of dying young. While he himself survived to the ripe old age of eighty-six, he experienced the sadness of seeing his only son, Joseph, die at the age of ten. Seeking solace in mathematics, Gompertz became an expert on human mortality and the actuary of a newly established insurance company—Alliance Assurance. His name lives on as a result of the equation he drew up to calculate the potential costs of insuring people's lives. The mortality model he produced in 1825 became known as Gompertz law.

Mortality rates rise with age—the older we are, sadly the more likely we are to die. Gompertz's claim to demographic immortality was his assessment of the rate at which mortality increases. In particular, he argued that mortality rates rise exponentially with age. The word "exponential" holds great potential to confuse but in simple terms the application of Gompertz law today suggests that after getting through childhood our risk of dying doubles roughly every seven or eight years.

At younger ages, this doubling doesn't make much practical difference. For example, in France, a thirty-year-old today has a mortality rate of 0.05 percent (i.e. the probability of dying is 1/20th of 1 percent).[17] By thirty-eight, this has almost doubled but is still only 0.09 percent. By the age of ninety, however, the mortality rate has reached 14 percent and at that level doubling leads to very high mortality rates. The upshot of Gompertz law is inescapable—if mortality rates rises continuously with age then there must be a limit to how long a person can live.

While Gompertz law is a powerful insight and explains a lot of the variation in mortality it doesn't explain everything. It doesn't, for instance, help explain higher mortality rates in early infant years.

There is also an active debate about whether mortality rates really do rise continuously with age. What if, as some studies suggest, mortality rates plateau around the age of 105 years?[18] This isn't just an arcane academic debate. If mortality rates continue to rise with age then there is a firm limit to a human lifespan—that is the upper bound for how long humans can live for. But if mortality rates plateau then there is no easily calculable limit to a human lifespan.

To see why imagine that mortality rates peak at 35 percent at age 105. Then as you celebrate your 105th birthday you would have a 35 percent chance of making it to 106, 12.3 percent (35 percent × 35 percent) of reaching 107 and a 0.5 percent chance of reaching 110 (at which point you would become a supercentenarian). As this example makes clear, very few people currently live this long. In fact, you are currently more likely to be a billionaire (globally estimated to total 2,640)[19] than a supercentenarian (estimated total 800–1,000).[20] If you were extremely lucky you would have a roughly one in 10,000 chance of making it to 122. That's the age Jeanne Calment was when she died in 1999 in Arles, in the south of France, making her the oldest person to have lived, or at least with the documents to prove it. She was born in the early days of the French Third Republic when Ulysses S. Grant was the US president and Benjamin Disraeli the UK prime minister. She died forty years into the Fifth Republic with Bill Clinton president and Tony Blair as prime minister. That is an extraordinarily long life. But if mortality rates plateau at 105 then you might live even longer than Jeanne Calment and make it to 150, albeit at very long odds (and if you are that lucky, it's probably worth financing this longer life by frequent trips to the casino).

While the odds of doing so remain tiny, the growing number of centenarians clearly increases the chances of someone breaking Calment's record. According to the United Nations, there were 95,000 people globally aged a hundred or more in 1990. Today there are more than half a million—around 100,000 in the US and Japan and about 25,000 in France and Germany. By 2050, it's estimated that there will be around 3.7 million. While the odds of living longer than Jeanne Calment are small for each of us individually, when the gamble is played by 3.7 million people the chances of someone beating her record is high. If Gompertz law doesn't hold at the oldest ages then we can expect Calment's record to be broken even without radical scientific breakthroughs.

Discovering exactly how long we could live for by determining the upper limits of the human lifespan is a fascinating question. Inferring it from what happens to mortality at older ages is however fraught with problems. There aren't that many people who currently live much beyond 105, making it hard to be confident about estimated mortality rates at that age. It is also plausible that those who do become supercentenarians may differ genetically from those who die at younger ages. Plateauing mortality rates may therefore reflect more a "survival of the fittest" effect than a genuine flattening of mortality rates with age.

Given the minuscule probability of outliving Jeanne Calment based on current medicine, a more pertinent question for most of us concerns not the outer limits of a human lifespan but whether we are close to a limit for average life expectancy. Given that current best practice life expectancy is eighty-seven, far off Jeanne Calment's 122, there is obviously scope for average life expectancy to increase still further. Indeed, the fact that best practice life expectancy continues to increase and most countries are still below best practice suggests that if there is a limit to average life expectancy then we still have some way to go to reach it.

That there is scope for further gains doesn't mean these will automatically occur. There are global concerns about rising obesity and the growing risks of antibiotic resistance and climate change. All these are genuine threats that may affect our future health and even our very existence. For now, though, it needs to be recognized that human lives have not reached any limit in terms of average life expectancy and have the capacity to become even longer.

But Will I Be Healthier for Longer?

In Greek mythology, the goddess Eos had a mortal lover, a Trojan named Tithonus. Eos asked Zeus to make Tithonus immortal but forgot to specify eternal youth. The result (given that Zeus had a mean streak) was that Tithonus lived forever while his body continued to age. According to Tennyson, "when loathsome old age pressed full upon him, and he could not move nor lift his limbs . . . she laid him in a room . . . there he babbles endlessly and no more has strength at all."[21]

The moral of the tale, of course, is to be careful what you wish for. Continuing to live while your body and mind fall to pieces is not an appetizing prospect. If lives are getting longer and your deepest fear is ending up like Tithonus, then focusing on the evergreen imperative to age well must be your priority.

The fate of Tithonus lurks behind the narrative of an aging society. That is because a new era where the young grow up to become very old in large numbers is leading to a significant shift in society's disease burden. When most of the population was young, and infant mortality was high, infectious diseases were the primary source of death. But as more and more of us live to old age, the danger to health has shifted to noncommunicable diseases such as dementia, cancer, diabetes, arthritis and pulmonary and cardiac-related illnesses. According to the World Health Organization, seven of the top ten causes of global deaths (before Covid-19) were noncommunicable diseases, accounting for roughly three-quarters of all deaths.

Noncommunicable diseases have two features. The first, as shown in Figure 1, is that the older you are the more likely you are to experience them. The second feature of noncommunicable diseases is that they tend to be chronic—in other words, they persist. Combine these two features and you get a third—the older you are, the more noncommunicable diseases you are likely to experience simultaneously (a condition known as "multi-morbidities").

If we live for longer, inevitably we are more likely to experience age-related diseases. In the UK, the cancer charity CRUK estimates that someone born in 1930 had roughly a 33 percent chance of experiencing cancer in their lifetime, whereas for someone born in 1960, the chance was up to 50 percent. The charity Alzheimer's Disease International calculates that every three

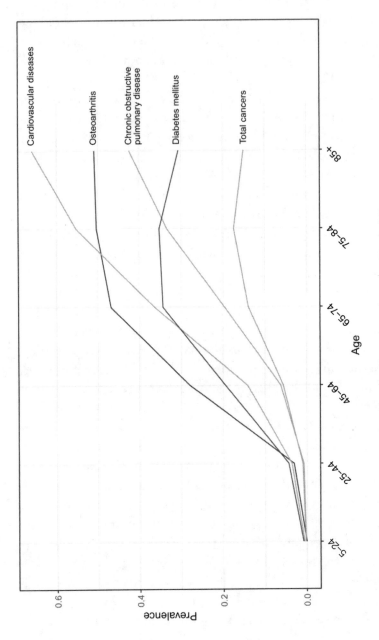

FIGURE 1: Incidence of Diseases by Age, United States 2019.

(Source: Global Burden of Disease)

seconds someone in the world develops dementia. That means while you read that sentence, two new cases were recorded. Already there are around 57 million people globally with dementia, the majority in low- and middle-income countries. That number is expected to increase to 153 million by 2050.[22]

It is undoubtedly a welcome family outcome to have four living grandparents (and growing numbers of great-grandparents) but it may bring an uncomfortable burden. Around three-quarters of people living with dementia are cared for by their family. The US Alzheimer's Association estimates that in 2010, 14 billion hours of unpaid care were provided by family members to their older relatives. Balancing family commitments with the demands of work and the need for leisure and other individual pursuits is becoming increasingly tricky for many people.

These unpleasant statistical realities cast a grim shadow over the prospect of getting old. But again, it's important to look at the facts carefully. Doing so leads to a different perspective and perhaps even grounds for optimism.

Dementia is a horrible disease, and its rising incidence is a serious problem. But not everyone will suffer impaired cognitive skills. One study of European and North American data estimates that around one in ten people aged between eighty-five and eighty-nine years develops dementia. Those odds are concerning but still imply that nine out of ten people of that age won't.[23]

There are two related factors here that need to be considered separately. The first is the probability of experiencing a disease. It is a truism that the longer you live, the more likely you are to experience any disease over your lifetime, especially if it is age-related. It is this increasing risk brought on by longer lives that explains the rising incidence of both dementia and cancer. The other factor is your probability of suffering from a disease at any given age. Here there is good news. The risk of getting dementia at any particular age seems to be declining, by around 13 percent each decade.[24] Because we are living longer we are more likely to experience dementia but at each age our risk of dementia has been falling. That is a powerful example of the malleability of age.

Similarly, while the lifetime risk of cancer is increasing so are the survival rates for many forms. In the US, between 1975 and 2016 five-year survival rates improved for twenty-one out of twenty-four types of cancers. In 1975 only half of these cancers had a five-year survival rate above 50 percent; now, it's 75 percent.[25]

Not all the news is good. Another disease where age is a significant risk factor is type 2 diabetes. The disease resulting from the body's ineffective insulin production has become one of the top ten causes of death globally and is estimated to double or triple mortality risk. Between 1990 and 2017, the global incidence of diabetes more than doubled. Around one in sixteen Brits and one in ten Americans are now diabetic.

Linked to this rise in diabetes is obesity—the body's accumulation of excessive fat. In 2016 more than 650 million adults globally were estimated to be obese—nearly one in thirteen of the adult population.[26] The worldwide prevalence of obesity is estimated to have tripled since 1975. It isn't just among adults that this has occurred. In 1975 around one in twenty-five children aged between five and nineteen were obese. Now it's nearly one in five.

So what are we to make of all these seemingly contradictory trends? Does living longer mean that on average we are healthier for longer? Or will we be living in poor health for longer? The good news is that the answer to the first question is yes. The bad news is that the answer to the second question is also yes. While more of our life is spent in good health, there has *not* been a reduction in the number of years in poor health. In other words, there has been an expansion rather than a compression of morbidity (years spent experiencing illness and disease).

That is because gains in overall life expectancy are currently outstripping our capacity to remain healthier for longer, and means there is a new imperative to age well. It is why tackling age-related diseases is paramount for all of us, and why as individuals we need to think hard about exercise, sleep, stress and nutrition. Governments need to think about a twenty-first-century public health initiative aimed at supporting healthy aging, especially given rising levels of obesity and the prevalence of diabetes. It also explains why the life sciences sector is getting ever more interested in developing treatments that help us age better. If our greatest fear is ending up like Tithonus, then it is obvious what our greatest priority should be. We must take evergreen steps to change how we age.

Underestimating the Capacity of Later Years

If an evergreen perspective focuses on changes in how we age, the aging society narrative instead concentrates on changes in the age structure of the population and the rising proportion of older people. That is never seen as a cause for celebration. We seem preconditioned to see old age only in terms of decline. Stock media photos emphasize wrinkles, frailty, loneliness, exclusion and loss of purpose. Government policies don't always help either, especially when the data that inspires them bears mournful titles such as the "old-age dependency ratio" (OADR).

The OADR is a measure of those aged over sixty-five years relative to those considered of working age (in this case, fifteen to sixty-four). The assumption made by officials is that the higher this ratio the worse the economy becomes as a result of fewer workers, more pension payments and higher health costs. As a result, the negative assumptions of unproductiveness, dependence and frailty become the starting point for government policy. It is hard to think of a better example of how we underestimate the capacity of older people and our later years. This definition runs counter to the fact that it is older workers who account for the majority of employment growth in richer countries,[27] and neglects the rising role of grandparents in caring for grandchildren and the substantial contribution older people make through charitable activities.[28]

Whether it is fears of Tithonus or concerns about an OADR, we suffer from negative preconceptions about aging. The irony of this bias is that study after study finds older people are happier than those in middle age. While Figure 2 shows the US data, the same U-shaped pattern is found across multiple countries.[29] Looking

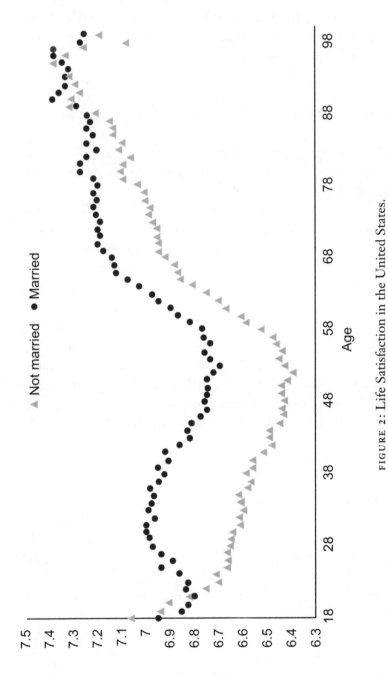

FIGURE 2: Life Satisfaction in the United States.

(Source: Danny Blanchflower and Carol Graham, "Happiness and Ageing in the United States," in David E. Bloom, et al. (eds.), *The Routledge Handbook of the Economics of Ageing*, Abingdon: Routledge, 2023)

at the data in Figure 2, you have to wonder why people in their late forties and early fifties fear old age given the years of happiness ahead of them. It is a powerful reminder that not everything declines with age.

None of this implies that older people don't have problems, but it is evidence that we shouldn't underestimate the capacity of our later years. It also leads to the obvious question of how we can use the extra time that a longer life brings to reduce the pressures in middle age. In an aging society we need to support older people, but a longevity agenda is about how we use longer lives to our benefit at all ages.

If old age isn't necessarily a burden for the individual, the same can also be said at a national level. Let's think about that apparently rather gloomy old-age dependency ratio. In 1922 the OADR for the UK was 11 percent; today, it's 32 percent and is forecast to reach 46 percent by 2050. What is striking is that every governmental analysis of future economic growth invariably starts with the negative consequences of that increase. But no economic historian starts with the past even larger increase in the OADR as an important factor in explaining previous British economic growth. There is a core inconsistency here—past increases in the OADR aren't seen as an important determinant of growth but future changes are. The twin senses of doom and gloom so frequently associated with an aging society simply aren't justified by the historical record.

The nineteenth-century French sociologist Auguste Comte once remarked that demography isn't destiny. The fact that past increases in the OADR weren't a key driver of economic growth reinforces this conclusion. It suggests that if we can make longer lives into healthier and more productive ones then we can create good news for the economy despite a rising proportion of older people. We can't do that if we start with the assumption that the older years are a burden and a problem, though. We need to change how we see the problem.

Whose Problem is It?

The longevity imperative requires moving away from the assumption that longer lives are only an issue for older people. I find this is one of the hardest points to get people to understand.

One example of this kind of thinking is the widely held perception that low- and middle-income countries don't need to worry about aging as their populations are younger and the numbers of older people smaller. In other words, only high-income countries have an aging society problem.

It is certainly true that high-income countries have higher *proportions* of older people. But the overall numbers tell a different story. In 2020 there are estimated to have been globally just over 1 billion people aged over sixty. Only around 300 million of them were living in high-income countries. That means some 700 million older people live in lower- and middle-income countries—the majority of the world's older population—and economic and social policies need to reflect this reality.

But that is still to look at the situation from the perspective of an aging society. Viewed from a longevity perspective the problem for low- and middle-income countries isn't so much the old as the young. Consider these examples. Germany and the United States currently have 22 percent and 17 percent of their populations respectively aged over sixty-five. South Africa and India have only 6 percent and 7 percent. It sounds as though South Africa and India don't have nearly as much to worry about. They've got plenty of toddlers and not so many old folks. Again the message seems to be that only rich countries have an aging society.

Yet by 2085, those toddlers will have grown up and will be over sixty-five. At that point South Africa will have 17 percent of people aged over sixty-five years and India 24 percent—similar to the United States and Germany today. If South Africa and India wait for the current young to become old before tackling an aging society it will be too late. The key thing is to ensure that the current young become the healthiest ever old people.

If a longevity agenda is not prioritized, countries will be trapped in a never-ending cycle of dealing with age-related issues based on norms, institutions and behaviors that aren't geared toward supporting longer lives. A longevity society requires focusing not only on the old but preparing the young for the challenges they face ahead of them. The need to develop a longevity society is not restricted to the rich world or the old. It is a global imperative for all countries and for all of us regardless of our age. Society needs to adapt not just to the changing age structure of the population but to help change how we age.

2

How We Age

You don't get to choose how you're going to die, or when. You can only decide how you're going to live.

Joan Baez

Both my maternal grandparents lived relatively long lives. My grandmother Rachel died aged eighty-eight and my grandfather Bill "Fingers" Palmer at ninety-one. They seemed very old to me from the moment I first met them and I'm sure many other children think of their grandparents in similar terms: grandparents are always "old," right? It seems to be part of the definition. Yet now I look back and I realize I'm not far off the age my grandmother was when I was born.

I always looked forward to their visits but my younger mind viewed them through a prism of age-related frailty. It's hard to recall my grandfather without thinking of the walking stick he used to aid his balance. When they arrived at our house, getting them comfortable in an armchair was always the first task. After lunch, there was usually a nap. Each visit would end with us helping them down the few steps from our door and into the car to drive them back home.

There were occasions though when I witnessed what seemed to me a miraculous reversal of the aging process. My grandfather had made his living as a pianist in the old British music halls (hence his nickname "Fingers"). When he sat down at the piano he was a different man, transported back in time to the melodies of another place and another age. His eyes shone brightly as his nicotine-stained fingers caressed the keyboard and he sang along to old familiar tunes as he entertained the whole family. I think he must have been in his late seventies then, but when he sang the years peeled away. I thought of "Fingers" recently when I heard the Rolling Stones perform in Hyde Park, London. At the age of seventy-nine, Mick Jagger was still Jumping Jack Flash, prancing and preening across the stage. "I'm 40 and I can't move like that," noted one fan on social media.

Bill and Rachel both lived long lives but their experience of later years was different. As Bill aged he grew more frail and tired easily. Yet every day he would dress smartly in his three-piece suit, a pocket watch in his waistcoat. He also carried an improbably large white handkerchief, which he would use for all manner of dabbing and polishing and wiping tasks. While his body weakened, his brain remained sharp to the end.

Rachel's last years were affected by Alzheimer's, resulting in her moving into care. She remained calm and kind most, but not all, of the time as the disease steadily robbed her of her memory and sometimes her character. Ultimately she couldn't recognize her family—those she loved and who loved her.

These family experiences amply illustrate the contrasting approaches to later life. In my early assumptions about my "old" grandparents and their fragile lives, there is the negative aging perspective. In Bill's pride of appearance and enduring musical skills, there is the evergreen imperative of aging well. There is also that key question—what is it that made Rachel's experience so different from Bill's and what, if anything, can be done to avoid her fate?

These memories also emphasize that aging better is about so much more than just health and age-related diseases. The essence of the evergreen agenda is about making the most of later life—not underestimating older people. All this requires rethinking how we age. It involves changing social attitudes toward older people and abandoning stereotypes. In this respect, Mick Jagger has done us all a big favor. The huge crowds in Hyde Park weren't drawn to watch Mick Jagger because he was seventy-nine years old. That was immaterial. His landmark musical accomplishments and enduring performance skills are what really count and are what drew the crowds. Jagger may be exceptional, but he isn't the only seventy-nine-year-old (or older) putting on an inspirational show. Once you start looking for them, you find them everywhere: entertainers, broadcasters, sportsmen, novelists, tycoons and world leaders.

Rethinking how we age also requires changes in our own internal attitudes toward aging. Were my grandparents old before their time? When I spoke with my grandfather in his final years he told me he had never expected to live so long. He hadn't prepared in any real sense for an experience he couldn't imagine. But now expectations have changed. As of today, we can look to the future with a reasonable expectation of being ninety. So how do you want to age and what exactly does aging better look like?

What is Aging?

Reduced to basics—at a risk of stating the obvious—the definition of aging is simple: it is the passage of time between birth and death. But as time passes things change. Some things hopefully increase with age (e.g. life satisfaction, experience, self-knowledge, etc.) while others might decrease (e.g. health, memory, etc.). Aging is clearly a multidimensional process yet the aging society perspective tends to focus on health and that inevitably warps our view by focusing only on what diminishes.

As an example, consider this definition from the World Health Organization (WHO). Scientifically impeccable but spiritually leaden, it describes aging as: "the impact of the accumulation of a wide variety of molecular and cellular damage over time. This leads to a gradual decrease in physical and mental capacity, a growing risk of disease and ultimately death."[1]

This is scarcely a positive description of aging in terms of increased experience and wisdom; of accomplishments achieved and failures felt; of loves won and loves lost; of the joys of friendship and seeing new generations emerge. Instead, it's a hard-headed medical focus on a biological process of decline ending in death. It is a technical version of the words of the English author Martin Amis in his novel

London Fields: "meanwhile time goes about its immemorial work of making everyone look and feel like shit."

T. S. Eliot remarked that the Jacobean playwright John Webster was "much possessed by death / And saw the skull beneath the skin."[2] The aging society narrative is similarly possessed. This is part of a long-running trend whereby the concept of "old age" has become increasingly medicalized. But if we medicalize old age then it becomes defined by age-related diseases and then not surprisingly old age becomes by definition a problem. That is an issue for a longevity society.

Yet this hasn't always been the case. Evidence for an attitudinal shift is found in a fascinating study of American newspapers, magazines and books (both fiction and nonfiction) from the last 210 years, making up a dataset of more than 600 million words.[3] Whereas in the 1800s narratives of old age were about long marriages, wartime heroism, extended family life and individual honor, in the twentieth century the emphasis switched to death, caregiving, nursing homes, illness and disability.

So over the last two centuries the number of older people has increased and the likelihood of the young becoming old has risen but our view of aging has become more negative. How can we explain these two discordant trends? Were older people traditionally venerated more because they were fewer in number and that gave them a scarcity value? Is it because medical science has found ways of suspending the survival of the fittest and keeping more of us alive for longer but not necessarily in good health?

The longevity imperative requires we tackle this negativity if we are to seize the opportunities of longer lives. Doing so involves recognizing that not everything declines with age and then finding ways to support even longer and more engaged lives. But it also requires directly tackling our fear of failing health and old age. It is this latter imperative that is the subject of this chapter.

Tackling those fears requires taking a hard look at how we actually age in practice. How does our mortality risk change each year? What can we expect to happen to our health as we get older? Armed with answers to those questions we can then assess whether we are right to fear getting old so much. But we can also do something even more important. We can start to identify what it actually means to "age better." That is crucial as otherwise the longevity imperative is just an ill-defined waffly platitude.

Understanding how we age also helps us broach the really crucial issue that underpins the evergreen agenda—what can you do to age better? Whenever I tell people I am researching longevity their eyes light up and they move in close to me and ask "What's the secret?" While no magic trick exists there are a number of important and reliable levers to pull that can help us all age better.

Intimations of Mortality

According to the UK government, the average British male of my age has a life expectancy of eighty-four years. That's a total of 4,368 weeks of which 3,000 have already passed leaving me with another 1,368 to go. That's a sobering thought. Planning next year's summer vacation? That will be fifty-two more weeks gone. Writing this book? Subtract another 104 weeks. What do I want to be doing in ten years? By that point, I will be down to 848 weeks of my life remaining, so I had better make good choices.

This forward-looking approach measures my thanatological (or prospective) age—the remaining life we can expect (in my case twenty-seven years, giving me those 1,368 weeks). That contrasts with the usual chronological way of measuring age—the number of years since I was born (fifty-seven years, or just under 3,000 weeks at the time I write this). Aging is like Janus, the two-faced Roman god of beginnings and endings, who simultaneously looked forward and backward. Because of this two people with the same chronological age but different thanatological ages may act very differently. Regardless of your current age, the more time you have ahead of you the more you need to invest in your future health, skills, purpose and relationships. A fifty-seven-year-old with a life expectancy of seventy will therefore behave very differently from one with a life expectancy of eighty-four. This forward- rather than backward-looking perspective is one of the key things that distinguishes a longevity society.

One of the reasons we fear becoming old is an awareness of moving closer to the end of our life. As our chronological age rises our thanatological age declines. Of course, we do not know exactly how many years we have left. Our chronological age is a fact (even if it is one people often lie about) while our thanatological age can only be an estimate. But because mortality rates rise with age, as we get older we sense an approaching ending.

So one way to age better would be to lower mortality rates at each age. That produces an increase in thanatological age and the gift of more time. Figure 3 shows how Japanese female mortality rates (the probability of dying at a certain age) have improved substantially over time. The mortality curves have shifted further and further to the right. The result is that a ninety-year-old in 2019 had the same mortality rate as an eighty-four-year-old in 1983 or a seventy-eight-year-old in 1947. In that sense ninety is the new seventy-eight.

Figure 3 shows that past shifts in mortality have been so substantial that, as with our earlier metaphor of a collapsible telescope, any further improvements will be driven mainly by reductions in mortality rates above seventy years of age given how close to zero they already are at younger ages.

It is at this point that the first longevity revolution starts butting up against the second. In the Bible, Psalm 90 famously states that "The days of our years are threescore and ten," and seventy years has featured throughout history as a natural assumption about the full extent of human life. It is a sentiment that has a contemporary echo in the WHO's definition of premature death as occurring before the age of seventy. After seventy, we should apparently be resigned to our fate.

As a result of the first longevity revolution 92 percent of Japanese baby girls can now expect to reach seventy. In 1947 only 40 percent could. That is a remarkable achievement but it doesn't challenge our concept of human life. Enabling a child to live through into adulthood seems a natural human progression. So does extending the life expectancy of the middle-aged so that they can now expect to reach

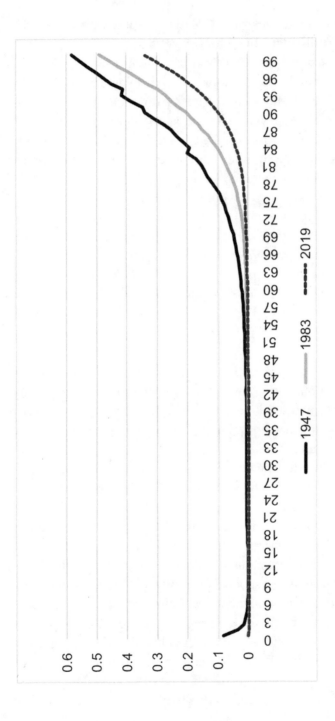

FIGURE 3: Japanese Female Mortality Rates.

(Source: HMD, Human Mortality Database: Max Planck Institute for Demographic Research (Germany), University of California, Berkeley (USA), and French Institute for Demographic Studies (France). Available at http://www.mortality.org)

seventy. But with 92 percent of Japanese baby girls now expected to
live to seventy this first longevity revolution of getting the majority
to live threescore years and ten is complete.

It is a second longevity revolution that is now underway as mortality rates continue to fall at the very highest ages. This second
longevity revolution is more radical as it increases our chance of
living to 100 and changes profoundly how we think about the length
of life. Today in Japan, one in ten seventy-year-olds is expected to
make it to a hundred. We are going well beyond threescore years
and ten.

The second longevity revolution makes many people uneasy.
It challenges our concept of what it is to be human in a way that
reductions in infant and midlife mortality didn't. Living to a hundred or beyond feels like pushing the boundaries of what defines
us as humans. This queasiness is increased by the progress being
made in geroscience, which seeks to understand the biology of
aging. This nascent field has made rapid strides in recent decades
such that it is now routine in the lab to slow down aging in a variety
of animal cells.

That is important because if the main causes of death are now
age-related diseases then if we could slow down aging it would lead
to substantial additional increases in life expectancy. It is estimated
that completely eliminating cancer would only increase life expectancy by around two years.[4] That's because cancer is only one of
several age-related diseases. If you do survive cancer there is still a
high chance of cardiovascular disease, dementia or other age-related
illnesses. But if we could slow down aging then all these diseases
would be postponed leading to large reductions in mortality for
those in their eighties or nineties. This is why the second longevity
revolution is so different from the first. The first was about getting
the majority to reach old age; the second will be about changes in
how we age.

The unease about aging better through reductions in mortality
such that more of us can expect to live to a hundred or beyond
takes many forms. One concern is that if people live too long society
would be governed by the very old and that would lead to a lack

of innovation and vitality. In the words of Elon Musk, the Tesla tycoon, "I don't think we should try to have people live for a very long time . . . if they [people] don't die, we will be stuck with old ideas and society wouldn't advance."[5]

The Musk quote also contains another major unease about further reductions in mortality—its reference to "if they [people] don't die" brings up the issue of immortality. It is remarkable how quickly talk about immortality emerges whenever further longevity gains are discussed. There is an enormous difference in improvements in mortality that lead to an increased chance of living to a hundred and the attainment of immortality. It is as if any debate about breaking Usain Bolt's world 100-metre sprint record of 9.58 seconds dissolves into an argument about whether humans will one day be able to fly. So much public debate on aging flips between a pessimistic aging society narrative where how we age is fixed and the opposite where aging is so malleable that we have the option of living forever. We need to focus much less on extremes and much more on the middle ground of an evergreen life if we are to have any hope of changing things in order to age better.

Another source of unease around further gains in life expectancy is the notion that dying of old age is in some sense "natural" and inevitable and so it is inappropriate to intervene. In other words, there is a notion that getting everyone to live a life of seventy years is natural, but taking efforts to go beyond that isn't. It is this sentiment that also lingers around the WHO's distinction of premature deaths.

The first longevity revolution was achieved by fantastic interventions that substantially reduced the risk from a multitude of diseases, such as typhus, smallpox, cholera, tuberculosis, scarlet fever and measles. It has also achieved dramatic improvements in how we treat cardiovascular disease and cancer. We have become so accustomed to these successes that we now think that experiencing aging is inevitable and natural.

But of course it once felt inevitable that scarlet fever or smallpox would kill a large proportion of those infected (30 percent for smallpox, 20 percent for scarlet fever). Historically mortality rates were so high at all ages that it was dying of old age that was seen as unnatural. That was the view of the sixteenth-century French humanist Michel de Montaigne, who thought that "dying of old age [is] a rare death, unique and out of the normal order and therefore less natural than the others." Dying of infectious diseases was "natural," but not dying of old age. That was also the view of the Brazilian-British biologist Sir Peter Medawar, who received the Nobel Prize for his work on tissue and organ transplants. For him, aging could only be achieved "by the most unnatural experiment of prolonging an animal's life by sheltering it from the hazards of its ordinary existence."[6] That is precisely what the first longevity revolution achieved. If a second longevity revolution is to be a success, we mustn't fall into the trap of thinking that how we age is inevitable.

How Does Health Change as We Age?

The other way to age better is not to lower mortality rates at each age but to enjoy better health for longer. As the late US President John F. Kennedy once remarked: "It is not enough for a great nation merely to have added new years to life—our objective must be to add new life to those years."[7] Aging better in this way is about increasing healthy life expectancy so that it closes the gap with life expectancy. If aging better through further reductions in mortality at older ages makes some uneasy, few reservations are expressed about aging better by compressing morbidity, that is shortening the gap between healthy life expectancy and life expectancy.

The increasing importance of understanding how we age has inspired researchers around the world. Many have developed datasets focused on people aged over fifty to understand the process better. I have spent time myself working with the English Longitudinal Study of Ageing (ELSA), which has collected data on more than 18,000 people since it started in 2002. I can testify to how fascinating and informative these datasets on how our capacities change with age are proving to be.

The cumulative nature of aging emphasized in the WHO definition is readily apparent in ELSA. In 2016 the following results were recorded: around one in sixteen participants had experienced cancer by the age of fifty-five; by sixty it was one in nine and by seventy-four one in five. Our health does tend to deteriorate with age.

ELSA also covers cognitive functioning. Pay attention in class, I'm going to start with a short test. I would like you to pass this book to someone else and ask them to read aloud the ten words found in this endnote at the back of the book.[8] Then write down as many of the words as you can remember and return to this page.

How did you get on? According to ELSA, fifty-five and sixty-year-olds recall on average around 6.5 words, seventy-four-year-olds 5.6, eighty-year-olds 4.7 and ninety-year-olds 3.8. If you are disappointed with your score, don't worry. There is plenty of evidence to suggest that cognitive activities, including reading or memory games, can improve your responses. Reading has been found to delay the onset of Alzheimer's by up to five years.[9] That's another example of how age is malleable and a really good reason to keep reading this book.

All this is interesting but aging is such a multidimensional process we need a broader measure to capture overall physical and cognitive capacity. One way to do this is to construct a "frailty index."[10] Datasets such as ELSA ask participants many different questions. Do you have problems walking a hundred yards? Climbing one flight of stairs? Getting dressed? Have you ever had high blood pressure? Do you feel lonely? A frailty index is calculated as the number of "Yes" answers divided by the total number of such questions. If a person answers "Yes" twenty times out of forty questions the frailty index would be 0.5. The lower the frailty score the better your physical and mental capacity.

If enough questions are included then the frailty index is more accurate in predicting mortality risk than chronological age.[11] It is therefore a useful summary of the extent cellular decline is impacting the ability of people as they age.

Figure 4 shows a frailty index based on 70,000 people from ten countries in the European Union.[12] On average frailty among Europeans rises by around 2.5 percent a year. At the outset when

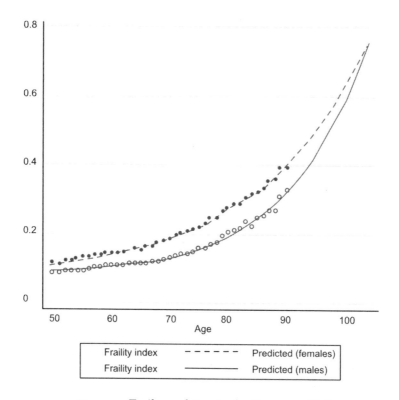

FIGURE 4: Frailty and Age in the European Union.
(Source: Ana Lucia Abelianksy and Holger Strulik, "How We Fall Apart: Similarities of
Human Aging in 10 European Countries," *Demography*, vol. 55, no. 1, 2018, 341–59)

frailty is low the increase is negligible, but over time it begins to climb. It is always rising at 2.5 percent a year—it is just that early on 2.5 percent is a smaller number than later on.

Lurking within all these averages is the glorious diversity of human life: some people are lucky enough to be active at eighty; others are sedentary at sixty. In England the healthiest ninety-year-olds (top 10 percent) have less than half the frailties of the frailest (bottom 10 percent) fifty-year-olds. Similarly, the top 10 percent of seventy-year-olds have a frailty index of less than the average fifty-year-old.

This diversity demands we recognize that people do not all age the same way. It also points to the inaccuracy of age-based stereotypes. That's a major challenge for the aging society narrative that assumes everyone over sixty-five is dependent, incapable of work and in poor health while everyone under sixty-five is the opposite. It also raises the possibility that aging may be far more malleable than we think. It can't just be luck that makes those healthy seventy-year-olds fitter than the average fifty-year-old. That illuminates the very essence of the longevity imperative. What can you do to increase your chances of being one of those healthy seventy-year-olds?

The good news is that, as with improvements in mortality, there is evidence for the United States, the EU and England that we are aging better in terms of health and frailty.[13] In the US, vulnerability to frailty is estimated to have improved by around 1 percent for each year of birth. That means a sixty-year-old born in 1958 has around 1 percent fewer frailties than a sixty-year-old born in 1957. An American born in 1950 can expect not just a longer life but a healthier one compared to those born thirty years earlier.

What lies behind these improvements in health and reductions in frailty among older people? Digging deeper in the ELSA data shows the main area of improvements relates to mobility and the ability to complete daily tasks such as getting dressed and washed, cooking meals and the like. That's good news as it reflects the importance of keeping mobile and active in later life as well as the role of technology and better design in facilitating greater mobility. There is also evidence of improvements in terms of mental health and cognitive functioning, partly due to the rising proportion of older people with better education.

Where there has been less progress is in the incidence of diseases such as cancer, diabetes and arthritis (even if survival rates have in general improved). This suggests that the extent to which these conditions have been improved by changes in behavior—such as reductions in smoking—has been offset by negative shifts, e.g. the rise in obesity. It also points to the idea that modern health systems have become more successful at keeping us alive but not in reducing the incidence of disease.

It is this lack of progress in terms of age-related diseases that makes developments in the biology of aging so interesting.

Throughout history a long list of characters, from the serious to the scandalous, have devoted themselves to the search for the philosopher's stone—the key to immortal life and the central symbol of medieval alchemy.[14] Even one of the greatest thinkers of all, the seventeenth-century rationalist René Descartes, decided in his forties to switch from philosophy and focus his research on aging. Alas, he died of pneumonia aged fifty-three before he could make much progress.

We have always been attracted to the idea of defeating the aging process; yet when the majority of people can now expect to become old, it has become too important a topic to be left to the charlatans and visionaries who flock to the subject. It isn't about the search for immortality but rather understanding why and how we age in the hope of developing treatments that can exploit the malleability of age, reduce the incidence of age-related diseases and further flatten the frailty curve. We can age better through changes in behavior but achieving dramatic compressions of morbidity will require scientific progress.

What Does Aging Better Look Like?

In Ernest Hemingway's bullfighting novel *The Sun Also Rises*, one of the characters explains that he went bankrupt in two ways: "gradually, then suddenly." That's a useful metaphor to think about how we age. The WHO definition of aging referred to the "accumulation of a wide variety of molecular and cellular damage over time." Think of your body as an interrelated system of multiple components. Each component experiences this accumulation of damage but not necessarily at the same rate. Eventually the damage reaches a level such that one or two components start to malfunction. The body can cope with this but as more and more components malfunction, increased stress is placed on the remaining parts accelerating their decline. The result is that aging happens "gradually then suddenly."

This pattern is clearly seen in mortality rates. For most of life mortality rates are low. Cellular damage is accumulating (starting, perhaps, with those first grey hairs . . .) but has not yet reached critical levels. At older ages, however, the cumulative damage across multiple components leads to sharply rising levels of mortality. It is this pattern that Gompertz law formalizes, whereby mortality rates double every seven years or so. When a small number doubles it is still a small number ("gradual") but after enough doublings the small number becomes large and the doublings become larger ("suddenly").

The "gradual but suddenly" pattern also shows up in the frailty curves. They start off flat and then get steeper with age. Aging is always happening and at the same percentage rate but it is only as our body becomes weakened cumulatively that it becomes more obvious. This "gradual then suddenly" nature explains why we tend to associate aging with end of life even if aging is a lifetime process. We become most aware of the aging process only when the "suddenly" bit commences. It is like only finding the iceberg when the ship hits the part above water. Its been there all the time under the surface but it's only when you face the most pronounced part that you realize it's there.

Based on this "gradual then suddenly" shape, there are two ways we can seek to age better. The first is to make the gradual part even more gradual by lowering mortality and reducing frailty at every age. In doing so we flatten the frailty and mortality curves and effectively stay younger for longer. That is why the mortality rate of an eighty-year-old female American in 2019 is the same as a sixty-eight-year-old in 1933 or an eighty-year-old in 2030 is expected to have the health of a seventy-two-year-old in 2020. In mortality terms "eighty is the new sixty-eight," in health terms "eighty is the new seventy-two." For all our fears of aging we are aging better.

In addition to making the gradual part more gradual there is another way we can improve how we age—make the suddenly part more sudden. That may seem paradoxical as you may well have concluded that aging better should mean slowing down aging, not speeding things up. In the 2021 film *Old*, directed by "M. Night" Shyamalan, the characters find themselves on a beach. Due to the nearby presence of electromagnetic material they age the equivalent of one year every half an hour. *Old* is a horror movie so the speeding up of aging is not seen as aging better but a horrific experience because they are young and aging prematurely. So why might aging more suddenly count as an improvement in how we age?

Take the case of frailty. The best outcome we can hope for is that all our years of life are spent in good health so that healthy life expectancy equals life expectancy. Achieving that requires, in the words of Professor Nir Barzilai, an aging expert at Albert Einstein College in New York, "living long, but dying young." If that sounds confusing think of the two necessary steps that are required if aging better is to make all of our life healthy. The first is we need to flatten the frailty curve so we are in good health all our life. That is how we compress morbidity and make healthy life expectancy closer to life expectancy. But for that to happen when we age it has to happen quickly—that's the second part of aging better. If it doesn't then we are back to a life where our final years are spent in declining health.

Those who are queasy about the prospects of ever longer lives in declining health are implicitly advocating improving how we age by making the gradual stage more gradual and the suddenly part more sudden. Back to Elon Musk again. When interviewed by *New York Times* journalist Andrew Ross Sorkin he remarked that he wasn't a huge proponent of longevity.[15] "I do think that having a good life for longer is better—we want to address things that can happen to you when you're old, like dementia, that's important—but I don't know, I definitely don't want to live forever." When asked how many years he wanted to live for Musk replied, "About a hundred good ones." That's a perfect description of aging better in terms of making the gradual part of how mortality and frailty deteriorate even more gradual, so that we are healthier for longer. It also requires the sudden part to happen more suddenly so that aged a hundred you die and there is no lingering end or uncertainty around time of death. If mortality rates remain low and then spike at a hundred, if our health remains high and then deteriorates rapidly at our end, then we can plan for a long life and enjoy good health all our years. Of course, whether a healthy hundred-year-old Elon Musk, or anyone else, would still feel keen on aging suddenly or would prefer to extend the gradual part even longer is another matter.

Implications of Aging Better

Armed with these depictions of how we age and what it means to age better in terms of mortality/frailty and gradually/suddenly, we can step back and take stock of some of the major consequences that an evergreen agenda has for how we think about our lives.

- *Chronological age*: The evergreen agenda requires changing how we age. That is a direct challenge to the aging society view with its monolithic concept of what being old is and its assumed immutability. It also implies the need to shift away from chronological age as the key concept for thinking about aging. Because chronological age is backward-looking it misses the extra future years longer lives bring and how they impact our decision-making. Also, chronological age is not malleable but how we age is. Chronological age may be an easily calculated fact. It just isn't the most useful way to think about age from an evergreen perspective. We need to focus more on thanatological age (how many years more we can expect to live) and biological age (reflecting how much damage your body has experienced over time) .
- *All of life*: It is very hard to tackle aging once the "suddenly" stage is underway. The focus has to be on extending the "gradual" part. Looking after the needs of an older population in poor health is obviously important. It just isn't a very effective way to improve how we age. We need to think about healthy aging from much younger ages. We need a greater focus on prevention early on rather than intervention later.
- *Recursive*: Aging is a recursive process. In other words, what you do today impacts where you are in the future. If you want to age

well in your sixties then it's better to reach sixty with a good level of health. That will be shaped by what you do in your fifties, which of course will be influenced by what you do in your forties, and so on. One study of 10,000 British civil servants found that the younger they first experienced multi-morbidities (more than one potentially threatening condition such as high blood pressure, diabetes, etc.) the greater their future risk of dementia.[16] For every five-year delay in experiencing one of these conditions, the probability of dementia declined by 18 percent. Don't wait until your sixties to think about aging well.

- *Better than average*: The recursive nature of aging has an important implication. If aging is about a gradual decline in health then the higher the level of health you give your future self the better. It is good to be in average health when you are fifty but it's even better to be one of the healthiest fifty-year-olds. An evergreen agenda requires a greater focus on health at all ages. Ironically, in a longer life it pays to be even healthier earlier.

- *Health not disease*: There is a certain irony in the fact that the International Classification of Diseases is the responsibility of the World *Health* Organization. Surely an organization responsible for health should not be so focused on disease? The same criticism of focusing on negatives can be made against the WHO definition of biological aging and the frailty index with its emphasis on decline.

The evergreen agenda takes aging better a step further. It isn't about negatives but positives. Its best outcome is to make the gradual part of decline so gradual it doesn't happen. That is quite a mouthful and involves an implicit double negative of "less decline." It would be a lot simpler to just say that an evergreen agenda is about staying healthy for longer. That after all is what it is really about. Because we see aging as natural we often draw a distinction between health and aging. We need instead to think about aging in pure and simple terms as being about health.

The psychologists Martin Seligman and Mihaly Csikszentmihalyi became known for criticizing their own profession over its focus on mental illness. They emphasized the need to focus on positive psychology and to study how to maintain and promote mental well-being. Similar measures are needed for our health system if we want to launch an evergreen agenda. Health is much more than the absence of disease.

When the WHO launched their Decade of Healthy Ageing in 2021 they defined their goal as "the ongoing process of developing and maintaining the functional ability that enables well-being in older age." That's an important shift as it makes aging part of health and not defined in terms of disease. A focus on aging better has to be about making the most of these extra years. That does require tackling age-related diseases but it is really about promoting health, purpose and engagement across all of life.

- *Inequalities*: The fact that aging is malleable is an empowering thought but it has an obvious corollary—inequalities in society will be reflected in how we age. In England a college graduate aged over fifty has a frailty rating around 35 percent lower than a fifty-year-old who left school before eighteen.[17] It turns out aging isn't so gradual if you have a low income or a poor education. In an evergreen society these inequalities need to be addressed.

What Can You Do to Age Better?

By now you have probably already arrived at a simple but helpful conclusion. You might call it an evergreen conclusion. It comes from the following logical syllogism:

Premise 1: I am now likely to live into old age.
Premise 2: My worst fear of living a long life is aging poorly.
Evergreen conclusion: I need to take steps *now* to maximize my chances of aging well.

This simple form of logical reasoning leads to an obvious question— what should you be doing now in order to age well? It is the question everyone asks me when they find out my interest in longevity and it's the subject of an increasing number of online articles. It isn't just the major newspapers that seemingly on a weekly basis give advice on nutrition, exercise and sleep. There is also a lively internet community interested in newly minted longevity "hacks." These often surface in intense online discussions on the relative merits of potential anti-aging drugs such as rapamycin or metformin.

Rapamycin is a fascinating drug developed from a bacterium found in a soil sample taken from Rapa Nui (or Easter Island) in 1965. It is widely used as an immunosuppressant for organ transplants and is generating much hope among longevity hackers as an anti-aging treatment. Metformin is a drug developed in 1922 that has its origins in French lilac. It is extensively used to help diabetics stabilize their blood sugar and is another popular treatment among those seeking a general treatment to promote healthy aging. Rapamycin and metformin are prescription drugs but there is also growing interest in a range of health supplements, such as resveratol, spermidine and NAD (nicotinamide adenine dinucleotide) or NMN (nicotinamide mononucleotide), all with varying claims about their ability to help slow down aging. These cutting-edge treatments sound exciting, some show promise, but their longevity benefits are so far mostly unproven.

Yet we don't need to cross our fingers and hope that someone comes up with a miracle pill or spends dollars on as yet unproven treatments. We can also do better than the advice of the vintage American comedienne Lucille Ball—"the secret of staying young is to live honestly, eat slowly, and lie about your age." There are plenty of things that you can do now to help you age better that we know work. Best estimates suggest that somewhere between 15 and 30 percent of our longevity and how we age is due to genetics. That is such an extraordinary statistic it is worth pausing to reflect on what it means. It implies that how you age is malleable and that there is an awful lot that can be influenced by your own behavior as well as your environment.

One of the ironies of entering a new era where for the first time ever we need to focus on aging well is that we tend to go straight to the new and the exotic and potential wonder treatments in seeking a solution, while much of current best practice advice isn't new at all but reflects basic wisdom passed down through the centuries.

That is one reason why there is a lot of interest in parts of the world that appear to have cracked the longevity imperative—the so-called "Blue Zones." Based on the work of Dan Buettner, they encompass five regions around the globe that have an unusually high proportion of centenarians: the Italian island of Sardinia; the Nicoya Peninsula in Costa Rica; the Greek island of Icaria; Okinawa island in Japan; and the town of Loma Linda in the San Bernardino Valley, in California.

These Shangri-las of longevity are valuable case studies and the inspiration behind a recent Netflix series. The characteristics they have in common (physically active populations, a high sense of purpose and community, mainly plant-based diets and so on) are all likely pointers as to how to age better. You can even buy Blue Zone cookbooks offering recipes for Icarian stuffed vine leaves and Californian cornmeal waffles. If you enjoy the taste of cornmeal waffles then go ahead and rustle them up in the kitchen. But if you are eating them for longevity purposes be aware that some critics think there is another factor that the Blue Zones have in common and which explains their remarkable number of centenarians. Bad recordkeeping. According to Saul Justin Newman, a senior postdoctoral fellow at the Australian National University, "relative poverty and missing vital documents constitute unexpected predictors of centenarian and supercentenarian status, and support a primary role of fraud and error in generating remarkable human age records."[18] Perhaps Lucille Ball was onto something after all.

Much current best practice advice largely centers around basic health hygiene. Getting enough good-quality sleep is important as sleep gives the cells of the brain and body a chance to repair themselves. Inadequate sleep is also linked to the incidence of Alzheimer's as well as to a range of other ailments such as cardiovascular problems, cancer and diabetes. It's also possible to sleep too much—a condition also linked to later cognitive issues.

A more difficult question to answer is what defines "good sleep"? How many hours, what time of the night or day you sleep and whether your sleep is continuous will all vary across individuals and will change as you age. The popular adage "eight hours a night" isn't likely to be right for everyone so finding your own optimal pattern requires experimentation. While a growing number of devices and their apps measure various aspects of your sleep, the bottom line is this: if you wake up feeling refreshed then you have been getting "good sleep." Your goal should be finding out what you need to do to achieve that.

Other obvious advice is to avoid tobacco, alcohol and obesity. Smoking exacerbates a large number of age-related diseases and accelerates aging. There has long been debate about the appropriate level of alcohol consumption and whether red wine is good or bad for you; most of us would probably accept that whatever the pleasures involved in drinking, modest levels of consumption are advisable (alcohol is after all a toxin). Modest, by the way, usually means less than what most "modest" drinkers think.

The alarming spread of obesity (measured as a body mass index (BMI) greater than 30) has become a literally oversized problem for future health. It is linked to a variety of debilitating diseases including diabetes, cardiovascular illness, cancer and dementia. In the US, obesity prevalence is estimated at more than 40 percent and severe obesity (BMI greater than 40—that is a weight of over 262 lbs for someone 5 feet 8 inches tall (122 kg/173 cm)) affects nearly one in ten of the population.[19]

It isn't just how much we eat but *what* we eat that matters. The American author Michael Pollan's advice to "eat food, not too much, mostly plants" summarizes succinctly a great deal of general dietary experience. From a longevity perspective, highly processed foods are to be avoided, red meat and sugar limited and the virtues of a Mediterranean diet embraced (NB Blue Zones and happy Sardinians). There is also evidence that a healthy gut containing a range of bacteria is important; experts tend to recommend a range of world foods and probiotics such as kimchi (fermented Korean vegetables); sauerkraut (Germany's national dish of raw fermented cabbage); tempeh (fermented Indonesian soybeans); kefir (a yoghurt-like drink that originated in the Caucasus); and miso (a traditional Japanese seasoning).

How often we eat and when also makes a difference. The first scientific study showing a link between calorie restriction and longevity in rats was published in 1935 and has since been shown to hold for a range of living organisms.[20] There are two problems with this approach for humans, though. The first is that it is impossible to do human trials to see if calorie restriction boosts longevity. It just isn't feasible to take different people and monitor them over their entire life and make sure the only difference between them is how much they eat. So following this approach requires assuming that results carry over from other organisms. The second problem is that the required level of permanent calorie restriction is substantial (25 percent or more). That's a difficult level for many people to sustain (it's certainly hard for me). It invites the vintage quip that this fierce a diet doesn't really make life longer; it just makes it appear so.

So calorific restriction seems to be beneficial but is a very difficult practice to follow. That's why there is great interest in finding ways of mimicking the effect without too much self-denial. As a consequence the refreshment breaks at longevity conferences tend to be notable for shared advice on intermittent fasting (while everyone pretends not to want to eat the pastries and chocolate biscuits). Diets such as the 5:2 (five normal days, two days of fasting) or the increasingly popular 16:8 (fast for sixteen hours a day, eat only in an eight-hour window before 8 p.m.) all lay claim to various health improvements and are followed by multitudes of longevity researchers.

The need to avoid discovering problems during the "suddenly" stage of aging highlights the importance of both general preventative health campaigns and, on an individual basis, monitoring your own health as part of a personal evergreen strategy. That might include annual check-ups with a health professional, monitoring your own blood pressure, pulse and sugar levels, checking for lumps or using your devices and their apps to track any number of health indicators. However you manage it, keeping an eye on your health is crucial in an evergreen world.

Equally prominent on the evergreen agenda is exercise and the immense benefits that regular workouts provide. It is hard to emphasize just how important a tool this is in helping us age better. Regular exertion, both cardio and muscular, is invaluable in helping to maintain balance and mobility in older years. Exercise also benefits cognitive health by reducing the incidence of depression and dementia.

Social and psychological factors also contribute. Sharing time and space with friends and family and having a sense of engagement and purpose all matter. There is plenty of evidence to suggest that people who have a positive concept of aging go on to live longer than others. One study that uses blood tests to measure biomarkers of aging finds that being lonely or unhappy adds up to 1.65 years on your biological age.[21]

Few will be surprised by these recommendations. When combined in an evergreen lifestyle they are likely to exert a significant influence on your own healthy longevity. To see the magnitude of these effects consider a review of twelve different European studies covering 116,000 people aged between forty and seventy-five.[22] The study looked at four lifestyle factors—alcohol consumption, smoking, physical activity and body mass index. Individuals scored 2 if for that factor they were behaving optimally, 1 if they were ranking intermediate/average and 0 if poor. The maximum number of points a person could score was 8 and the lowest 0. Those who scored full marks live ten more years free of chronic disease compared to those who scored 0. If scoring top marks across the board is too hard, take comfort that each additional point on average gives you around one more year free of chronic disease. Worth thinking about if you are reading this book while smoking and enjoying a drink.

That none of this advice is new doesn't mean it isn't relevant (although exactly how best to sleep and exercise, and what and when to eat is increasingly coming under a scientific lens). The novelty of the longevity imperative means simply that it has never been so important and so we have never had such a large incentive to follow it. The challenge to society and individuals is how we create a lifestyle that makes these healthy behaviors easy to choose. Think, for example, about how you work, how you structure your day and what options you face when you shop. Precious little of our daily experience is supportive of an evergreen lifestyle. The goal is to make the good choices easy and natural.

Finally, as so often with longevity, there is the issue of inequality. Many of the above lifestyle shifts require time and money. Not everyone has the time to sleep longer or cook healthy meals; nor the money to sign up for a gym. It is why an evergreen economy has to be mindful of not just improving best outcomes but making sure more people have access to its benefits, an issue we return to later. When it comes to longevity a rising tide definitely doesn't lift all the boats.

Into the Red Zone

If we are aging better in terms of health and mortality, why is there such a fear of an aging society? Why is the evergreen imperative so important? This brings us to our final dimension of aging better—the relative speed of changes in mortality and morbidity.

The problem is that improvements in mortality have been greater than reductions in frailty. That wasn't too ominous when the improvements in survival meant a higher chance of living into your forties and fifties. Those are years of low frailty, so the extra years gained were mainly healthy. But now the falls in mortality represent more people living into their eighties and nineties, which increases the probability of living into years of worse health. Society is entering what Chicago demographer Jay Olshansky calls the "red zone"—the period at the end of life characterized by high levels of frailty. The evergreen imperative is to turn this red zone green—to convert it into years of good health.

It is the red zone that fuels those fears of an aging society. The red zone also explains why we begin to worry that gains to life expectancy are not a good thing. The concern is that we have created a health system that keeps people alive but doesn't keep them healthy. The faster mortality rates improve relative to frailty, the more time we spend in the red zone. The gains from the first longevity revolution are coming to an end.

This raises difficult questions. Are further gains to life expectancy valuable or does the existence of the red zone mean that further reductions in mortality rates no longer equate to aging better? Is our health system making things worse by keeping people alive rather than healthy? Have we reached a limit to desired human life expectancy?

At this point we need to move on from pinning down the precise trajectory of biological aging or metaphysical discussions about immortality. We need to move from the philosophical and medical to the economic. We need to shift from discussion of years of life and health to the impersonal metric of money. To do so, the next chapter turns to using economic tools to provide a monetary answer to two questions:

How valuable is it to age better?

How do we value life expectancy gains relative to healthy life expectancy?

3

All's Well That Ages Well

The modern meaning of life's end—when does it end? How does it end? How should it end? What is the value of life? How do we measure it?

Don DeLillo

My father died from motor neurone disease (ALS) at the age of seventy-seven years. For a man who had always been a good athlete it was a particularly cruel illness, afflicting nerve cells in the brain and spinal cord and progressively diminishing muscle activity. His final weeks were spent in hospital where he eventually ended up needing a ventilator to breathe. Those were raw and difficult times but during one visit I learned a powerful truth that made me see his circumstances differently. As my mother sat there holding my father's hand, wrapped in the easy silence that only lifelong companionship can bring, she turned to me in reassurance to remind me that despite my father's reduced circumstances there was pleasure in being together. "Life is sweet," she said in a voice that was both profound and sorrowful.

My mother died ten years later at the age of eighty-five from an infection picked up in hospital after a hip operation. She was warned that the operation was risky and I had long conversations with her about the dangers. But she was adamant she wanted to proceed. She'd had enough of the pain and immobility that stopped her from doing the things she wanted, and I suspect she had also had enough of widowhood. Life wasn't as sweet anymore.

Today, increasing numbers of us will face decisions like these: how to balance the quality and quantity of life. This is where Medawar's "unnatural experiment" of prolonging life becomes personal. At what point do the negatives of battling on outweigh the positives of staying alive?

That's why the longevity imperative is so important. It seeks to mitigate these difficult personal dilemmas by improving the trade-off between the quantity and quality of life. But aging better demands significant investment from both individuals and governments. The trouble is, as we know only too well, time and money are limited so choices have to be made and goals prioritized. Why should aging better be prioritized over multiple other goals that we all have?

Right now in the UK there is widespread media coverage of the "worst ever crisis" in the National Health Service (NHS). The NHS was founded in 1948, and it is now a seventy-five-year-old that is not aging well. A system stretched by Covid is struggling to deal with backlogs, seasonal flu and an aging population, and this is interacting with staff shortages and underinvestment to create enormous pressures. The result is an increase in deaths above what should be expected based on the age of the UK population.[1] That is a very long way from an evergreen agenda. But perhaps, given all the competing demands for government money, it is just inevitable. Perhaps the wish to age well is a "nice to have" rather than a crucial priority. Just where should the evergreen agenda rank in your and the government's list of priorities?

Governments routinely wrestle with the problem of how to allocate resources and have developed a variety of tools to decide what represents "good value" when it comes to health interventions. It is these tools we turn to in this chapter, to place a dollar value on the different ways of aging better. It may be that you don't need to be convinced just how important it is. In that case you may want to skip some of the intricacies of the economic calculations outlined below. But the economic tools provide two distinct sets of insights.

In arriving at dollar values they provide answers to the key questions—how valuable is the longevity imperative to age well? and which is most valuable, the quantity or quality of life? These answers are foundational for everything that follows in this book. They also point to multi-trillion-dollar benefits for society. It really is a case of "all's well that ages well." Based on the analysis of this chapter, the evergreen agenda should be at the top of everyone's priorities—far from where it currently stands. These answers also show resoundingly that it is healthy life expectancy we should focus on and not life expectancy. Life may be sweet but it is made sweeter by being healthier rather than simply longer.

The economic tools also provide a qualitative insight. They show us we need to focus less on treating specific diseases and more on improving our health by targeting how we age. In doing so they provide a glimpse into our future. A virtuous circle exists whereby the better we age the more we want to live for longer and age even better. The consequence is humanity is at a take-off point. This new stage will transform what it means to be old both in terms of health and longevity but also for how long we will want to live.

Characterizing Aging

Since the earliest times humans have been fascinated with the prospect of defeating aging. As far back as three thousand years ago the earliest surviving epic tale was describing the search by the Sumerian King Gilgamesh for a plant that bestows immortality. In this chapter I will use literature's obsession with the topic to consider four different ways of aging better, each offering different combinations of improvements in the quantity and quality of life. This gang of four is made up of Jonathan Swift's Struldbruggs, Oscar Wilde's Dorian Gray, J. M. Barrie's Peter Pan and the Marvel Comics' antihero Wolverine.[2] Together they provide a convenient means of summarizing different ways that we could age better through different combinations of shifts in the mortality and frailty curves of the previous chapter. I'll start by climbing in a boat and setting sail for the island of Luggnagg.

A Journey to Luggnagg

In 1726 the Irish clergyman Jonathan Swift published *Gulliver's Travels*, a multilayered satire of human nature that became a classic of English literature. Among the imaginary destinations that Gulliver reaches—from Lilliput and Brobdingnag to the Land of the Houyhnhnms—is the distant island of Luggnagg, 100 leagues south-east of Japan. Some of Luggnagg's inhabitants bear a red mark on their foreheads. These are the Struldbruggs, and what distinguishes them is that although they age in the same way as everyone else, they do not die. The Struldbruggs are immortal.

Gulliver is at first impressed by the notion of immortality, but that changes when he discovers the reality. The Struldbruggs revisit the Greek myth of Tithonus and Swift spares no mercy in recounting the horror of their existence. The French philosopher Simone de Beauvoir refers to it as "the cruellest portrait of old age that was ever drawn."[3] The Struldbruggs may live forever, but they lack eternal youth. They go blind, their hair falls out, and they suffer from all the ailments of age. In this way the Struldbruggs live on enduring "all the follies and infirmities" of normal humans, but also knowing that they will continue to endure them forever. At the age of eighty they are declared legally dead even though they continue to live. They are not allowed to work, own assets or take decisions. That is because "otherwise, as avarice is the necessary consequence of old age, those immortals would in time become proprietors of the whole nation, and engross the civil power, which, for want of abilities to manage, must end in the ruin of the public." Swift's account of the Struldbruggs is a devastating eighteenth-century account of an aging society.

Viewed in modern demographic terms, this Struldbrugg scenario represents an improvement in how we age only in terms of mortality. Using the terminology of the previous chapter, the mortality curve shifts to the right but the frailty curve remains unchanged. The result is an ever-increasing red zone as the gap between healthy life expectancy and life expectancy widens. What the Struldbruggs' experience emphasizes is that eventually there comes a point when longevity gains alone are not desirable. For Swift, who was in his late fifties while writing *Gulliver's Travels*, that point arrives at the age of eighty.

Swift died not long before his seventy-eighth birthday. His last few years of life were marred by cognitive impairment, probably dementia. Even before that, though, Swift found his old age a burden not just in prospect but in reality: "I never wake up in the morning without finding life a little more devoid of interest than it was the day before."

A widespread concern today is that our current health system is propelling us along this Struldbrugg path. In the words of Eileen Crimmins, professor of gerontology at the University of Southern California, we haven't yet managed to slow aging but we have slowed the dying process. A hospital system based on treating illness is keeping people alive, but not necessarily keeping them well. More and more people are surviving cancer, more people are living after a stroke, but often with their health and functionality impaired. That may seem better than the alternative—patients dying sooner—but it leads to a world where further investments in longevity can legitimately be questioned.

Swift's satire captured the essence of an intractable human dilemma: we want to live for a long time but we don't want to be old. Yet for all the mockery he aims at longevity, Swift is making the same point as the evergreen imperative. If lives are going to be long, we need to age well.

Dying Young at an Old Age

Let's now consider the polar opposite to the Struldbruggs. Mortality stays the same but this time it's health that improves at every age. In terms of the previous chapter only the frailty curve shifts to the right while the mortality curve remains fixed. As a consequence, the quality of life increases but its quantity remains unchanged. Let's call this the Dorian Gray experience, after the lead character in Oscar Wilde's 1890 novel, *The Picture of Dorian Gray*.

In *The Picture of Dorian Gray*, the handsome young hedonist of the book's title makes a Faustian bargain to cling to his physical beauty, as captured in a painting by one of his friends. He wishes the Dorian in the painting to age while he remains young and beautiful in body. He quickly discovers that the more he indulges in debauchery and vice, the older and uglier his face in the painting appears while his own looks are preserved.

Returning to our modern longevity analysis, the focus in this Dorian Gray scenario is not on living longer but on maintaining your health for longer. The result is the red zone shrinks as healthy life expectancy catches up with life expectancy, reducing the years spent in poor health at the end of life and so compressing morbidity. Taken to its extreme, this Dorian Gray scenario leads to Nir Barzilai's "living long but dying young." The gradual part of how health deteriorates with age becomes so gradual it is nonexistent and the suddenly part becomes so sudden it happens in an instant and at a much older age.

Compared to the chilling prospect of the Struldbruggs' desolate immortality there is much to like about *Dorian Gray*. With its focus on improving health as we age it tackles our main fears while avoiding concerns about living too long. Yet drawbacks remain.

In emphasizing staying young and healthy the Dorian Gray scenario can slide into a cult of youth. In his dialogue *On Old Age*, Cicero thought that a major advantage of becoming older was freedom from passions and sensual appetites. With those distractions behind him he could focus on the language and letters that led Voltaire to describe him as "the greatest as well as the most elegant of Roman philosophers." It is this perspective that underpins long-standing views that wisdom accumulates with age. By the end of Wilde's novel even Dorian Gray understands that there's more to life than youth, beauty and hedonism. He ends up destroying his portrait and in so doing destroys himself. It is a powerful reminder that aging isn't only a biological phenomenon. Extending health may be foundational for making a long life a good life but so is the accumulation of wisdom, experience and friendships.

Slowing Down Aging

The Struldbruggs and Dorian Gray represent either/or options: improvements in mortality but not health or improvements in health but not mortality. But what if we could slow down aging itself? If we could make "seventy the new sixty" then seventy-year-olds would have the health and mortality of sixty-year-olds. That involves shifting both the mortality and frailty curves to the right. That would lead to a double dividend—improvements in both life expectancy and healthy life expectancy. It is precisely this double dividend that happens when someone stops smoking or starts exercising and which materializes if geroscience successfully develops treatments that slow down how we age biologically.

In the limiting case where biological aging doesn't happen at all, we would be forever young. Inspired by that thought, let us call this the Peter Pan scenario, after J. M. Barrie's play about the boy who never grew up. In the most extreme case of Peter Pan your health and mortality would remain unchanged throughout your life. But in general the Peter Pan scenario is about slowing down the rate at which you age biologically so that you live not just longer but in better health at every age.

While Peter Pan is obviously a work of fiction, the experience of mortality and health being minimally affected by age is a reality for some animals. One obscure creature in particular is of endless fascination to longevity scientists. The naked mole rat is found in East Africa. Its wrinkled skin, absence of fur and large pointy teeth win it no beauty contests. But what makes it a winner is its mortality rate, which barely rises with age. That makes it remarkably long-lived (seventeen years in the wild, thirty in the laboratory) for a small mammal.[4] That is impressive because in general larger animals live longer lives than smaller animals. Relative to its size the naked mole rat lives around five times longer than expected,[5] raising the intriguing prospect that we might be able to learn something from its genetics about how we can age better.

Slowing down aging in a way that achieves a constant mortality rate doesn't mean that we would live forever. A naked mole rat isn't immortal—it has a near constant mortality rate, not a zero one. But if we do end up flattening the rate at which mortality rises with age then it would lead to dramatic changes in life expectancy.

To see the magnitude of the effect consider my eldest son, who will soon turn thirty. Imagine a scientific breakthrough happening on his birthday that stopped him from aging. That would be quite the birthday present. As each year passed his chronological age would increase but his mortality risk and frailty would be locked into whatever they were when he was thirty. How many more birthdays could he expect to experience?

The chances of dying aged thirty are happily very small—around 0.07 percent for British males. If that remained his mortality rate forever then crunching through the maths leads to the result that his life expectancy would be a rather daunting 1,462 years. If the chance of dying each year is less than one in a thousand then life expectancy stretches far out into the next millennium. This simple but fantastical example shows the impact aging has on our lifespan. It is only because mortality rates rise with age at the rate they do that our current life expectancy is below three figures. Under Peter Pan and a slowing down of biological age that all changes and so does life expectancy.

But not all cases of a constant mortality rate lead to such long lives. It obviously depends on how old you are when aging ends. At 0.4 percent, mortality rates are higher at fifty than at thirty. So if aging were stopped from fifty onward then redoing the calculations leads to a slightly more manageable but nonetheless startling life expectancy of 303 years. If you were 303 years old as I write, you would have been born in 1720—the year that saw the bursting of the first stock market bubbles (the South Sea Bubble in England and John Law's Mississippi scheme in North America), Jonathan Swift start work on *Gulliver's Travels* and the birth of Anna Maria Mozart, mother of Wolfgang Amadeus. You would have been in your fifties for the American War of Independence and in your sixties at the time of the French Revolution. You would have taken your place on the longevity scale alongside the Greenland Shark, which is esti-mated to live for more than 300 years; but you'd still be far behind the ocean quahog, a species of North Atlantic clam with a lifespan of 500 years or more. Longevity is all relative.

What if instead mortality rates stop rising when you reach seventy and thereafter remain the same? At that point the gains to average life expectancy will be much more modest as the UK male mortality rate at seventy is 2 percent. In this case life expectancy would be 106. It turns out that making "hundred the new seventy" in a Peter Pan way is what delivers Elon Musk's "good hundred."

These are of course merely mathematical calculations and not serious conjectures about the future. But they do help provide some insight. Halting biological aging doesn't produce immortality. It doesn't even necessarily lead to preposterously long lives. It all depends upon the age at which aging is frozen. These conclusions hold all the more if instead of halting aging we manage only to slow the process.

There is, though, another way that flattening frailty and mortality at older ages will change our sensibilities around aging. In fact this effect is already at work today since it doesn't require 1500-year-long lives to reveal itself.

It is because mortality rates rise with age that we expect the old to die before the young. If instead mortality rates were constant then thirty-, fifty- and seventy-year-olds would all have the same remaining life expectancy. It would no longer be the case that you would expect to outlive your parents or even your great-great-grandparents. That might seem strange but historically it isn't so unusual. My parents grieved the loss of their infant son and in the eighteenth century Benjamin Gompertz did the same. After centuries of tragically high levels of infant mortality it is only relatively recently that the young can *expect* to outlive the old.

The combination of diversity in how we age and flattening mortality curves at older ages will lead us to see more radical variations of traditional family aging patterns. Take the case of ninety-eight-year-old Ada Keating from Liverpool, who decided to go into a care home in 2017. She did so not because she needed care for herself but in order to support her eighty-year-old son Tom, who was already in the home. In Ada's words: "I say goodnight to Tom in his room every night and

I'll go and say good morning to him. I'll tell him I'm coming down for breakfast. When I go out to the hairdressers he'll look for me to see when I'm coming back. When I get back he'll come to me with his arms outstretched and give me a big hug. You never stop being a mum!"[6]

Reversing Aging

The idea that we might achieve Peter Pan lives by slowing down aging may sound far-fetched, but it's not totally remote from our experience. We all know friends and acquaintances who have been careful with what they eat, who don't drink or smoke, who exercise frequently and who "look good for their age." We therefore know already that biological age is malleable and can be slowed even if extreme Peter Pan outcomes are as yet beyond us.

But what if we were able to not just slow aging but reverse it? Could we somehow make ourselves carry on living healthily as if we were years younger? Not by going backwards in time, as in so many Hollywood films, but by tinkering with your body clock to regain biological youth. It's far easier to wind a watch back in time than it is to slow it down. What if our aging system is the same?

Geroscience is looking at the possibility of winding back the aging process. In January 2023 Rejuvenate Bio, a San Diego biotech company, reset the cells of mice to a younger state and extended their lifespan by around 10 percent. Alkahest is an American biopharmaceutical company targeting neuro-degenerative and age-related diseases. Based in California, its clinical trials involve transplanting young blood plasma into older human patients. Another American company, Lygenesis, is conducting trials using stem cells to regenerate livers as an alternative to transplants.

Perhaps not surprisingly, Hollywood got to the subject of rejuvenation first, as any fan of superhero movies will know. The popular Marvel Comics character Wolverine possesses the ability to reverse the effects of any injuries he suffers by regenerating organs and tissues to their original healthy state. So let's refer to reversing the aging process as the Wolverine scenario. Wolverine demolishes conventional ideas about aging by reversing the flow of time and replacing the inevitability of decline with the possibility of renewal.

As with the naked mole rat, nature gives examples of animals with the potential to do this. The axolotl, an endangered species of Mexican salamander, regenerates its limbs, skin and most of its body parts. Perhaps even more intriguing are hydra—spindly fresh-water polyps that grow to be about half an inch long with protruding tentacles. Their name echoes the Greek myth of the many-headed monster that grew new heads when existing ones were chopped off. Hydra are mostly made up of stem cells, enabling them to constantly renew their bodily cells. As a result, they appear to remain forever young with no signs of aging.[7]

Wolverine completes our quartet of characters depicting different ways of aging better. Each proposes a different mix of changes in mortality relative to frailty. All four are literally fantastical, drawn as they are from literature; but each in more moderate guise offers insights as to how we could age better.

The Struldbrugg case is closest to the path we are currently on, where increases in life expectancy are outpacing healthspan. The Dorian Gray scenario highlights the appeal of healthy aging and compressing morbidity by boosting healthspan. The power of Peter Pan and Wolverine is that they bring biological aging explicitly into the analysis, leading to a boost in both healthy life expectancy and life expectancy.

You may already have formed a view as to which of these four scenarios is most appealing. But to rank each of them and determine exactly how high they are in our priority lists we must now turn to economics in order to place a dollar value on each. We want to determine just how valuable aging well is and which matters most—quantity or quality of life?

The Price is Right

Exactly how much we value health and life became a central issue during the Covid-19 pandemic. In early 2020, as the virus began its malign spread, individuals and governments were aghast at the potential scale of the problem. According to one influential report, the UK faced the prospect of more than 500,000 Covid-19-related deaths and the US over 2 million if no corrective actions were taken.[8]

In response to these dire projections, we changed our behavior and governments introduced emergency policies which produced dramatic economic declines. In the UK, GDP fell by 20 percent in a single quarter, with widespread predictions of the worst recession since the Great Frost of 1709. You would need to be a geriatric Greenland shark to remember that far back. The UK's economic experience was a common one internationally—across sixty-four countries the average initial impact of lockdowns was a fall of 30 percent in GDP.[9]

These punishing declines swiftly led to a hesitant but inevitable discussion of competing priorities, of trade-offs between health and money. Was the alarming cost of combating the virus worth the number of lives saved? That's a bleak question to ask, let alone answer. For many it sounded obscene. The then New York governor Andrew Cuomo was one of many who refused to be drawn into so painful and potentially acrimonious a debate. For him, there was only one possible answer: "I say the cost of a human life is priceless, period."

Politicians answer to voters. Economists, on the other hand, are experts on trade-offs. That is because at the heart of the subject is the allocation of scarce resources. If you spend more money, time or resources on X there will be less available for Y. Economics specializes in understanding these trade-offs and how to quantify them, invariably in terms of money.

To non-economists, this need to quantify everything in monetary terms is unnecessary and often distasteful. In Oscar Wilde's play *Lady Windermere's Fan*, one of the characters poses the question "What is a cynic?" The famous reply is that a cynic is someone "who knows the price of everything, and the value of nothing." Perhaps Wilde also had economists in mind.

The same Wilde play, though, contains a less famous definition. Wilde describes a "sentimentalist" as someone "who sees an absurd value in everything and doesn't know the market price of a single thing." There are lots of things in life that we value highly but limited resources means we can't have them all. We might want to live in a larger apartment as well as work less, but most of us will end up having to make trade-offs. On a grander scale, during Covid governments around the globe were forced to make trade-offs between policies that saved lives and those that kept the economy strong.

The point of all this should be clear. The case for aging well is obvious. No one wishes to age badly. The issue then is around the cost of achieving it. Just how important a priority is aging well compared with all the other demands hollering for your time and money?

Because government trade-offs involving money and health are so routine, the language of economics is used extensively in health systems across the world. In the UK total health care expenditure in 2021 was £277 billion, more than £4,000 per person.[10] Yet even a sum that substantial isn't enough to meet all our health needs. That means decisions need to be made on which treatments to perform and which drugs to buy and which ones are not value for money.

In the UK these are based on guidelines established by the National Institute for Health and Care Excellence (NICE). At the heart of these guidelines are elaborate calculations that effectively place a cash value on human lives. Key is a metric called quality-adjusted life years, or QALYs—the number of years of remaining life adjusted for the level of a patient's health. If a treatment can add one more QALY to a patient's life, it is deemed to represent good value if it doesn't cost more than £30,000. The consequence of this NICE approach is that a treatment that offers a patient an increase of ten QALYs will get a green light provided it costs less than £300,000. The choice of £30,000 lacks an obvious theoretical justification but is probably chosen to ensure that total drug expenditure is in line with overall health budgets.[11]

In 2021 the drug Zolgensma was approved by the UK's National Health Service. Zolgensma is a remarkable drug in many ways. Most notably, it halts the progression of spinal muscular atrophy (SMA), a genetic condition that makes the muscles weaker, in children. Tragically, babies with SMA have a life expectancy of only two years.

The drug is delivered in a single dose and replaces the faulty gene SMN1 that causes SMA.

The other remarkable feature of Zolgensma is its price—at £1.79 million for a single treatment it is the world's most expensive drug.[12] Yet because life expectancy for the average British newborn is eighty-three years, its use creates so many QALYs the drug was approved by NICE. In other words, budgeting rules don't prevent large amounts of money being spent on individual treatments that are proven to extend lives. Our health is incredibly valuable.

How to Value Health

The NICE guidelines offer a consistent way to allocate drug expenditure. But there is a deeper issue—how should we calculate the economic value of improvements in health or longevity? One way would be to calculate how aging better impacts the economy. To start with an obvious example, if we live longer in better health, we would be able to work for longer which in turn would boost GDP. We could therefore measure the dollar value of aging better in terms of this resulting increase in GDP. Alternatively, we could calculate the savings that aging better would produce from reduced expenditure on treating diseases such as dementia or cancer. That would free up funds for other pressing issues such as education, housing or cleaning up the environment.

While both these approaches are valid they don't really capture the full value to us of aging better. It's a mistake to believe that the economic value of something depends only on its impact on the economy. A parent doesn't value the health of a child on the basis of its future earning power. Improving the health of a ninety-year-old isn't unimportant just because they may no longer be working. Similarly it can't all be about cost. Consider, for example, a treatment that cures dementia but which costs 10 percent more than the current charge for dementia care. Surely we would pay that and consider it a good deal? Health is valuable to us in its own right regardless of its financial implications.

To capture this broader value for health, economists resort to a concept known as the value of a statistical life (VSL).[13] It is important to stress the "S" in VSL—this is a statistical concept, not a moral one. The VSL is not a calculation for how much a particular life is worth. Instead it is an answer to a subtler question: How much should we spend to reduce the risk of dying? If you are prepared to pay $10,000 for a safety feature in your car that reduces your mortality risk by 1 percent then your VSL is $1,000,000 ($10,000 × 100).

In 2022 the United States government pegged the VSL at $11.4 million per life.[14] Life really is sweet! To see what this means let's say a government calculates that installing safety barriers on a treacherous stretch of road will save ten lives. The value of those lives saved in VSL terms is $114 million. If the barriers can be installed for less than $114 million, they would represent a worthwhile investment.

How does the Environmental Protection Agency (EPA) arrive at a VSL of $11.4 million? By looking at the trade-offs individuals make in terms of income and the risks they face at work; at how much they pay for safety features in cars, smoke detectors, etc. All these decisions reveal how we value reductions in mortality and can be used to measure the VSL. The fact the resulting VSLs are so large points to just how valuable health and life are to us. At that rate the number of lives saved by restricting the Covid death toll represented a bargain, despite the negative impact of lockdowns on GDP.[15]

This VSL approach can be used to calculate the value of the various improvements to health and longevity that each of my gang of four fictional characters represents. Each scenario changes the VSL in one of two ways. One is through changes in the *quantity* of life due to increases in life expectancy. Generally speaking, the more time we have the better. But not all time is equally valuable. That is why the *quality* of life, reflected in your health and your standard of living, also impacts the VSL. Years where health is good, consumption is larger or you enjoy lots of leisure time are more valuable than years spent in poor health, with low consumption and long working hours. Each of our four scenarios leads to different combinations of quantity and quality of life and produces different VSLs. We can use these changes to pin down the dollar value of aging better in each case.

An important part of the VSL analysis is the recognition that if your health or life expectancy changes then you will make different decisions about work, spending and saving over your lifetime. So in thinking about making life longer we don't just have to think about the quality and quantity of the extra years. We also have to think about how they affect the quality of life in the years beforehand. At the heart of the VSL calculus is a model that works out the optimal economic response of the average American to changes in health or longevity and which can be used to recalculate the VSL.[16]

Take the case of an increase in life expectancy. If you don't change when you retire then you will be living for longer but still earning the same amount of money over your lifetime. That requires you to cut back and spend less every year. The result is you end up with more leisure time (in retirement) but have less money to spend each year. If you like leisure a lot then this may be a great outcome. But it might be that you would prefer to work a few more years rather than see your spending cut. Either way the introduction of more years at the end of life has changed the quality of life in earlier years—either through reductions in spending or making people work for longer. It is these complex adjustments over the life course that the VSL allows for.

Because You're Worth It

Having explained the mechanics behind this VSL analysis it is now time to turn to the insights it delivers based on our four characters. The results below are all drawn from a paper published in *Nature Aging* that I wrote with Martin Ellison of Oxford University and David Sinclair at Harvard Medical School.[17]

Longer Lives Are Valuable (for a While)

The Struldbrugg scenario is the least appealing of our quartet as it means living longer but in declining health. However, according to the VSL analysis it is still valuable. Based on an initial US life expectancy of seventy-nine years, increasing life expectancy by one year in this way is worth just under $100,000. Swift may be right that there comes a point where living in failing health is no longer desirable, but this analysis suggests that that happens at a much later age than eighty for the average American.

An extra year of Struldbrugg life is beneficial but there is a problem. With a VSL of $11.4 million and a life expectancy of seventy-nine the average year of life is worth around $150,000. So with an extra year of Struldbrugg life at seventy-nine valued at $100,000 that makes it significantly less valuable than a typical year of life.

The reason for that provides insight into why we fear an aging society. One reason that extra year of life at seventy-nine is less valuable is because it is a year lived in below-average health. That reduces the quality of life. But that is only part of the story. The other reason is that living for an extra year requires a mix of either saving or working more earlier in life in order to finance this additional year. That reduces the quality of life in earlier years. An extra Struldbrugg year is a benefit but it also effectively acts as a tax on earlier years. The result is that increasing life expectancy in this way leads to diminishing additional benefits and greater demands are placed on earlier years. That explains why in high-income countries there is growing concern around an aging society and further extensions to life expectancy.

Healthy Aging is What Really Matters

If the VSL analysis tells us that simply living for longer is of diminishing value, it also provides the insight that the most important priority is to improve how we age in terms of our health. While US life expectancy is seventy-nine years, healthy life expectancy is only sixty-nine. If through improving health at each age you could generate one more year of healthy life expectancy, our VSL analysis of Dorian Gray says that's worth $216,000. That's more than twice the value of an extra Struldbrugg year at age seventy-nine. As explained above, the Struldbrugg case gives one more year of life but in poorer health, and while this is a benefit it also acts as a tax on past years. The Dorian Gray scenario gives us no additional time but it makes each existing year better by improving our health and all without acting as a tax on earlier years. We don't need to work more to finance these extra healthy years.

In fact the analysis goes even further. It isn't just that first extra year of healthy life expectancy that is more valuable than an extra year of life itself. That holds for each and every year of healthy life right up until healthy life expectancy equals life expectancy. Our VSL analysis reaches the strong conclusion that the most important health priority right now is not extending life but rather getting healthspan to match lifespan. That signals the transition from a first longevity revolution based on extending life to a second longevity revolution aimed at changing how we age.

That is a radical message given the bias of current health systems and modern medicine toward life extension. It is perfectly understandable that doctors respond to patients by trying to keep them alive. But if all it leads to is more patients surviving in diminished health, they are providing a one-way ticket to the red zone of aging badly. The Dorian Gray analysis shows that eliminating this zone has to be our number one health priority. Governments need to place healthy life expectancy as a key measure of their success and much less emphasis on life expectancy.

The same conclusion to prioritize healthspan over lifespan also holds for us as individuals. I often have people tell me that they would rather not live a long life given the effort and sacrifice required. Watching your weight, restricting alcohol and regular exercise all require effort and there are always more appealing options available. I understand those sentiments only too well. Life is full of trade-offs and it is perfectly reasonable to trade years of life against enjoyment. The only catch here is that we live in a society that is pursuing Struldbrugg outcomes. We have health systems that are very good at keeping you alive through a range of operations, drugs and emergency procedures. Because of that the trade-off you face is not between more quality of life today and less quantity in the future. The choice may be between better health now and better health later or worse health now and even worse health later. In an evergreen world even the Faustian bargain changes. Just ask Tithonus.

The Benefit of Slowing Down Biological Aging

This Dorian Gray analysis however is not the end of our story. Supporting good health for longer is incredibly rewarding. But we also value living longer too. That makes the double dividend of Peter Pan especially valuable. By slowing down the rate at which we age biologically we get the joint benefit of better health and more years. That makes Peter Pan even more attractive than Dorian Gray let alone the Struldbruggs.

If we could increase life expectancy in the United States from seventy-nine to eighty by slowing down biological aging so that mortality and frailty rates were lower at each age, it would be worth $180,000 according to the VSL analysis. That isn't just higher than the $100,000 Struldbrugg gain; it is greater than the value of an average year of life (which we calculated at around $150,000). Under Peter Pan the quality of each additional year of life expectancy gained is higher than that of the Struldbruggs because of better health, but Peter Pan also makes the quality of earlier years better by increasing their health levels too. Thus, far from acting as a tax on earlier years Peter Pan actually improves their quality. That makes an extra year of life produced via Peter Pan worth a lot more than an extra year produced by the Struldbruggs. Similarly an extra year of healthy life expectancy produced by Peter Pan is worth more than an extra year produced by Dorian Gray. If you gain another year of healthy life expectancy by slowing biological aging, it is worth $294,000, more than the $216,000 of Dorian Gray. That is because with Peter Pan you get a double dividend of better health and also more time in the form of extra life expectancy.

What about the Peter Pan vs. Wolverine smackdown? Even though slowing and reversing aging sound radically different, in many cases there isn't a great deal of difference between the two. Explaining why would take us on a lengthy detour, but they both effectively keep you younger but in different ways. Consider the case of two different treatments: a Peter Pan intervention that slows down my son aging from his thirtieth birthday or a Wolverine drug that he takes at sixty and which reverses his biological age back to thirty. Between thirty and sixty the Peter Pan treatment is more desirable; he will be in better health than under Wolverine. From sixty onward the Wolverine outcome is preferred. The net result isn't that they are the same but that each has different pros and cons and so the differences aren't that substantial between them. Ultimately which is more preferable will be about which one is easiest/possible to achieve, the cost of any treatment and the efficacy and repeatability of any drug.

There is, though, one very important reason why Wolverine and regenerative medicine, if feasible, is more appealing than Peter Pan outcomes. Who knows if or when a geroscience breakthrough will occur, but when it does I would prefer it to be of a Wolverine kind. While my son at thirty may benefit similarly over his lifetime from both, I prefer Wolverine. If a treatment that successfully slows down aging appears when I am eighty, that's a lot less valuable to me than a treatment that lowers my biological age. It could be welcome news to discover at eighty that you will be healthier at ninety than you previously imagined. But it is even better to be told you will return to the health you enjoyed when you were fifty.

On the Importance of Targeting Aging and Not Disease

The Peter Pan and Wolverine scenarios also reveal something else. The gains from slowing down how we age far exceed those from eradicating any single disease. That is a perspective which demands that we put aging and not disease at the center of our debate on health.

There are two reasons that make this shift in focus so important. The first is a simple arithmetical one: if aging is the root cause of so many age-related diseases then attacking the cause makes more sense than chasing its individual effects. If reducing the incidence of cancer or dementia or cardiovascular disease is substantial—if we can slow down biological aging so that we reduce the incidence of all three of these age-related diseases – then the gains will be even larger as you sum across them all. In other words, the gains from slowing down aging are large because you would benefit from slowing down multiple diseases.

But it turns out that the gains from slowing down aging are even larger than the sum of the impact on each individual disease because of a phenomenon called "competing risk." Eradicating cancer would be a wonderful achievement but the gains to health and life expectancy it produces are limited by the existence of multiple other age-related diseases. The same goes for eradicating dementia or heart disease. This isn't just an issue for the quantity of life but also its quality. If we survive cancer but then suffer from dementia we may gain extra years but not in good health. When it comes to aging and age-related diseases, Claudius's words in *Hamlet* are appropriate—"when sorrows come, they come not single spies, but in battalions." The result is that the gains from slowing down aging are greater than the sum of the gains from eradicating each age-related disease due to these synergies.

These two effects, impacting multiple diseases and the synergies that unlocks, make the benefits of slowing down aging much larger than the benefits gained from tackling just one specific disease. This is a profound shift and emphasizes the importance of preserving health and aiming at delaying aging rather than persisting with a disease-based model focused on illness. Rather than intervening when a patient develops a disease, it would be better to keep the patient healthy by helping them age better. We need a health system genuinely focused on health and prevention, not disease and intervention. We need to look more holistically at our health as we age rather than see health as driven by separate diseases.

A Multi-Trillion-Dollar Opportunity

There is one final reveal from our VSL analysis—just how important the longevity imperative is for society as a whole. We have already seen how large the gains are to individuals, so it should come as no surprise that when we add these up across hundreds of millions of citizens we get vast numbers.

Let's start with a Peter Pan example of slowing down biological aging so as to produce one extra year of life expectancy with improved health at all ages. Our VSL analysis calculates that for most countries that is worth the equivalent of around 3–4 percent of GDP in a single year. If that seems a lot, recall that it is broadly in line with the falls in GDP governments were prepared to allow in order to save similar reductions in life expectancy during Covid.

But that 3–4 percent of GDP is the benefit accruing in just one year. If it is a permanent increase in life expectancy then we need to add this up over all future years (but we give the future a discount because money in the future is worth less than money today). Doing that for the United States leads to the staggering amount of $51 trillion—that's more than double the 2021 GDP ($24 trillion). In the UK the benefits add up to $6.5 trillion and to $11 trillion in Japan (both countries have smaller populations so the gains are less).

The gains from slowing aging are enormous because saving lives and improving health are extremely valuable, and the biggest contributor to global deaths and disease is now age-related illnesses. We took dramatic measures in order to prioritize life and health in the face of a Covid pandemic. These calculations argue that the same prioritization should be made to support healthy aging. When aging better generates $51 trillion of welfare gains the longevity imperative needs to be right at the top of government priorities.

So why isn't it happening already? That is because the challenge is a new one. It hasn't always been important. It is only now, when the young can expect to become the very old, that the gains are so substantial. If we repeat these VSL calculations for earlier times then we get much smaller numbers. Back in 1922, when a twenty-year-old Briton had a one in five chance of making it to eighty, the longevity imperative lacked urgency. Why worry about an outcome with such long odds? Why worry about age-related diseases when you are unlikely to become old. Today a newborn Brit has a more than 75 percent chance of making it to eighty and a better than evens chance of reaching ninety. If longevity wasn't an issue in 1922, it certainly is today.

The sad truth is we have fashioned a society that doesn't invest enough in later years because for most of human history only a minority reached those ages. That is no longer the case. The gains from an evergreen agenda have become too large and important to ignore.

Our VSL analysis therefore points to two key results. The first is the overwhelming importance of compressing morbidity and improving healthy life expectancy relative to life expectancy. We need to change how we age. That links to the second. We need to shift from looking at specific age-related diseases and instead focus on prevention and maintaining health by slowing down biological aging.

A New Era for Humanity

One hundred years ago, one in eight children born in the UK didn't make it past the first five years of life. That made improving infant mortality the most important health challenge. By 1970, that battle was being won and attention turned to improving midlife mortality—half a century ago, only one out of three fifty-year-olds made it to eighty. Today we have reached the point when four out of five children are expected to live into their eighties.

This time, though, the experience will be radically different. There is a virtuous circle around improving how we age that there isn't around the diseases of early years and midlife. As the Struldbrugg results show, us simply increasing life expectancy without improving health leads to diminishing returns. The priority has to be Dorian Gray—boosting healthspan to catch up with life expectancy. But as that happens so the benefits of living for longer rise. In other words, if we live through our eighties in poor health the value of living to ninety is low. But if we can be healthy through our eighties then the prospect of living into our nineties becomes more valuable. The consequence is the better we get at aging the more we will want to age better for longer. With all previous diseases, the better we have become at treating a disease the less we are interested in it. That isn't the case for aging. That is why the Peter Pan scenario is so valu-able—it increases health at the same time as it raises life expectancy and in doing so sidesteps diminishing returns.

This is, in short, a take-off moment in human history. We are entering a whole new era. With global life expectancy already over seventy years, we might be tempted to feel the aging challenge is over. A longevity revolution has been achieved. But it is precisely this achievement that marks the arrival of a second longevity revo-lution. What matters now is to age well but as we age well we will then want to live longer, and as we live longer we will then want to extend healthspan further.

There is, of course, no guarantee of success in any attempt at slowing down aging and certainly no expectation of instant progress. Scientific breakthroughs might be slow and incremental or rapid and transformational. It could take decades, it could take centuries or it may never happen at all. But finding breakthroughs in how we age needs to be our focus. Success will depend on the depth of human ingenuity, the allocation of sufficient resources and the com-plexity of human biology.

Pursuing this evergreen agenda is likely to be expensive, but given how valuable aging better is, that isn't a problem. It is worth it. Health is what economists call a "luxury" good—the richer a country gets the greater the proportion of income is spent on it. That's cer-tainly been the pattern of the past hundred years. Between 1950 and 2020 US expenditure on health services increased from 5 percent to 20 percent of GDP (substantially higher than most other countries). That may well rise in future years to as high as 30 percent.[18] Our VSL analysis says that is money well spent so long as the money is used to keep ourselves in good health rather than supporting us to live with disease. Right now, though, that isn't what is happening in the US.

Throughout this chapter the longevity imperative to age well has been defined in terms of health. But ensuring that the quality of life matches the quantity of life clearly goes far beyond medical issues. It means planning how to finance a longer life and filling it with activity and purpose. We will need to keep engaged, preserve our relationships and find ways of forging new ones, and avoid boredom and seek challenges. All that requires more than a revised health regime and the development of new drugs; it involves changes to career planning, to financial management, to how we think about old age and to every aspect of how we live our lives. That is why there is a lot more to the evergreen agenda than trying to understand the genetics of the naked mole rat and whether its aging skills might be adapted by humans.

Without achieving the fundamental goal of extending healthspan to match life expectancy, we will struggle to match the quality of our future years with their quantity. But achieving this goal will require and enable many other changes to society, our behavior and our way of thinking. It is time to turn to the building blocks of an evergreen life.

PART II

Building an Evergreen Economy

4

A Health Revolution

Health is the state about which medicine has nothing to say.

W. H. Auden

In Terry Gilliam's film *12 Monkeys*, set in 2035, Bruce Willis plays a convict who is offered a chance to earn a pardon. To succeed he has to go back in time to 1996 and discover the source of a virus that has killed 5 to 6 billion people, forcing the remnants of humanity to shelter underground in order to survive. If the virus can be prevented or a vaccine found, life can go back to normal. That is Bruce's mission.

Gilliam's film comes to mind for multiple reasons when discussing the need for a health revolution. With a world population of more than 8 billion and global life expectancy of over seventy, we are in need of our own action heroes to save us from a future where billions suffer from age-related illnesses. If the multi-trillion-dollar gains of aging better are to be realized then we mustn't rely on time travel but take radical action now. As with *12 Monkeys*, the key is to take preventative measures rather than wrestle later with entrenched disease. As with pandemics, aging is best tackled early on rather than later.

For all its focus on the future and science fiction, Gilliam's film taps into two features, one historic and one contemporary, of how we view health. The historic is our deep-seated psychological fear of viruses. That fear was revealed only too recently during the Covid pandemic as modern society found itself grinding to a halt. But Covid is just the latest battle in a long war against viruses. The reason why historically only a minority lived into old age was our vulnerability to a raft of diseases. Plague, smallpox, typhoid, cholera, tuberculosis and malaria have each killed hundreds of millions, if not billions, of people. It is communicable diseases such as these that have been our greatest threat.

But *12 Monkeys* also taps into a more contemporary belief—that we can conquer disease. The story of the first longevity revolution is one of continuous progress through improvements in prevention, diagnosis and treatment that dramatically reduced the threat from these diseases and many more. Take the case of smallpox, the "speckled monster," which can be traced back to at least ancient Egyptian times and is believed to be the cause of the demise of pharaoh Ramesses V. More contagious than Covid and with a mortality rate of 30 percent, it is estimated in its last hundred years to have been the cause of at least half a billion deaths.[1] But thanks to vaccines, on May 8, 1980 the World Health Assembly declared smallpox eradicated. A phenomenal achievement.

The long lives we can now expect are a result of this progress. Scientific methods (e.g. the discovery of germ theory), medical breakthroughs (e.g. vaccination, antibiotics, blood transfusion, radiology), public health (e.g. sanitation, anti-smoking campaigns, seatbelt wearing) and improvements in the standard of living (e.g. better diets, cheap washable fibers, soap, indoor toilets) have together transformed life expectancy.

But we now stand at the threshold of the second longevity revolution where the focus has to be on aging better. The scientific advances behind the first longevity revolution need to change substantially. We now need a health system with a much greater emphasis on prevention rather than intervention. We need scientific research to investigate the biology of aging rather than specific diseases.

When the UK's National Health Service was founded in 1948 around half the population died before the age of sixty-five and the most common causes of death were infectious diseases. Today only one in eight deaths occur before that age and infectious diseases are no longer their main cause.[2] We now live in a world where people die late in the second half of their lives from noncommunicable conditions that are slow to develop but long-lasting. The result is a health system under increasing financial pressure and which is becoming separated from the promotion of the nation's health with more of a focus on the treatment of illness.

That means it is time for a health revolution. Our health systems need to heed the career advice of the California-based leadership guru Marshall Goldsmith, known for his maxim "What got you here, won't get you there." Having got to "here"—a world where the majority of children born today can expect to live a long life—we need to get to "there"—a world where long lives are accompanied by lasting good health.

To see the challenge consider the three components that define health systems: public health, health care and long-term care. Public health is about the health of the whole population rather than particular individuals. Included in its remit are campaigns for healthier lifestyles—such as those based around reduced tobacco and alcohol consumption and compulsory wearing of seat belts—and the monitoring of infectious diseases. Health care focuses on our individual health and consists of the primary and secondary care provided by doctors, nurses, surgeons, clinics, pharmacies and hospitals. Long-term care is about helping those in need of support in dealing with a range of age-related illnesses either in their own home or in an institution.

All three components need to change radically to deal with the second longevity revolution. Public health systems tend to be underfunded, which is a serious problem given the need to shift behaviors and make it easier to pursue healthier living. Health care (primary and secondary) swallows most of the funding but is focused on the diagnosis and treatment of specific diseases rather than prevention and maintenance of health. Currently, only around 2.5 percent of total health expenditure in high-income countries is focused on prevention.[3] It is this emphasis on intervention that generates Struldbrugg outcomes, which are in turn overwhelming a long-term care system that is underfunded, expensive and not properly integrated with the health care system. As a consequence, a health system that brilliantly supported the first longevity revolution is not set up to achieve the second and is unsustainable.

But the second longevity revolution will need more than just a new health system. It will also require scientific progress and medical breakthroughs that help us age better. This means investing in geroscience, the study of the biology of aging.

Creating an Evergreen Health System

Currently health systems are dominated by health care. In the United States nearly 80 percent of all medical expenditure is on clinical care—primary, secondary and pharmaceutical.[4] But based on a study of health across US counties, 80 percent of the systematic variation in health outcomes is due to the combined effect of socioeconomic factors (nearly half) and individual behaviors (around a third).[5] Only 16 percent is due to clinical care. A shift from intervention to prevention requires more expenditure on nonclinical health policies aimed at improving the environment in which we live and the choices we make.

In an evergreen world maintaining our health will increasingly be influenced by actions happening further away from doctors and hospitals. How we age is affected by everything from the built environment to the nature of work, public transport, loneliness, what we eat, financial security, agism, education, design, water and sanitation, and much more. The health system becomes much wider in an evergeen world.

Public Health

This broader agenda demands greater investment in public health. If health care focuses on treating individual patients, the aim of public health is to support the health of the population as a whole. It is about identifying and reducing the risks to our health through changes in the environment and shifts in our collective behaviours.

As the recent Covid pandemic showed, public health is an important first line of defense against many diseases. In the absence of a reliable medical intervention, either in the form of vaccination or treatment, the only hope was prevention through public health measures. That took the form of analyzing data to see where the pandemic was spreading, encouraging the washing of hands and the wearing of masks, providing tests to self-diagnose and lockdown policies aimed at preventing the spread of the virus.

Covid also showed public health to be a complex and controversial issue. It requires shifting individual habits and social customs and in doing so brings itself into conflict with vested economic interests. It is an area rife with problems regarding the role of the state and individual freedom. Also, when the public health system intervenes to prevent loss of life the gains often go unnoticed. Preventing a problem doesn't get the same recognition as intervening to solve a problem. Perhaps that explains why public health has shrunk as a share of health expenditure, now accounting for around 3 percent of overall US spending.[6]

Despite all these complications, public health has had multiple successes. From better sanitation to improved road safety, a variety of measures have collectively saved hundreds of millions of lives. A recent example is the policies that have reduced tobacco smoking. Smoking lowers life expectancy by ten years and expands the gap between life expectancy and healthy life expectancy by six years.[7] It is estimated that in the twentieth century 100 million people died prematurely because of smoking.[8] Since employing a variety of measures the number of deaths from smoking have declined substantially. In the US the probability of dying from smoking fell by around a half between 1990 and 2019.[9]

When it comes to aging, public health once more needs to be a first line of defense. Six areas should be the major focus—smoking, alcohol, air pollution, social isolation, lack of physical activity and obesity. Each has a substantial negative impact on both health and life expectancy. Success will require altering our own individual behavior as well as changing the environment in which we live. Progress is likely to be hard-won and cumulative rather than dramatic and sudden.

While there have been improvements around smoking there is still much to be done, especially outside high-income countries.[10]

Globally around one in four adults smoke, contributing to approximately 8 million deaths annually, about one in seven due to passive smoking.

The impact that air pollution has on our health is also becoming increasingly apparent. Globally air pollution accounts for nearly 9 million deaths and there is increasing evidence that air pollution is linked to dementia.[11] Tackling environmental pollution isn't just important for the planet, it's also important for our own health.

Loneliness and social isolation are bad for your mental and physical health and how you age. The impact is substantial, as Noreena Hertz brutally summarizes in her book *The Lonely Century*: "If you are lonely, you have a 29% higher risk of coronary heart disease, a 32% higher risk of stroke and a 64% higher risk of developing clinical dementia. If you feel lonely or are socially isolated you are almost 30% more likely to die prematurely than if you are not."[12]

Probably the most urgent of all public health issues is the need to tackle rising obesity. Based on a study of nearly 1 million people, moderate obesity (a BMI of between 30 to 35) lowers life expectancy by around three years while severe obesity (a BMI of between 40 and 50) lowers it by ten years.[13] Healthy life expectancy is much reduced also as a whole host of diseases, such as diabetes, cancer, heart disease and arthritis, become more likely. It isn't just an individual's health that is affected. In the UK it is estimated that obesity accounts for more than £50 billion in terms of lost productivity, lost taxes and higher welfare spending not to mention the additional health care costs that result.[14]

Tackling obesity as a health problem will be far from easy but then neither was achieving reductions in tobacco use. The same issues of freedom of choice, the power of vested interests, understanding the triggers that determine individual behavior as well as the need to reach a consensus on the science are all present.

Success will therefore depend on the same mix of policies that successfully reduced tobacco use. That means a combination of taxation and cessation support programs, marketing campaigns (both on the dangers of certain behaviors as well as explaining the advantages of healthier habits) and restricted availability of harmful foods.

Just as the tobacco industry became the focus of public health in the drive to reduce smoking so the food and beverage industry will become an area of focus in a longevity society. Hippocrates said: "Let food be thy medicine." One of the great successes of the Industrial Revolution was the provision of cheap food. But as we move away from a Struldbrugg world so there will be much greater focus on the link between what we eat and our health. Sugar, salt and additives in particular will be subject to growing taxation and regulation.

In identifying factors that put the population at risk it is important that public health has an emphasis on subgroups who are most vulnerable to aging poorly. We have already stressed how those with lower income have lower life expectancy and higher levels of frailty. Covid revealed in both the UK and US how much more exposed certain ethnic groups were to health risks at the same time as facing inadequate access to health care. When it comes to preventative health, those gaps are likely to be even more pronounced and will require proactive policies if inequalities are not to be compounded and longevity is to be a gift for all.

A Shift to Prevention

Sir John Bell is the Regius Professor of Medicine at the University of Oxford. He is a worried man. "There is no health system in the world that I think is currently sustainable, it's all going to fall over," he declares.[15] Britain's National Health Service (NHS) is one of his examples. "You only have to look at the NHS numbers, it's bloody awful," Bell adds. "You have massive waiting lists, hospitals are full, everybody's unhappy, so what do you do? Train 40,000 new nurses and 10,000 new doctors. Really? How does that work? That's what they did in the [the Battle of the] Somme, they just sent more people in, and they get slaughtered by the system. There's a fundamental problem with how we're trying to solve the problem."

Bell's analogy with the Battle of the Somme is a striking one. The four-month-long First World War battle saw more than a million soldiers killed and was described by the poet Siegfried Sassoon as a "sunlit picture of hell."[16] The British lost nearly twenty thousand men on the first day; the generals on both sides concluded that the only way forward was to send more to their deaths. Bell's argument couldn't be clearer: if we are to win the war against age-related diseases we need a new approach. Sending in more people to do the same thing won't produce different results. Bell's analogy brings to mind Philip Roth's dismal words in his novel *Everyman*—"Old age isn't a battle; old age is a massacre."

One part of the problem is finding enough people to provide the care and support that an ever-rising number of older people need. In the United States, the Bureau of Labor Statistics predicts that nursing will be the fastest-growing occupation between 2020 and 2030, growing in number by 275,000. In Japan, the number of nursing homes has risen nearly 50 percent over the last decade. Similarly in the UK there is a growing need for nurses and carers but as of 2022 there were 165,000 unfilled vacancies for adult care workers. Finding the trained staff to take on what are difficult and often not well-paid roles is going to be hard. But it isn't just a shortage of professional nurses and carers that makes the situation unsustainable. Caring also makes huge demands on families. In the UK around one in five adults aged over forty are providing some form of adult care.[17]

As well as generating an inexhaustible demand for carers, Struldbrugg outcomes also generate unsustainable health costs. In the UK, average annual health care costs per person are £1,000 for someone with no long-term condition, £3,000 for someone with two conditions, £6,000 for three conditions and £7,700 for more than three conditions.[18] Given that so many chronic diseases are not just treatable but avoidable, there must be a better way. To achieve Dorian Gray or Peter Pan outcomes we need more of this clinical expenditure to be spent on preventative measures. In 2020 total US health care expenditure was $4.1 trillion.[19] That is $12,516 per person but only $363 per person of that was spent on prevention.[20] Even if preventative care is expensive surely it is better to spend money on promoting health rather than just treating sickness?

The trouble is that while there has been plenty of innovation around prevention of infectious diseases, especially with vaccinations, there has been hardly any when it comes to noncommunicable diseases. That is why public health so often stresses the importance of remedies such as diet and exercise.

But it isn't only lack of innovation. Clinical tests aimed at detecting susceptibility to a disease are expensive as there are so many diseases to focus on. There are programs aimed at early detection of breast and prostate cancer but to do the same for every possible condition is not an option. That leads to the financial decision to choose to intervene when a disease manifests itself but it is harder to treat illness when it is entrenched and the focus is then on sickness not health. We are backed into a Struldbrugg world.

Perhaps now, though, there is genuine scope for innovation. Your DNA can be processed for as little as $100 and developments in big data and AI provide enormous amounts of information to monitor and predict your health. That opens up new possibilities. We can't offer a full set of preventative health measures to everyone, that is too expensive. And we wouldn't want to provide a full set of measures to just a few, that is too elitist. But we can think about providing to all people some preventative checks targeted at their individual risks.

For instance, genetic screening can determine if you have a greater chance of becoming diabetic, experiencing dementia or getting breast cancer. Rather than perform preventative tests on all these diseases, armed with the genetic screening information the health system can keep measuring you in the areas where you are most at risk.

The advantages of this approach are twofold. The first is that rather than wait until a disease is entrenched, measures can be taken to tackle the disease early on or even prevent it. That moves us away from Struldbrugg outcomes and toward Dorian Gray ones. The second advantage is that through targeting these measures costs can be kept down and earlier interventions achieved and so better health is produced. That's quite the hat trick.

Central to all this is the extraordinary amount of data that can now be collected about your health as well as your genes. Your smartphone can provide you with masses of data about how you slept, how much exercise you have taken, your walking speed and gait. It is increasingly easy to monitor your own blood sugar levels and blood pressure at home. The hope is this data can be used not just to improve the efficacy of preventative policies but also to improve diagnosis and treatment.

To help achieve this the UK has launched an initiative entitled Our Future Health. Its aim is to recruit 5 million adults who will provide information about their health and lifestyles as well as blood samples for detailed genetic analysis. In the US the All of Us program seeks to do the same based on 1 million Americans. This is the beginning of a new health system.

Menopause

An important component of any preventative health program aimed at healthy longevity will be a focus on menopause. Because of menopause, women face a long gap between the loss of their reproductive ability and their life expectancy. There is plenty of evidence that this exerts a significant impact on women's later health.[21]

Occurring usually between forty-five and fifty-five, menopause lasts for an average of seven years but can last as long as fifteen. It brings about significant bodily changes: a decline in estrogen production and an increase in body fat which produces higher insulin resistance as well as an adverse shift in lipids (triglycerides and cholesterol). This leads to changes in health risks. Below the age of fifty-five cardiovascular illness is a more likely cause of mortality in men than women. After fifty-five the reverse is the case.[22] The increase in insulin resistance increases the risk of diabetes and falling levels of estrogen raise the risk of osteoporosis.

Given the central importance of health to longevity it is striking how little attention is given to menopause as an issue in an aging society. There is much that remains unknown about menopause. Even why humans are one of only five species to experience menopause (the others being all whales—beluga, narwhals, killer and pilot) is uncertain.

Menopause occurs at ages the vast majority of women can expect to reach and who now can expect to live ever more years afterwards.

In 1933 a twenty-year-old American woman had a 80 percent chance of living to fifty-five and experiencing menopause. Today they have a 94 percent chance of doing so. In 1933 a fifty-five-year-old American woman had an expected twenty years of remaining life. Today, assuming no further progress, they have an average of twenty-eight years left. The likelihood of experiencing menopause and the consequences of its impact on future health has never been greater. It is an obvious component of an evergreen agenda.

It isn't only health that is affected by menopause. A variety of symptoms combine to disrupt working and family life and lead to withdrawal from the labor market with all the financial implications that entails. If we are seeking to make the most of our later years, we need to heed the words of Oprah Winfrey: "So many women I've talked to see menopause as an ending," says Oprah. "But I've discovered this is your moment to reinvent yourself after years of focusing on the needs of everyone else."

Person Focused

A longevity society involves maintaining health rather than treating disease. But too many aspects of our current system point the other way. For instance, many modern health systems are financed by budgets based on patient statistics such as the number of operations performed in hospitals. In other words, budgets are linked to the number of ill people rather than just the population as a whole. But if instead funding is provided based on the size of the local population then spending money successfully on prevention means fewer operations, fewer patients and less pressure on budgets. That was the change initiated in Singapore in March 2022. In the words of Singapore's health minister Ong Ye Kung: "With this shift in the basis of funding, there will be a natural incentive for hospitals to try to keep residents healthy through preventive care."[23]

A disease-based approach is also increasingly problematic, with an older population experiencing multi-morbidities. Treatment becomes fragmented, requiring numerous specialists focused on a particular disease rather than the individual patient's needs and welfare. The consequence is considerable duplication of effort, overprescription of drugs and expensive and often inefficient treatments. The overprescription of drugs (polypharmacy) is a major problem not just in terms of financial wastage but because interactions between drugs lead to adverse health effects or reduced effectiveness. Greater use of gerontologists rather than disease specialists, single clinics with teams of specialists and better integration of primary and secondary care are all needed to provide a more integrated service.

Supporting this will require creating community-based ways to engage across a range of health issues. That means local pop-in centers, mobile resources and scattered health clinics rather than a reliance on large hospitals and medical facilities. Linked to this is the need to understand individual patients and their personal goals. We all want to remain healthy but we also want to live the life that matters most to us. Which aspects of our health we value most and want to target will vary from person to person. The illnesses I fear as a largely deskbound academic who likes to read may differ from others employed in outdoor work or who enjoy mountain climbing. Given that everyone ages in different ways, health care should be flexible enough to respond accordingly.

Whose Responsibility?

This shift to preventative health places a much greater responsibility on the individual. David Cutler, professor of applied economics at Harvard University, notes that "the single most unused person in healthcare is the patient." That is all set to change. Right now, once they have presented themselves at the doctor's or the hospital, patients tend to become passive participants in a process. Measurements, diagnosis and interventions become the responsibility of trained medical staff.

In a world where preventative care is crucial, the patient will need to become much more engaged. They could scan whatever information their smartphone provides and note changes, and make use of new consumables that provide information or monitor their own blood sugar.

There is much that can be done to delay seeing your doctor. Rather than go to a doctor when you have diabetes, it is best to take action before then. Diabetes is defined by a fasting blood sugar level of 7 mmol/L, but as with so many medical measures it isn't simply about a particular threshold that defines you as healthy or unhealthy. Keeping your sugars low for as long as possible is key. You don't need to be a medical expert but you could invest in understanding your health and know what key indicators to look out for and what steps to take.

These reforms are far-reaching and require a great deal of coordination. The scale of change required is considerable and that points to a role for government. Precisely what that role is will vary from country to country as the institutional specifics of health care vary enormously. Everywhere public health is part of a government's agenda, but health care is a mix of public or private provision. And the broad range of influences on how we age means that much of our health is determined outside the health system. Governments need to set healthy life expectancy as a target and create longevity councils with the responsibility for closing the gap between healthspan and lifespan. The US has a Council of Economic Advisers and the UK has its Monetary Policy Committee. We need similar groups overseeing the health of the nation, advocating change and chasing targets.

The Scientific Solution

As well as changes to the health system, the second longevity revolution will also require advances in scientific methods. Progress has already been made with several age-related illnesses, especially cardiovascular disease, diabetes and some forms of cancer. But given the increasing importance of age-related diseases, a greater focus on the biology of aging and efforts to directly influence the aging process itself will be needed.

Over the last twenty years there has been remarkable progress in geroscience, the study of the biology of aging. It turns out that aging may be a lot more malleable than we imagined. But what exactly has been learnt and what does it mean for our future? Can we really manipulate our rate of aging and are we about to discover a cure?

Why We Age

The Greek mathematician Archimedes may have been the first but he wasn't the only scientist to experience a "eureka" moment while sitting in his bath. Professor Tom Kirkwood was pondering the mysteries of aging while taking a bath at his Newcastle home in 1977. The English biologist's insight was how even if an animal was not genetically designed to age, evolutionary forces would work to make aging a reality. This is important for geroscience as it suggests that biological aging may not be as hardwired into genetics as previously thought.

Behind Kirkwood's insight is a difference between two types of cells. Cells crucial to the perpetuation of the species—known as the germline and represented by the sperm and the egg—survive forever through reproduction. All the other cells in the body, collectively known as somatic cells, are nonreproductive. They are prone to constant threats of damage, mutation and other forms of disruption, which eventually lead to death.

The evolutionary imperative is to ensure that germline cells survive through reproduction so that the species continues. Kirkwood recognized that that makes the body crucial only to the extent that it helps transfer the germline across time—from parents to children. The body is like an envelope carrying an important letter. So long as the letter arrives the envelope can be thrown away. Hence the phrase "disposable soma."

Cells require energy in order to function. Given that the body's energy supply is limited, decisions have to be made whether to allocate this energy at a cellular level toward either growth, reproduction or repair. Imagine an animal that is genetically designed not to age. That means its body directs its cellular energy to ensure maintenance and youth. Despite not aging the animal still faces a mortality risk due to infectious diseases and predators. Let's assume that because of these threats the animal has only a 50 percent chance of surviving each year.

Now imagine it develops a genetic mutation that means less energy is used in maintenance (thereby speeding up the aging process) but more is allocated to growth and reproduction. On the plus side the animal will grow more quickly (fending off predators and disease) and will reproduce more quickly (ensuring the germline is extended). On the negative side, the longer the animal lives the more frail and vulnerable it becomes. That sounds like bad news but if the animal has only a 50 percent chance of surviving each year this downside will have limited impact on reproduction. Only about 6 percent of animals make it to age four and so older animals of this species make only a small contribution to passing on the germline. Much more advantageous to the survival of the species is the boost to growth and reproduction occurring in the early years. Therefore, thanks to natural selection, over time animals with this particular genetic mutation will outnumber those who don't.

Kirkwood's "disposable soma" logic is effectively the inverse of the evergreen imperative. The "body as envelope" approach suggests that faced with a low probability of reaching older ages, it is better for evolution to focus on growth and reproduction rather than aging and maintenance. It is an explanation of why we age but one which has an important corollary.

The point is that aging has never been a priority for the evolutionary process. Evolution selects toward genes that help boost reproduction but it doesn't select against things that affect us after reproduction. If aging were programmed in our cells to convey an evolutionary advantage then it wouldn't occur at ages which so few humans used to live to. That suggests aging is more a consequence of evolutionary neglect rather than intent.

This creates both a challenge and an opportunity for the evergreen agenda. The challenge is that while there are many things we can do to support healthy aging there is still a biological reality at work. If we want to age better, major breakthroughs in geroscience will be required. The opportunity is that if aging is a bug and not a programmed genetic feature then there are grounds to be optimistic that we can find ways to manipulate how we age. This is the scientific solution to the evergreen agenda.

How We Age

If Kirkwood provides an insight into why we age, the search is on to understand how we do so. To provide answers major universities have established new centers based on the biology of aging, with high-profile professors engaged in pioneering work. Both *Nature* and the *Lancet*, prestigious academic publications, have launched specialist journals devoted to the topic. Fame, fortune and immortality (at least reputationally) await anyone who makes a major breakthrough.

An additional sign that an established field is emerging is a newly minted consensus on what have become known as the "hallmarks of aging"—the diverse biological processes that collectively constitute biological aging.[24] The hallmarks are twelve in number: (i) genomic instability; (ii) telomere attrition; (iii) epigenetic alterations; (iv) loss of proteostasis; (v) disabled macroautophagy; (vi) deregulated nutrient sensing; (vii) mitochondrial dysfunction; (viii) cellular senescence; (ix) stem cell exhaustion; (x) alterated intercellular communication; (xi) chronic inflammation; and (xii) dysbiosis.

Each of these hallmarks in different ways explains the cellular and molecular damage that leads to biological aging. Explaining how each hallmark works would take us far beyond the longevity imperative, but consider as an example the eighth hallmark—cellular senescence.[25]

Normal human cells continually replicate and divide in order for the body to grow and repair itself. A famous finding by the American biologist Leonard Hayflick in the 1960s established that there was a limit to how many times a cell can divide (somewhere between forty and sixty). Once cells have reached their replication limit they enter a zombie-like state and become senescent. The older you get, the greater the accumulation of these senescent cells. Like bad apples in a bowl, these worn-out cells fuel inflammation in the body causing other cells to become senescent. The immune system becomes steadily less effective at countering them. All of this is part of the cellular process that characterizes biological aging and its "gradual then suddenly" nature. Exploiting a growing understanding of this hallmark, researchers are now trying to develop a new class of drugs—known as senolytics—that target and remove these senescent cells. The hope is such treatments may, for instance, help tackle arthritis. That would be a welcome Dorian Gray outcome.

Another area full of potential involves stem cells (the ninth hallmark). When stem cells divide they either form other stem cells or assume a specific cellular function in different parts of the body—the liver, the heart, the brain, the skin and so on. However, the more they divide the more they suffer from stem cell exhaustion. The result is effectively coding errors such that new cells fulfill their function less well. In an extraordinary result, Nobel Prize winner Shinya Yamanaka showed it is possible to reverse this process and convert adult cells back to their "pluripotent" form (stem cells with the ability to take any cellular form in the body).[26] That raises the possibility of using an individual's own cells to create pluripotent stem cells which could then replenish aging parts of the body—a Wolverine type of treatment.

All this is incredibly exciting and there is a real and justified sense of progress being made, both in theory and in the lab. But reaching an understanding about how biological aging happens doesn't necessarily mean that we will be able to control the process. The fact that there are twelve hallmarks, all of which may interact with one another, points to just how complicated the aging process might be.

I have spent much of my career studying another forbiddingly multidimensional system—the economy. Like the human body, a national economy runs on complicated networks of interconnected systems and is vulnerable to external shocks. As a result, predicting economic outcomes is a difficult if not foolish task. Yet governments have found that a limited number of policy instruments—notably tax rates, interest rates and government expenditure—can exert an outsize influence on the economic future. What if a similar approach was applied to aging and a few key pathways could transform how we age?

That is exactly what Cynthia Kenyon, an American molecular biologist at the University of California—San Francisco discovered in 1993. She found that altering just one gene (*daf-2*) in a species of roundworm (*C. elegans*) was sufficient to make them live twice as long as normal.[27] They also appeared to remain healthy to the end. In other words, they were Peter Pan not Struldbrugg worms. It is a long way from worms to humans—our genetic frameworks are much more elaborate than theirs—but Kenyon's reaction to her discovery was notable: "You just think, 'Wow. Maybe I could be that long-lived worm.'"

Kenyon's finding is of critical importance as it shows that aging may be strongly influenced by just a few key pathways rather than manipulation of the entire system. And Kirkwood's disposable soma suggests why aging may be more malleable than previously thought.

To see what this might mean in terms of future treatments that make us age better, let's pursue the comparison between the economy and the biology of aging. The economy is vulnerable to multiple shocks and interactions between different parts of the system create instability. Further, when economies are struck by larger shocks, the ability of governments to smooth their impact is limited. Exactly the same holds for the body and so while breakthroughs in geroscience may improve how we age there's no guarantee of instant success and certainly no promise of immortality. The nature of aging will always create challenges. As Stanford's Professor Tom Rando notes: "It's not A causes B causes C causes D causes aging. It's a network diagram of nodes and links—all subject to feedback loops where consequences become causes—that gradually become more and more destabilized."[28] As with the economy, we may be able to influence aging to achieve better outcomes but that doesn't mean we will be able to perfectly control it.

There is also no single magic trick for fixing a troublesome economy. Governments use multiple policy levers to address inflation, unemployment, trade and growth. Similarly, there is unlikely to be a single treatment that tackles all the hallmarks of aging. There may be different patterns of aging for the brain, the heart, the skin, the immune system, and so on. The fact that the incidence of a number of diseases rises with age and that they can therefore be called age-related diseases doesn't mean that the same biological pathway of aging is at work in each case.

That suggests—just as governments use a combination of broad measures (interest rates, exchange rates) and more targeted combinations of policies (investment credits, capital tax relief and employment subsidies)—that we can expect something similar whenever geroscience leads to successful drug development. Kenyon's findings that a limited number of genes can change aging in a worm is an amazing insight. But aging in humans is likely to involve more pathways. As a result, the more complex the biology of an animal the less impact on longevity can be expected from any one specific intervention.

Finally, economic interventions in one area often have an impact elsewhere. For instance, when trying to control inflation central banks raise interest rates. That may lower inflation but it also leads to slower growth and higher unemployment. Similarly, any treatments targeting biological age will need to be assessed for adverse side effects. For example, cancer can be less of a threat at older ages as all cells grow more slowly, including malignant ones. If we age better, this might no longer be the case. Sometimes solving one problem creates a dilemma somewhere else.

But despite these caveats there ought to be little doubt that the potential treatment of the hallmarks of aging opens up exciting prospects for geroscience. This is reflected in the bracing optimism of many researchers. David Sinclair, a professor of genetics at Harvard Medical School, says: "I believe that aging is a disease. I believe it is treatable. I believe we can treat it within our lifetimes."[29]

The British biogerontologist Aubrey de Grey is similarly optimistic. With his flowing beard, striking turns of phrase and fondness for intellectual combat, de Grey is a distinctive and controversial figure in longevity research. His Twitter account has the simple but ambitious statement: "I'm spearheading the global crusade to defeat ageing." He has invented terms such as "The Methuselarity" (the march toward a rejuvenation breakthrough which will spare us from age-related ill-health) and "longevity escape velocity" (the point at which life expectancy increases by more than a year every year).

With this mix of heady concepts, hard numbers and relentless logical projections, de Grey's views get a lot of attention. De Grey's concern is that unless the message is conveyed loudly and dramatically not only will insufficient research funding be forthcoming to tackle the most urgent health problem society faces but we will also be unprepared for the scientific breakthroughs which, he believes, are about to unfold. According to de Grey, "there's going to be absolute total pandemonium as soon as this technology becomes widely anticipated."[30]

But these arguments are dangerous for others in the longevity camp. While they raise interest in the topic they also raise expectations and the risks of both overpromising and mockery. In addition they trigger a sense of public queasiness over achieving immortality rather than a sense of excitement about targeting the most pressing health problem of today—age-related diseases. This group prefers to emphasize the gradual emergence of a second longevity revolution, driven by the cumulative progress of academic paper after academic paper, animal trial after animal trial before finally shifting to human trials. They avoid the "I" word (immortality) and stress the "H" word—(healthspan), focusing on the Dorian Gray scenario of looking and feeling good at all ages. In scientific terms, they emphasize the importance of achieving a full compression of morbidity—reducing the onset of chronic illness to the very end of life. They talk of "healthy aging" rather than "longevity," stressing the evergreen insight tells us that healthy aging is our most urgent imperative.

Measuring Biological Age

In Greek mythology there were three female Fates, usually depicted as celestial seamstresses, who together determined the length of our individual destinies. Clotho spun the thread of life, Lachesis used her measuring rod to determine its length and Atropos, eldest of the three, determined when to cut it. You couldn't deny your fate. Chronological age might tell you how long you have lived but it didn't tell you how soon you would fall victim to Atropos' blade.

A similar problem afflicts chronological age in an evergreen world. A host of everyday expressions (such as "they look good for their age" or "I am feeling my age") suggest a subtle difference between the number of candles on our birthday cake and our intuitive sense of aging. It is this underlying concept of aging that is crucial for an evergreen agenda. If aging is malleable then it is this more subtle underlying concept of aging that we wish to manipulate, not the candles on our cake. That means that if preventative health is to succeed then we need a way of rivaling Lachesis' measuring rod and to find ways of quantifying how we are aging.

Recognizing this, geroscience is building on the hallmarks of aging and developing ways to measure biological age. Discovering the hidden secrets of our body is a powerful idea. Even more powerful is the thought of acting in response to this measure by slowing down aging and claiming control over our fate.

The current state-of-the-art approach is that of German-American geneticist Steve Horvath, one of the elite scientists recruited by Altos Labs, the California-based cellular rejuvenation research company. Horvath has developed a sophisticated DNA-based test known as the Horvath aging clock, which accurately estimates biological age based on DNA methylation levels.[31] Our DNA changes due to epigenetics—that is interactions with our behavior and the environment. DNA methylation is part of that process whereby methyl groups attach themselves to certain segments of DNA and turn some genes off. For Horvath, aging "is a bit like rust on a car . . . as we age, things change . . . and these changes are methylation, so by measuring the amount of 'rust' you can measure the age." For the record, this particular test is linked to the third of our hallmarks of aging: epigenetic alterations.

The potential of these biological measures of age is substantial, but as with so much geroscience there are still numerous issues to be resolved before we can claim a victory. In the television series *The Simpsons* Dr. Hibbert tells Marge: "Well we can't fix [Homer's] heart but we can tell you exactly how damaged it is." Unless we can learn how to regulate our biological age, measuring it has limited benefits.

Equally, we also need to be sure that lowering *measured* biological age is the same thing as genuinely lowering our biological age. A thermometer records room temperature but if I lower the thermometer reading by wrapping it in a cold towel I will have done nothing to impact the room temperature itself. Only the measurement has changed, not the underlying reality. We need to be sure that the biomarkers used to measure biological age aren't just correlated with aging but are causally connected with how we age. The good news is that there are promising early signs that measures of biological age are both malleable and do accurately reflect our underlying health. It is just an irony that only the passing of chronological time will enable us to know for sure whether my measure of biological age is a reliable estimate of my longevity.

The other challenge is whether there really is a single number which summarizes how you are aging. We know people age differently. For some people, it is their immune system that ages more rapidly, for others their cardiovascular system or their skin or their cognitive processes. There may be separate measures of biological age for different parts of our body. If this is true, we can then focus on the ones that need the most attention. Discovering which parts of your body are aging most rapidly will be invaluable for improving preventative health.

Drug Development

The ultimate aim of geroscience is to develop drugs to support the evergreen agenda. That means either "geroprotectors" that help ward off aging (prevention) or "gerotherapeutics" that tackle age-related diseases (intervention). But unlike research focused on cancer or dementia, geroscience focuses on the process of aging itself rather than a single disease. The dominance of the disease paradigm in our health system means that this shift of focus requires major changes in drug development.

The average time it takes to develop a successful drug from start to finish is around twelve years.[32] Most drugs don't even make it that far. Only around one in a thousand drugs makes it through preclinical trials (conducted in laboratories and usually based on animal testing). Of those that pass the first hurdle, only one in ten survives through the next three stages of clinical testing aimed at establishing safety and effectiveness. All this makes drug development an expensive business: the average cost of taking a drug to market is $1.3 billion.[33] As a result, new drugs appear much less often than doctors and patients would like.

The development process needs to be quicker, cheaper and more reliable. The two great hopes here are artificial intelligence (AI) and repurposing existing drugs. Pharmaceutical companies are investing billions of dollars in AI research programs. The hope is that AI can search through all past research and trials and find previously undiscovered patterns that can help with drug design and drug testing.

The second area of rich potential derives from our improved knowledge of the hallmarks of aging. It is possible that drugs used to treat one age-related disease may also be effective against others. The best-known example here is metformin, a drug that was first described in the medical literature in 1922. It has since become one of the world's most widely used anti-diabetic medications. A number of studies have suggested that it may have potential as a geroprotector.[34] Diabetics who took the drug have in some studies been shown to live longer and be less likely to experience age-related disease than non-diabetics not taking metformin. But before you rush off to place an order for metformin be aware that this finding is controversial and not yet proven in a drug trial. Nonetheless it does offer the tantalizing prospect of a cheap drug (metformin costs around 30 cents per pill) that could help us age better and be taken as regularly as statins and aspirin.

Even so, geroscience's focus on aging hits problems when it comes to drug trials. The aim of a drug trial is to provide evidence of success—or otherwise—in treating a disease. That is a problem because aging isn't recognized as a disease. Whether it should be is controversial. In 2022 the WHO updated its International Classification of Diseases and replaced "senility"—a word that over time had become pejorative—with "old age." So great was the resulting protest that they backtracked, replacing "old age" with a more nuanced definition:

"the decline in intrinsic capacity associated with aging."[35] The change may seem subtle but it is important. If our evergreen aim is to avoid underestimating the capacity of our later years then it is clearly problematic to define people as diseased simply because they are old. Yet not everyone agrees with this. David Sinclair argues that it is prejudicial *not* to classify aging as a disease. He argues: "The current view that aging is acceptable is agism in itself."[36]

Others point out that the fact that aging is a driver of many diseases does not mean that aging itself is a disease. Similarly, if aging is multidimensional then it may not reflect a single process or be defined as a single disease. In short, this debate reveals many fault lines. "Aging" is a portmanteau term capturing many different meanings. The sense in which scientists see "aging" as a disease is radically different from the sense "aging" has in other contexts. That makes it almost inevitable that the phrase "aging" triggers misunderstanding in any debate on how to age better.

Within geroscience, the fact that there are twelve different hallmarks of aging suggests there is plenty of room for argument about what exactly comprises aging. From this perspective, the refusal to recognize "aging" as a disease is really a challenge to geroscientists to assess, describe and rank the hallmarks of aging more precisely.

Yet there's another problem with drug trials aimed at therapeutic treatments for aging—they can't be done in a hurry. Ideally, you would track a group of young and healthy people over many years in order to chart the long-term differences between those who used geroprotector drugs and those who didn't. Given that pharmaceutical companies chafe at the expense of long-term trials, waiting for young people to grow old isn't an appealing commercial prospect. Randomized control trials, the most established way of assessing the efficacy of any treatment, can't easily be done on treatments aimed at healthy longevity.

But this is another reason for excitement about biological measures of aging. If they are reliable, they can bypass the need for lengthy trials. That is why biomarkers of aging are a key component in a proposed trial, handily entitled TAME (targeting aging with metformin), set up to assess metformin's ability to act as a geroprotector. Led by Professor Nir Barzilai and designed in consultation with the US Food and Drug Administration (FDA), the TAME trial will track 3,000 individuals aged between sixty-five and seventy-nine over a six-year period.[37] Barzilai's team will be charting not the incidence of a single disease but a composite of various age-related conditions—including cancer, dementia and heart disease. Accompanying this conventional monitoring will be measures of biological age to assess the impact of metformin on the aging process itself.

Not everyone is enamored by metformin. Some doubt its effectiveness. Others argue that it works but its effects are small and more powerful treatments should be tested instead. But even if the TAME trial concludes that metformin is ineffective all will not be lost; its methods have been designed to provide an FDA-approved template for the evaluation of drug targeting aging.

If you are keen to follow progress in developing aging therapeutics, keep an eye on treatments for dogs. Those of us who have pets usually want them to stick around as long as they possibly can in comfort. That helps explain why annual expenditure on pets in the United States is worth nearly $110 billion and around $1,400 for each dog. But as anyone who has ever owned a dog will know, their lives are long enough for us to fall helplessly in love with them but short enough to break our hearts. Most dogs live for ten to thirteen years. That makes an attractive market for longevity treatments as testing can be done more quickly and much more free of regulatory oversight. That is the aim of Matt Kaeberlein, a professor at Washington University in Seattle, and his Dog Aging Project. It is remarkable how swiftly talk of slowing down aging in humans leads to concerns about immortality. I have never heard that concern expressed around interventions for dogs. Watch your pooch for early indications of aging breakthroughs.

This Time it's Different

For all its recent progress, the longevity sector has a problem—a long-standing tradition of overpromising. As far back as 1317, Pope

John XXII condemned alchemists, with their search for the philosopher's stone and an elixir of life, because "they promise what they do not produce." A lot more overpromising has happened since then and it is likely a lot more will be done in the years ahead. Geroscience has a millennial-long credibility problem that affects its perception as we begin a second longevity revolution.

Because there is always money to be made in promoting longevity there has never been any shortage of gurus claiming to possess the secret. In their book *The Quest for Immortality*, Bruce Carnes and Jay Olshansky pungently write that "the life extension industry begins with a grain of truth but quickly gets mixed with a tablespoon of bad science, a cup of greed, a pint of exaggeration and a gallon of human desire for a longer, healthier life—a recipe for false hope, broken promises and unfulfilled dreams."[38] Olshansky went on to establish the Silver Fleece Award for Anti-Aging Quackery for the "product with the most ridiculous, outrageous, scientifically unsupported or exaggerated assertions about aging or age-related diseases." The prize? A bottle of vegetable oil relabeled "Snake Oil."

In every financial bubble, investors invariably fall for the belief that "this time it's different." Whether it is the South Sea Company, railroad mania, the Dot-com revolution or the recent surge and fall in cryptocurrency prices, investors believe that something new is happening that will radically transform the future and justify surging expectations and asset prices. Sir John Templeton, described by *Money* magazine in 1999 as "arguably the greatest stock picker of the century," famously said that "this time it's different" were the four most dangerous words an investor could hear.

Similarly, each generation finds new ways of believing that a cure for aging is within its grasp based on tantalizing reports from the scientific frontier. Given the history of visionaries, quacks and charlatans, there is an understandable tendency to be skeptical. It is like the Aesop's fable of the little boy who cried wolf. If you cry wolf too many times eventually no one listens to you.

It is, though, too easy to look back and mock. The frontiers of science are murky. No one at the cutting edge knows for sure what might work and what won't. In the 1920s Eugen Steinach became a celebrity advocating partial vasectomy as a means of slowing down aging and preserving vitality. Steinach's clients included Sigmund Freud and the "gland old man" W. B. Yeats. Eventually Steinach's longevity methods were revealed to be worthless, but he was a serious endocrinologist who was nominated nine times for a Nobel Prize. While his ideas on slowing aging were proved wrong his work on hormones directly led to the discovery of insulin, which has led to substantial improvements in both healthy life expectancy and life expectancy.

Current research in geroscience will similarly lead to three distinct paths. One path will be frontier science that leads to genuine breakthroughs that help us age better. Another path will eventually lead nowhere. Then there will be a host of treatments with little scientific merit that capitalize, sometimes fraudulently, on the promise of current scientific breakthroughs. This is an area where there will always be headlines that run ahead of reality and plenty of candidates for the Silver Fleece Award. In fact the more that geroscience appears to be making genuine progress the louder will be the claims of Silver Fleecers trying to hitch a ride. It is worth bearing that in mind in the years ahead as more stories and more products emerge claiming evergreen properties.

But the reason we keep thinking that "this time it is different" is that history also tells another story. Not of swindlers and fraudsters but of scientific heroes overcoming challenges with breakthrough technologies that have led us to the reality of the young now expecting to become the very old. Why should we expect that progress to end? Surely tackling the mysteries of aging is just the next of nature's secrets that science will reveal? Even if it doesn't happen now, eventually it will, so that one day things really will be different. When as serious an authority as Francis Crick, the Nobel Prize-winning discoverer of DNA, says that "eventually, the process of aging, which is unlikely to be simple, should be understandable . . . Hopefully, some of its processes can be slowed down or avoided," it is reasonable to believe.

There are certainly some signs that this time it really may be different. The first is the recent progress geroscience has made.

Slowing aging in the lab is now a routine event.[39] That has never been possible before. At the moment the promise is still greater than the achievement but undeniable progress has been made.

Secondly, serious money is beginning to flow into geroscience. Funding of longevity companies is increasing rapidly, reaching $5.2 billion in 2022. That is small change compared to an overall pharmaceutical research and development budget of $83 billion, but the longevity trend is unmistakably positive. With this funding comes a number of trials for longevity treatments. At the time of writing, there are ninety-nine preclinical trials for longevity therapeutics focused on the biological pathways of aging, an additional fifteen in phase one (focusing on safety and dosage), twenty-five in phase two (effectiveness and side effects) and nine in phase three (comparing new treatment to existing treatments). Given the risky nature of biotech investments, it is to be expected a large number of these will fail. But a pipeline is emerging.

Thirdly, there are signs that some of the science is making its way into the mainstream. The National University of Singapore is collaborating with the health system to open a Longevity Clinic at Alexandra Hospital. The aim is to design individualized plans to slow aging that incorporate geroscience developments and biological measures of aging. With the goal of providing five more years of healthy life to the average Singaporean, this is a first attempt at a new evergreen approach to health provision. A health revolution has begun ushering in a second longevity revolution.

What Will Happen and When?

So what does the future hold for geroscience? Given the current scale and ingenuity of research on aging, it is hard to deny that something will happen. But the key questions are what and when?

But first the caveats. A lot needs to happen before effective anti-aging treatments become widely available. More progress needs to be made in understanding the twelve hallmarks and how they work separately and jointly. Regardless of recent work, geroscience remains a work in progress. Even when the biology of aging is understood, research will have to be done on medicines and treatments. That too will take time. Then there are the long lags involved in drug trials, further delaying the rollout. Nor should we overestimate the speed at which intellectual progress will happen. The search for cancer cures has made great strides but after decades of research we still haven't declared victory even if now there is optimism it will happen one day. Much less progress has been made in tackling dementia.

There are also reasons to be cautious about the progress made to date. Felipe Sierra is chief scientific officer at the Hevolution Foundation, which supports aging-related research, and is the former director of aging biology at the US National Institute on Aging. "None of this is ready for primetime," he warns. "The bottom line is I don't try any of these [anti-aging products]. Why don't I? Because I'm not a mouse."[40] We may share 92 percent of our DNA with mice but when it comes to translating clinical trials that were successful on mice to clinical trials on humans there is a statistical echo—the failure rate is also close to 92 percent.

One problem is that mice are renowned for their "shortgevity." Getting an animal that ages quickly to age more slowly might not provide a useful benchmark for humans who already have long lives. As Steve Austad, who has the unusual distinction of listing the title of both professor of biology and lion tamer on his C.V., argues in his 2022 book *Methuselah's Zoo*, more attention should be devoted to studying animals which have exceptional rather than limited longevity.

In terms of future progress for geroscience, there are broadly three possibilities. One is that the field turns out to be totally barren. Given recent progress this seems unlikely—something will emerge that will help in some way. A second possibility is step-by-step advances where science builds cumulatively toward an evergreen goal. The third and final possibility is radical breakthroughs that lead not to incremental changes but to dramatic improvements in how we age in terms of both healthspan and life expectancy.

The experience of our battles against cancer and dementia—billions of dollars invested, years of continuing research—suggests caution is the wisest approach. The likeliest outcome for geroscience is the steady accumulation of knowledge and the gradual development of specialized therapeutics tackling different but potentially limited aspects of aging.

Seán Ó hÉigeartaigh, executive director of Cambridge's Centre for the Study of Existential Risk, summarizes this form of progress neatly when he says, "Extending max lifespan significantly in the near-term seems unlikely to me; but identifying and arresting aging-related factors that increase preponderance and severity of age-related conditions is more plausible."[41]

In other words, progress will happen, it will happen cumulatively and its first stage will be in improving healthspan. That seems at least intuitively right. We saw in chapter 2 that there are already many eighty- and ninety-year-olds in reasonably good health. There aren't however any 130-year-olds. That combination of facts suggests that extending lifespan beyond 122 will be more challenging than improving healthspan for those in their seventies, eighties and nineties. For now the evidence points to a Dorian Gray outcome as not only the most valuable but also the most plausible.

How might these improvements in healthy life expectancy show up? One realistic near-term goal is to develop senolytic drugs that might delay, prevent or reverse age-related diseases such as arthritis. Even some form of rejuvenation is a realistic prospect given our growing ability to use stem cells and cellular reprogramming to repair human organs such as the liver. In both these cases, potential treatments are already in Phase II trials and it is not unreasonable to expect them to come to market within the next ten years. Existing drugs, such as metformin or rapamycin, mentioned in chapter 2, could also be repurposed as geroprotectors within that time frame if they are shown to be safe and effective in trials. Nothing is guaranteed in terms of any particular treatment, but the idea of progress being made in the short run is more than possible.

As a fifty-seven-year-old I find it perfectly reasonable to expect that I will still be around to benefit from these developments in terms of healthspan and maybe even lifespan. As knowledge accumulates and a virtuous evergreen circle demands more investment into healthspan and lifespan, it is reasonable to expect greater progress further out. Drug development isn't quick. There are sure to be more failures than successes and optimism may waver en route. Yet the younger you are the more these cumulative gains will add substantially to your healthspan and lifespan.

How Far Can We Go?

In 2001 Steve Austad, the lion tamer, and Jay Olshansky, the hunter of snake oil merchants, attended a conference in Los Angeles. In reply to a reporter who asked when we will see the first-ever 150-year-old human, Austad woke the conference up by claiming that they had probably already been born. Olshansky disagreed and the pair settled on a wager. Each of them arranged for $150 to be paid into a special fund each year for the next 150 years (their annual stake has since increased to $300). If by the year 2150 someone makes it to 150 years old, the contents of the fund will be paid to Austad (or his descendants). If no one has lived that long, the money will go to Olshansky's family.[42] Based on historic rates of return, by 2150 the fund should be worth around $1 billion (compounding interest works wonders on a 150-year timescale). The same might be said for the cumulative impact of scientific discoveries. An awful lot can happen in a century and a half.

The choice of 150 was interesting. It's just the right length to seem thoroughly improbable yet at the same time not ludicrously impossible, given Jeanne Calment reached 122. We probably all sense that we'll need more than sound lifestyle choices to survive that long. However much broccoli and fermented cabbage we eat, however well we sleep or exercise, getting to 150 will depend entirely on major breakthroughs in geroscience. If Austad is to win his bet, his future 150-year-old will today be twenty-two. That gives

Austad roughly a sixty-year window for the development of gero-therapeutics that will effectively slow an eighty-year-old's further aging and put them on a path for being alive in 2150. Whether that is achievable depends on the limits to both human ingenuity and human biology. History points to the power of human ingenuity, but for all the excitement about recent progress in geroscience there is currently zero evidence that the human lifespan can be increased by even a day.

Regardless of who wins Austad's wager, the very notion of a 150-year-old life shows just how radical the evergreen era is. The evergreen virtuous circle demands that we contemplate the possibility. Dorian Gray outcomes are what we currently most value and are what are probably most likely from a scientific perspective. But if we can understand the biology of aging sufficiently to achieve Dorian Gray outcomes then the chase will move on to further extensions in life expectancy and Peter Pan outcomes. Whether that is achievable at all, let alone by 2150, is today unknowable. But an evergreen logic demands we consider the prospect of a future 150-year-old life. It will, though, be biology and not logic that determines whether it will ever be a reality.

The American futurist Roy Amara, president of the impressively named Institute for the Future, remarked that "We tend to overestimate the effect of a technology in the short run and underestimate the effect in the long run." Amara's law, as it is known, is an interesting take on current geroscience development. For the first time ever as humans we can expect the young and middle-aged to become the old or very old. Investing in how we age and trying to improve how we do so will become increasingly important. It is early days and many disappointments, advances and setbacks will occur. Short-term pessimism combined with long-term optimism seems a good lens through which to view the exciting progress geroscience is making. Get ready for fundamental change in what it is to be human.

5

Seizing an Economic Dividend

Retirement at sixty-five is ridiculous. When I was sixty-five I still had pimples.

George Burns

"I'm going to work until I die, if I can, because I need the money." Those are the words of Richard Dever, a seventy-four-year-old American who traveled 1,400 miles from his home in Indiana to work at a campground in Maine cleaning showers and cutting the grass.[1] Mr. Dever is not alone in stretching his working life out as long as he can. One in six Americans his age are still working and their numbers are rising, as they are throughout the OECD economies.[2]

If declining health in old age is our primary fear of living longer, it is closely followed by worries about running out of money. Short of winning a lottery there are two main remedies for this fear, but neither is especially appealing. The first is to spend less and save more, spreading your lifetime income more thinly over the years. The other is Mr. Dever's path—keep working in order to keep earning. Depending on how much you can save that may mean working until you die. If neither option appeals, you could always follow the advice of an old *New Yorker* cartoon and mix the two: "If we take a late retirement and an early death, we'll just squeak by."

Which of these two paths you follow will depend on your individual circumstances. How much money do you need? How physically demanding is your job? Do you enjoy your work? Will your health be good enough to support working longer? Will your employer support you in continuing to work?

As that list of questions reveals, the outcome won't be the same for everyone. But one thing is for sure—you can't duck this either/or situation. You will either have to spend less or work more. For most people, in my view, the result is going to involve working for longer. While a dwindling few may be lucky enough to retire on a decent company pension, for the vast majority of us longer lives require longer working careers.

That is why Richard Dever finds himself working on a campsite aged seventy-four. It is also why governments around the world are raising the age at which a state pension is payable. If you're in your twenties and reading this in Denmark, I hope you're prepared: you will be Richard Dever's age before your state pension kicks in.[3]

I often get a lot of resistance to pointing out the logical implication that longer lives require more years of work. The resistance I get, though, is nothing compared to that which President Macron received in 2023 when, motivated by rising life expectancy, he increased France's retirement age from sixty-two to sixty-four. One million protestors took to the streets as Paris saw riots in response. As we shall see, though, even from a longevity perspective there are valid reasons to protest against simple-minded increases in the retirement age. They simply aren't sufficient to deal with the challenge. Yet it is hard to move away from the conclusion that as a result of the first longevity revolution we need to extend our working lives.

To see why, let's run some numbers. Assume that you can increase how much you save by 1 percent every year for thirty years. In other words, instead of saving 10 percent of your income each year, save 11 percent. An alternative which provides the same financial boost is to delay your retirement date by an additional six months.[4] Which of those options appeals the most? Reducing how much you spend for the next thirty years or working six months more? Most of the time when I ask people which they prefer it's the additional six months that they reluctantly go for. They simply don't feel they have spare money lying around to increase their savings.

There is also another reason why working longer is likely to be the path for most of us. The amount you need to save from your monthly income to fund retirement depends on when you start saving. If you (or the government in the case of state pensions) haven't spent the last twenty years saving that extra 1 percent then you will need to save three times more over the next ten years in order to catch up. By contrast, the financial benefit of those extra six months of work at the end of your career is always the same. The result is that if you are behind in your savings then the working for longer option becomes more attractive over time. That is why longer careers end up being the most likely route to make the finances of a longer life add up.

We seem once more to be back in a gloomy world where longer lives are a problem. Retirement and state pensions were one of the great innovations of the twentieth century. No longer was it necessary to work until you died or became incapacitated and dependent on the goodwill of your family. But the fear is that this is all being washed away. If working life extends into later and later years, how do we avoid the prospect of endless toil and ennui? Once more Samuel Beckett has the appropriately weary and dismal words. When it comes to working in a world of rising longevity it seems to be a case of: "You must go on. I can't go on. I'll go on."[5] It is an economic version of the Struldbruggs, living longer but in a weary, unhappy way.

But surely there is a better way? As with health systems, trying to make existing policies and practices work in the face of longer lives is unsustainable. Just as hiring more doctors and nurses doesn't solve the health problems of an aging society neither does simply stretching out careers and postponing retirement solve the economic challenge of longer lives. If the key challenge for the health system is how to maintain our health for longer, for financing a longer life it is how to maintain our earning capacity for longer. Simply raising the retirement age does little to achieve that. Far more substantial reforms are required.

That is why in this chapter we turn to how to achieve the third dimension of a longevity dividend. The first longevity revolution provided us with one dimension—additional years of life; the previous chapter focused on a second dimension—how to make longer lives also healthier ones. We now focus on the economic dimension—how to pay for longer lives by extending the years we remain productive and engaged.

Being productive, of course, is about far more than just paid work. That is important to stress given that older people are disproportionately involved in volunteering and caring (both for their grandchildren and their spouses).[6] Those are key resources that many of us benefit from and the fact that they go unpaid doesn't mean they aren't productive or valuable. Work also performs many roles other than providing a salary. At its best it can provide a sense of identity, purpose, challenge, enjoyment and community. There is even evidence that finding engagement and community through work helps achieve evergreen outcomes by extending healthy lifespans.[7]

But it is the narrower sense of productivity in terms of paid work that is the focus for now. While longer lives provide more years to spend across a range of different types of activity, it is deciding the number spent in paid work that is most controversial and urgent. We need to find policies that help us finance our longer lives by being productive for longer. Achieving the health revolution outlined in the previous chapter will be a key component of this. If we don't maintain our health then we can't work for longer. But it will also require investing in adult education, redesigning jobs to support the needs of older workers, tackling agism and revamping retirement. This will have radical consequences for how you think and plan your career. Another major challenge will be grappling with variations in health and life expectancy. Not everyone has seen the same improvements in health and longevity or has the same capacity to carry on working. We need policies that deal with this heterogeneity.

So President Macron was right in recognizing that longer lives require more years of work. But supporting that will involve multiple policy innovations. In many ways raising the retirement age is not the most important policy lever to move first. For instance, if you aren't working at retirement age it is highly unlikely you will find work after that time.[8] That makes tackling the problem of employment before retirement a more important policy than raising the retirement age.

The benefits of being productive for longer are not just tied to the individual but spill over to the whole economy. The aging society narrative, with its focus on a rising "old-age dependency ratio," warns of declining economic growth. But if lives are healthier and productive for longer then the evergreen agenda will lead to a boost to GDP growth. That increase in our collective resources is what constitutes the economic longevity dividend.

We have long recognized the benefits to economic growth of investing in health and education for young people. We want them to grow up economically productive because it benefits both them and broader society. But we also need to recognize that the same principles hold for older people. Investing in health and education at older ages will be part of how we realize this economic dividend.

The economies that perform best in the years ahead will be those which unlock this economic longevity dividend. The importance of doing so is already apparent. Over the last ten years workers aged over fifty accounted for the majority of employment growth in the world's richest nations.[9] In the words of leading American social entrepreneur Marc Freedman, "old people are the only natural resource that is increasing in the world."[10] Maintaining productivity through our life and finding ways to tap into this potential are key for our future standard of living.

The Bad News Story of an Aging Society

The question of how to finance a long life may worry us as individuals but it's an even bigger headache at a national level. That is because governments are facing a dual problem. It isn't just that people are living longer but also that right now a very large generational cohort, the babyboomers, are aging. The result is a dramatic increase in the number of people aged over sixty-five, which is putting a lot of pressure on pensions and health care.

It is at this aggregate level that the tendency to underestimate the capacity of later life leads to the most negative conclusions. At the heart of the problem is resources. The standard economic assumption is that older people don't produce them but only consume them. In other words, they don't work or earn money but they do need a pension. Things are made worse by declining health in old age, which demands even more resources to fund health systems. As a result, older people are seen as a burden and bad news for the economy. The main concerns are falling GDP growth, rising government debt, low returns on investment and rising inflation. The consensus is that these negative consequences are already affecting the economy and are only set to get worse in the years ahead.[11] We stand on the precipice of an economic "Agemageddon."

For an evergreen agenda to succeed, we need to understand why an aging society leads to these negative conclusions so as to identify how a longevity society can alleviate them. That involves a quick dive into understanding the determinants of GDP—the size of the economy.

In its simplest form, GDP is driven by two factors—the number of people working ("employment") and the output each worker produces ("productivity"). The number of people working in turn depends on the size of the overall population, what proportion of that population is of working age and, finally, what fraction of the people of working age are employed. An aging society is seen as negatively affecting these components of GDP.

One component of an aging society is declining fertility rates, which reduces the population and makes the potential workforce smaller. That in turn leads to lower GDP. If nothing else changes, a 1 percent fall in population leads to a 1 percent fall in GDP—1 percent fewer people means 1 percent fewer goods and services produced. Take the case of China and Japan, both of which face sharp population declines over the next fifty years. According to the United Nations, China's low birth rate will reduce its population by a quarter and Japan's will shrink by nearly a third. As a result, both countries are staring at substantial declines in GDP growth.

But lower economic growth on its own isn't necessarily a problem. If both GDP and the population fall by 1 percent then the amount of resources available to each person (GDP per capita) doesn't change at all. The real problem comes when there is a shift in the population structure so that there are fewer people of working age. In that case GDP falls by more than the population so there are fewer resources to go around resulting in a lower standard of living and less GDP per capita. This problem is particularly worrying for China and Japan, where working-age populations are set to decline by 22 percent and 14 percent respectively between now and 2070.

The final negative component of an aging society concerns productivity rather than employment. The usual assumption is that older workers are less productive (spoiler alert—assumptions are often wrong). In this case, as the average worker becomes older, even if they are still working, productivity declines and so does GDP growth.

The combined effects of these negative forces—slowing population growth, fewer people of working age and a greater number of less productive older workers—create the pessimistic vision of an economy weighed down by an aging society. For all the economic terminology, the underlying logic is simple. If our later years are not productive then spending more of our life in those years lowers our average lifetime standard of living. Similarly if at any point in time we have more people alive living in those less productive years then the economy will be producing less and GDP will be lower.

The economic problems are not restricted just to GDP growth, though. In a recent book, the London-based economists Charles Goodhart and Manoj Pradhan argue that a "great demographic reversal" is underway.[12] Their thesis is that the world is shifting from a net demographic dividend, caused by a rising number of working-age people, to a demographic burden as the number of older people increases. Combined with the assumption that the glory days of globalization are over, Goodhart and Pradhan add rising wages, higher prices and inflation to the problem of lower GDP growth.

Why rising wages if the overall story is of a weaker economy? That is because both an aging society and a reversal of globalization, which cuts off low-wage economies, leads to a shortage of workers. These higher wages in turn push up both costs and prices, generating higher inflation. Inflation is further fueled by the growing number of older people who are consuming but not producing, leading to higher prices as demand outstrips supply. Again stripped of the economic mechanisms the logic is simple. Fewer workers means higher wages. A battle for resources as more people become unproductive means higher prices.

As if that wasn't enough, an aging society is also believed to explain why interest rates are so low in real terms—that is, relative to inflation. Back in 1985, money in a UK savings account would increase by around 4 percent a year above inflation.[13] By 2012, that rate had fallen to zero and since then has turned negative. Your savings are effectively being shrunk by inflation. Even though interest rates have risen since 2022, this problem still remains. In most countries inflation remains stubbornly high so that the real return on savings remains low. According to Andrew Bailey, governor of the Bank of England, about half of this long-term decline in the real interest rate can be attributed to the effects of an aging society.[14] This isn't an isolated UK phenomenon but a global shift.

Why does an aging society lead to lower real interest rates? The reason is twofold. Firstly a shrinking workforce requires less equipment and smaller premises than are currently supplied, putting downward pressure on the return on capital. The second reason interest rates are kept low is a high level of savings. If you retire at sixty-five but expect to live to ninety, you need a lot more money than if you expect to live only to seventy. Combine this with the large size of the babyboomer cohort and the result is a lot of savings flowing into financial markets to fund retirement but chasing fewer investment opportunities as firms seek to borrow less. The net result is meager interest rates and a host of problems for savers.

While low interest rates might be a problem for savers they are of course good news for borrowers. But that too comes with a sting. Fueled by access to cheap mortgages many countries have experienced a surge in house prices. That is great if you own a house but not if you haven't yet climbed on the housing ladder. Further, it wasn't just house prices that benefited from lower interest rates but a whole host of asset prices, such as equities and bonds. The consequence is that years of low interest rates ended up exacerbating wealth inequality between the haves and the have-nots and increasing intergenerational problems as the value of parents' homes soared while their children became priced out of homes of their own.

That is quite the litany of economic woes, all triggered by demographic factors. It is a worrying economic backdrop but also a convenient one for policymakers to blame so many of today's economic problems on external factors beyond their control. It's all the old people's fault. In this aging society story the dismal science of economics is hard at work turning the good news—we will live longer lives—into bad news—the economy shrinks, inflation rises and we are all worse off.

Investing in Productivity

These negative aging society predictions have something of a Malthusian strain to them. Born in 1766 into a well-to-do family, Thomas Malthus became one of Britain's most influential thinkers. He was a teacher at the East India College in Haileybury, Hertfordshire, where such was his obsession with demography and population that he was known to his students as "Pop." His claim to literary immortality resides in his 1798 book *An Essay on the Principle of Population*.

The main theme of this work is best summed up by his view that "the power of population is indefinitely greater than the power in the earth to produce subsistence." The consequence of this assumption is that rapid population growth would lead to outbreaks of poverty, famine, war and disease, otherwise known as Malthusian catastrophes.

Whereas Malthus focused on the inevitability of population overwhelming our resources, the aging society narrative points to the danger of expanding life expectancy doing the same. Longer lives in poor health and more time in retirement will exhaust our resources. If Malthus argued that society couldn't support a large population, the argument now is that we can't support long lives.

Recent concerns about climate change and environmental sustainability have given new legitimacy to and insight into Malthusian fears. But what is striking about Malthus's warnings is that for all their influence their predictive power has to date been woeful. When Malthus wrote the world's population was near 1 billion. It reached 2 billion in 1927, 3 billion in 1960 and 4 billion by 1974 and today has surpassed 8 billion.

To be fair, like any sensible economic forecaster, Malthus shied away from being too specific about numbers, such as what is the maximum attainable size of the earth's population, as well as dates, such as when any limit will be reached. But given the growth of the global population over the last two hundred years, Malthus clearly overemphasized the limitations on population size.

What defeated Malthus's logic was the surge in productivity arising from the Industrial Revolution. Institutional reform, improvements in technology, investment in physical capital and increases in education and health meant each person could produce more. The result was output and GDP expanded creating the resources that a growing population required. In fact, output grew even faster than the population. That provided even more resources for further investment in technology, health and education, propelling humanity on a virtuous circle to longer, healthier and more productive lives. Malthus, in other words, underestimated human ingenuity and our capacity to provide for ourselves.

Similar innovation and investment will be required if we are to overcome the gloomy prospects of an aging society. The inability to support longer lives has to be overcome by increasing our lifetime productivity. Doing so will once again require investing in technology, health, education and institutional reform with a particular focus on the second half of life. If we live for longer then we need to create more resources to support those additional years and to pay for the investment in health outlined in the previous chapter. If we don't then we will see a decline in our standard of living.

The reason why the aging society analysis is so negative is because it focuses only on the rising proportion of older people. It assumes older people are not productive and destined for bad health and that that cannot be altered. But if the longevity imperative succeeds in making more of our life spent in years of good health and when we are productive then our standard of living increases rather than diminishes. In an evergreen world, GDP is boosted by a longevity dividend rather than diminished by an aging society.

It is the balance between these two forces—the strength of an aging society with its changing age structure versus the longevity imperative's focus on changing how we age—that will determine future economic growth. The balance between these two forces is far from being the same everywhere. In countries such as China and Japan, which are seeing more dramatic increases in their older populations, the aging society effect is much more pronounced than in the US and UK. To mitigate that effect they will need to invest even more in the longevity imperative than the US and the UK if they are to overcome the bleak predictions of Goodhart and Pradhan.

There is perhaps one more thing I should have mentioned about Goodhart and Pradhan's insightful work. *The Great Demographic Reversal* was published in 2020, when Goodhart was eighty-four years old. Some of us are already evergreen and being productive for longer.

Towards an Evergreen Economy

Delivering a longevity dividend by raising our productivity over a longer life will require three distinct sets of government policies: increasing the retirement age, raising the proportion of people working in the years running up to retirement and boosting the productivity of older workers.

Let's start with the first—raising the retirement age. There are limits to how far you can raise the retirement age as well as how effective the policy is, but undeniably it has the potential to boost GDP and provide us with the extra resources longer lives require.

Take the case of the US, where one in three Americans aged sixty-five to sixty-nine is still at work compared to one in two aged sixty to sixty-four. If sixty-five- to sixty-nine-year-olds were as likely to work as sixty- to sixty-four-year-olds, that would add 4.3 million people to the workforce—a 3 percent increase in total employment. The potential gains in other countries are even larger. There's a big employment slowdown in Germany after the age of sixty-five—only one in five Germans aged sixty-five to sixty-nine is still at work, compared to two out of three aged sixty to sixty-four. Extending retirement age has the potential to lead to large increases in GDP.

That is why governments are so keen on raising the retirement age, despite the backlash that politicians inevitably receive, as President Macron can testify. But there is an additional reason governments are so keen on this measure. Every extra year of work is another year of taxes received and one less year of paying a state pension. But while that double financial blessing may be attractive for the government's fiscal position it doesn't do anything to support an evergreen agenda. It does nothing to actually make it possible for people to work for longer. It doesn't tackle their individual health, employability or productivity. A genuinely evergreen economy requires being productive for longer, not forcing people to work for so long they end up feeling like Struldbruggs.

The problem with relying extensively on raising the retirement age becomes apparent when you look more closely at what happens to employment as people turn fifty. At age forty-nine, around four out of every five Americans are working. By the time they reach sixty to sixty-four, only three out of five are working. After the age of sixty-five, it's down to two out of five. The result is that as many Americans stop working between the ages of fifty and sixty-five as do so at retirement age. The problem is particularly acute for those with lower levels of education. At age fifty around nineteen out of twenty American male college graduates are employed, by sixty that has fallen to around fifteen and by sixty-five only about ten of them are. But for those who didn't graduate from high school the corresponding numbers are fifteen, eleven and four. The process of leaving the labor market begins for everyone, regardless of education, years before a state pension is payable.

For a few, leaving employment may be a choice of early retirement, but for the vast majority it is a decision forced upon them.[15] For some, it is about work becoming too physically demanding or difficult. For others, it is about caring responsibilities for partners or parents or their own bad health. Age discrimination also plays a role, making older workers more likely to lose their job and it harder for them to find a new one. Even those who find subsequent employment usually do so at a lower wage. The net impact is that employment after age fifty is far more precarious than many expect and that creates major problems in financing retirement. Helping people to remain productive for longer has to start well before retirement age.

If you are reading this and you are in your forties and fifties, you need to be aware that you are heading into a danger zone. Your main problem isn't what work you'll be doing after you're sixty-five; it's making sure you get to sixty-five and still have a job. Your chances of working into your sixties are heavily influenced by what you get up to in your fifties. If you maintain a steady employment record in this key period then you have an 80 percent chance of still being at work aged sixty-four. If you are only employed 50–80 percent of the time, your chances fall to 42 percent. If you get through your fifties without a job then you're left with only a 4 percent chance of working between sixty-two and sixty-six.[16]

Preventing a post-fifty fall-off in employment is therefore an obvious way to create a longevity dividend. It is less fraught for governments than courting controversy by extending the retirement age. It also makes a larger impact on the workforce. If the fifty to sixty-four age group enjoyed the same rate of employment as the forty-five to forty-nine cohort, America would gain an additional 8 million workers, or 5 percent of total employment. Based on average productivity statistics, that would add around $1.15 trillion to GDP each and every year. That is a very sizable economic longevity dividend.

Harvesting that dividend requires multiple changes, all aimed at raising the productivity of older workers. In order to keep working, people in their fifties and over will obviously need to maintain good health. In the UK, one in six people of working age report themselves as long-term sick (long-term disability in the US). That shows a direct link between investing in the health of older adults, especially reducing health inequality, and boosting GDP. A better focus on adult education and lifelong learning is also needed, so that workers can update their skills as well as learn new ones for new roles.[17] With automation becoming more common, individuals will need to learn new digital skills or learn the non-digital skills required for new roles. Similarly those who previously worked in physically demanding roles will need support and training to adapt to new occupations requiring different skill sets. To support older workers firms will also need to redesign the workplace to accommodate a range of age groups and utilize their different skills and attributes. Also important will be greater use of existing legislation to stamp out age discrimination in hiring and firing.

Raising the retirement age is part of an evergreen agenda in response to growing life expectancy. But on its own its impact will be limited. Just as living longer without improving health is not what we want, so lengthening working careers without extending purpose and increasing productivity is undesirable.

An End to Retirement?

Sir William Osler was a brilliant Canadian physician and one of the founders of the elite medical school at Johns Hopkins University in Baltimore, Maryland. In 1905 he achieved a certain notoriety as a result of a farewell speech he made before taking up the post of regius professor of medicine at Oxford University. He startled his audience by remarking on the uselessness of older men, recommending that they be forced to retire at sixty and euthanized soon afterwards. Osler, who was in his mid-fifties at the time, referred to *The Fixed Period*, a satirical novel by Anthony Trollope set in 1980, which proposed that men in their sixties be "peacefully extinguished by chloroform."

While Osler's speech displayed a misplaced sense of humor the popular press took him seriously and front-page mayhem ensued. For some in his audience, which presumably contained a high number of older men, the real upset was not his unwise joking about chloroform but his emphasis on the uselessness of older men and mandatory retirement. In 1905, the vast majority of men aged over sixty-five still worked as there was no state support for retirement in those days. It wasn't until 1908 that the UK government introduced a state pension and in 1935 that the US Social Security was introduced (both a long way behind Prussia's social security program, introduced by Otto von Bismarck in 1889).

The impact of state pensions on older workers was dramatic. In the UK and US in 1880, around three-quarters of men aged sixty-five years were still working.[18] Over the next hundred years this proportion declined continuously, reaching around one in six in the US and one in twelve in the UK by 1990. In France, only one sixty-five-year-old in fifty was working by 2000. Since then the trend has begun to reverse with one in four now working in the US, one in seven in the UK and around one in twenty in France.

As the pendulum swings back, where, exactly, are we likely to end up? Governments are keen to raise the retirement age, so is Richard Dever mowing lawns at seventy-four in Maine a sign of all our futures? Should governments index retirement age to life expectancy? If an evergreen agenda leads to further increases in life expectancy, will retirement cease to exist?

In order to begin answering these questions we can start with some basic financial arithmetic. That's what I did with my London Business School colleague Lynda Gratton for our 2016 book *The 100-Year Life*.[19] Start with the cautious assumption that when you retire you want to have a pension that pays you 50 percent of your final salary. Further, assume you save 10 percent of your income every year and that your savings are invested half in equities and the other half in a bank account. Based on historical rates of return you can calculate how long you can afford to retire for. If you work until your early seventies, you'll be financially OK until you're eighty-five. If you think you're going to live to be a hundred, you would need to keep working until eighty if you want to hit that 50 percent salary target. Even if you enjoy your work and are fit and able to keep going that long, a sixty-year career probably isn't a very appealing option.

It is important to stress these calculations are not intended as investment advice. That isn't just a necessary legal disclaimer, but a really important point. Long-term financial planning is far too important and individual circumstances much too diverse to base your financial behavior on these simple calculations. But they do help to provide some simple back-of-the-envelope calculations about the link between life expectancy and retirement age. However, their major limitation, other than restrictive assumptions, is they only consider financial motivations.

In reality the choice of when to stop work involves many more trade-offs. When it comes to retirement there are benefits to continuing to work. You earn some money, which is of course useful. You may (or may not) also find your work fulfilling, promoting a sense of identity and purpose as well as providing a community of friends and acquaintances. But there are also costs. Some of these are financial—commuting costs, buying work clothes, paying for lunch or for someone to look after the family. There are also non-financial costs such as commuting time, the physical discomfort and difficulty of work, the stress involved or the psychological loss you feel from not spending time with your family.

If these negative costs increase with age (due to declining health, increasing caring obligations and the like) and the benefits decline (your pay diminishes, work becomes boring, you encounter agism or have less need of money), there will come a point where the costs of working outweigh the benefits. That is when you will want to retire.[20] We can use this broader framework to answer our earlier questions about the future of retirement and how governments should adapt to longer lives.

The Perils of Average

The first obvious conclusion is that there isn't a single retirement age that works for everyone. If you are in poor health, perform a physically demanding job or have accumulated the funds you need, you will want to retire earlier. If you need money, are in good health or enjoy work and it provides you with a sense of community and purpose, you will want to keep at it. This diversity is why it is unwise for governments to run one-size-fits-all retirement policies based on average life expectancy.

Consider the Struldbrugg case where life expectancy increases but health continues to decline with age. Living an extra year of life means you need more money if you aren't going to see your standard of living fall. But working for another year, especially in poor health or in a difficult job, is unattractive. You will need to balance the prospect of a lower standard of living against the unpleasantness of another year of work. The better your health, the higher your wage and the more enjoyable your work, the more this trade-off pushes you toward being prepared to work for longer.

Now consider what happens when a government raises the retirement age in line with average life expectancy. If you are in a well-paid job and have above average life expectancy, this is not a problem. The increase in retirement age is less than the gains to life expectancy you have experienced and so the time you can expect to spend in retirement still increases. You also find work more enjoyable and so the costs of working for longer are less. If instead you have lower life expectancy and poorer health and work in a more physically demanding job then the increase in retirement age is detrimental. The time you can expect to spend in retirement reduces and if your health is worse and your job more physically challenging then you would prefer to work fewer years with less income rather than work the additional years in discomfort.

All this explains why there are legitimate reasons to protest against increases in retirement driven by improvements in average life expectancy. The greater the degree of health inequality the greater the protest will be as more people will lose out from increases in the retirement age. If governments want support for raising the state pension age, they need to narrow health inequalities, improve health and working conditions and help individuals maintain their productivity.

This also has sharp implications for you as an individual. Given that governments have already raised retirement ages, you will need to adapt to these changes. In simple terms that requires taking steps to lower your costs of working longer and raising the benefits. That means investing in your health, switching to occupations that are more age-friendly, seeking easier commutes, updating your skills so your wage is higher or changing to work that is more rewarding.

There is also another reason why governments shouldn't link retirement age to average life expectancy. It is really healthy life expectancy that matters. Consider our Struldbrugg and Dorian Gray cases again. Under Struldbrugg life expectancy increases but health diminishes. If health deteriorates swiftly or if caring obligations spike then you will not be able to work for longer. Under Dorian Gray there is no increase in life expectancy but health remains higher for longer. That means working for longer makes longer careers more viable. It is imperative therefore that governments should link retirement age to healthy life expectancy, not life expectancy. This has an added benefit. It provides governments with a strong incentive to invest in the health of the older population.

If we want older workers to work for longer then ensuring they remain in good health is important. That is the opposite of what is currently happening. The postponement of retirement has left many older workers in OECD countries struggling to work in poor health (defined as at least one chronic condition).[21] The United States in particular is experiencing a workforce double whammy: a rise in the number of working years in poor health and a decline in working years in good health. Over 8 million people in the US claim social security disability insurance.[22]

More Leisure Time

There is one further reason why rising life expectancy doesn't have to lead to a higher retirement age. After all, for most of the twentieth century life expectancy increased but the retirement age declined. To understand why we need to do some more economics. The reason we think living longer means working for longer is we need more resources to finance a longer life. Working more years is a way to do that. But there is another way—make each year we work more productive so we need to work fewer years. Productivity growth can provide the extra resources longer lives need without having to work for longer.

Productivity growth makes us richer and when we are richer we want to buy more of the things we like.[23] Leisure is one of the things we value highly and so rising incomes in the twentieth century saw the rise of weekends, shorter working weeks and longer vacations. It also saw the introduction of retirement at age sixty-five and more leisure in later life.

So when it comes to pinning down retirement age there are two contrasting effects. The first is longer lives which lead to working for longer. The other is productivity gains that lead to you earning more and not having to work for so long. What will happen to the retirement age going forward will depend on the balance between these two elements. If life expectancy continues to increase and income growth continues to disappoint, the retirement age will rise further. If instead life expectancy gains stall and income growth increases, there will be no need to raise the retirement age.

This logic points to an interesting possibility. The more successful an evergreen agenda is the more health and productivity are maintained for longer. That makes working for longer more feasible. But it also gives other options. Consider two scenarios, each with the same life expectancy. In one you follow the Struldbrugg case and experience declining health and productivity while in the other you follow a Dorian Gray outcome of more years in better health and higher productivity. Because in the Dorian Gray case you are more productive for longer you can work for fewer years and still earn the same lifetime income. That means you could retire earlier than under Struldbrugg. That is our punch line—higher productivity helps finance more years of leisure.

But there is another option with this Dorian Gray case. You take the extra years of leisure not only at the end of life. In other words you retire later and have a shorter retirement so that rather than waiting for a big block of leisure at the back end of life, you bring some of it forward and spread it over your lifetime. That might take the form of a four-day working week, caring for a family, longer breaks for annual vacations or flexible part-time working, especially in later years.

This shift to taking more leisure this side of retirement is apparent in a change that is already happening. Rather than see work come to a hard stop, retirement is becoming a continuous shift moving from full-time to part-time to eventually no-time. Retirement is no longer an event but a process—a glide path where work becomes increasingly more age-friendly. Such an easing helps to extend working careers and productive life expectancy while supporting healthy life expectancy.

But this shift in the timing of leisure is likely to go even further in an evergreen world. George Bernard Shaw, the Nobel Prize-winning Irish playwright, famously observed that "youth is wasted on the young." In a similar vein, this Dorian Gray thought experiment raises the possibility that leisure is wasted on the old. Does it make sense to start work at eighteen or twenty-one if you know you might have to keep at it nonstop for the next fifty or sixty years? A better form of lifetime management might be to take time to go traveling or pursue your passions before you step onto the treadmill of work and responsibilities. Or to take time off in your forties or fifties and plan on postponing retirement to pay for it. That midlife break could be used to avert the middle-aged dip in happiness we saw in chapter 1. Or it could be used to update skills for the next stage of a longer career, either to pursue something new or defending yourself against technological obsolescence. In addition to these voluntary breaks, your career path may entail involuntary stumbles if you lose your job or circumstances shift. The overall result will be careers incorporating multiple breaks between different stages.

This is the real gain with an evergreen agenda. Not the promise of endless drudgery and drawn-out careers but greater options as to how to benefit from the time a longer life provides. An evergreen society shifts the balance between work and leisure. In the twentieth century, increasing life expectancy resulted in more leisure spent after retirement; as the age of retirement increases, the twenty-first-century trend will be more leisure before you retire.

This brings us back again to a stark contrast between a longevity society and an aging society. The more successful the evergreen agenda is (in other words the longer we retain our health and productivity) the later retirement happens, the more career breaks occur, and leisure is taken this side of retirement. The more an aging society unfolds (Struldbrugg), the smaller the shifts in retirement age due to ill-health and inability to work, and the more leisure is forced to be taken later in life when health is poorer. That is why we should resist efforts to raise the retirement age unless they are backed up with evergreen measures.

So should we retire retirement? Retirement still exists and the concept of retirement age remains an important policy variable for governments, but the twentieth-century concept of a single age at which everyone comes to a hard stop has long since gone. To adapt to longer lives we need far more extensive policies than a simple-minded link between retirement age and life expectancy. A focus on health and a wide range of measures aimed at maintaining productivity (from adult education through job redesign) are all required as is a realization that how we age is so diverse that a single set of policies aimed at older workers is far too blunt. Retirement will still exist in an evergreen world but becomes a much more fluid and varied experience and plays a less critical role in determining the boundary between work and leisure.

There is, though, one set of circumstances that might lead to an end to retirement. Take the extreme Peter Pan case where health and mortality remain the same at every age. Let us also assume in this miraculous world that your wage is the same each year. Under these assumptions every year is the same and so you make the same work decisions each year and never retire. Intuitively, this makes sense. If retirement is a period at the end of life when you no longer work due to declining health and productivity, then in this Peter Pan case there are no old people, no declining productivity, no deteriorating health and so there is no retirement.

This extreme Peter Pan case is clearly fictitious but it captures a world where as we age better and if jobs are more age-friendly then retirement may never actually happen and work will continue until you die. Retirement disappears. I know of several university professors who seem to be pursuing that course. The more your older years resemble your younger years, the more choice you will have about when to retire. Boredom or the sense of an approaching end might trigger eventual retirement; or you may just keep working to the end. That isn't a case for a general policy but for some it will be the way to respond to longer lives.

Age-friendly Jobs

My mother-in-law lives on Long Island, New York. She recently stopped working aged eighty. Her last job involved planning tours of notable gardens in New York State and acting as a guide during the visits. Working as a tour guide ranks among the top ten jobs in terms of "age-friendliness."[24] By contrast, jobs that involve working with cement and concrete rank in the bottom ten—they require strength and stamina and are physically taxing. While I wouldn't dare bet against my mother-in-law's abilities, I doubt she would last long shoveling cement.

The point here is that if the evergreen agenda is to succeed, we must create more "age-friendly" jobs. We can't just rely on making older workers "younger" by improving their health, we need to adapt the working environment to support older workers. Comparisons of workers of different ages show that older workers place a higher value on occupations with greater autonomy, the ability to set their own schedule, flexible hours, fewer physical demands and lower levels of stress.[25] They also value better working conditions, a slower pace, less target-driven jobs and less responsibility for others. It is these characteristics that make a job more age-friendly.

Of course it isn't just older people who value those features. We all do, but the key is that older workers value them even more. For example, workers under sixty are prepared to take a 7–10 percent lower wage for a job that enables them to set their own schedule but workers over sixty would take a 15 percent cut.[26] Similarly, younger workers would take an 8 percent pay cut for a job that required only moderate rather than heavy physical activity. But workers in their fifties would sacrifice 18 percent of their wages for easier work while those in their sixties would accept 30 percent less.

Creating age-friendly jobs makes working for longer easier and so supports an economic longevity dividend. There is also a subtler benefit. It helps minimize a common concern of older workers: that by clinging to their jobs they are denying career advancement opportunities for the young.

There's a term for this old–young conundrum: economists call it the "lump of labor fallacy." Only if there is a fixed number of jobs does older people working longer lead to unemployment for the young. But if older people work for longer they will spend more money which will support higher employment creating jobs for younger workers. There's a useful precedent in the substantial rise in women's employment over the last hundred years. More women in the workplace did not mean fewer jobs for men, despite the fears of many.

But there are other ways older people working affects the young. When a larger group of people is hunting work, employers will offer lower wages knowing they'll be able to fill the jobs. The more that young and old compete for the same work, the more intense this effect will be and the more the career prospects of the young are affected by the extended careers of the old. These problems would be reduced if younger and older workers were not competing directly for the same jobs. So policies aimed at creating age-friendly jobs also reduces the impact on other ages.

The good news is that between 1990 and 2020 three-quarters of US occupations became more age-friendly, i.e. jobs with greater autonomy, the ability to set your own schedule, flexible hours, fewer physical demands, lower levels of stress, etc.[27] Part of this is due to rapid growth in office jobs compared to manual labor, but it also reflects fundamental changes in how we do our work due to new technologies. Employment in the most age-friendly of these jobs increased by 49 million. That helped create a supportive environment for workers over fifty, who have gone from being one in five of the workforce to one in three. Even before working from home became commonplace during the pandemic, it was becoming easier for older workers to keep going longer as jobs become less physical and more flexible.

But it isn't all good news as not every industry is age-friendly. Major industries including construction, manufacturing and agriculture score the lowest on measures of age-friendliness. The skills needed to work in these sectors are very different from those needed in age-friendly jobs such as finance. That leads to some older workers being stuck in less age-friendly industries so that the fast-growing occupations with more age-friendly jobs have turned disproportionately to younger workers. That is what happened in the US where over half of the new age-friendly jobs went to younger workers. That isn't necessarily bad. For instance, the characteristics that make a job age-friendly overlap with those that Harvard's Claudia Goldin suggests reduce gender disparities in the labor market.[28] More flexibility, less physicality and stress, and better working conditions also appeal widely, which is why younger graduates have also been enticed into them.

But this broader take-up of age-friendly jobs has adverse consequences. It means older and younger workers are competing for similar occupations after all. Working for longer may not create unemployment among the young but it does affect their wages and their career prospects. Businesses and governments have to think hard about policies supporting older employment while enabling career progression for younger workers.

Another challenge derives from a particular type of older worker who is losing out in terms of access to age-friendly jobs. Older men without a college degree remain predominantly employed in the least age-friendly occupations with the worst record of improvement, such as construction and manufacturing.[29] The double challenge is how to make their current jobs more age-friendly and how to ease them into more suitable occupations. The former can be achieved through the greater use of robots that take on more physically challenging work, a process already underway in manufacturing.[30] In a much-cited case the car manufacturer BMW instituted numerous changes to the production process in their Dingolfing plant in Bavaria. The idea was to make work more age-friendly and the result was higher productivity. Relatively simple measures such as installing new floors to reduce knee pain, providing new footwear and chairs, workstations with adjustable heights and job rotation to avoid repetitive strain all help to make work age-friendly.

More challenging is how to help older males with less education move into different roles as they leave more physically demanding ones. A rising number of jobs in the future will be based around caring and social interaction and that is a major shift from construction or manufacturing. Success will require significant focus on training and retraining as well as changing social norms that make transitions to more age-flexible work more acceptable.

What Does it Mean for Your Career?

Just as it is a mistake for governments to only aim at changes in the retirement age so it would be wrong for you to think the most important career implication of longevity is a longer working life. Far more profound changes are underway. If retirement is delayed, you need to behave differently well before then.

Collectively, the changes required for a beneficial longevity dividend add up to a redesign of careers. In the twentieth century, we divided our lives into a canonical three stages: a triptych of education, work and retirement. It is this structure of a three-stage life that forms the building block of the aging society narrative. In combination with a changing age structure it leads to fewer workers, more pensioners and economic doom and gloom.

An evergreen agenda requires moving away from this three-stage structure. Unfortunately, governments have so far tended to look at changing the parameters of this three-stage life—raising the retirement age, lowering the pension and increasing taxes to pay for it all. None of this supports an evergreen agenda of maintaining health and productivity for longer. So what is the alternative and what does it mean for you?

Ensuring that you extend your career to be productive for longer requires taking a deep breath and pondering the following:

1. *Mix it up*: As careers lengthen they will become multistaged.[31] Maintaining health, skills, relationships and purpose over a longer time will require shifts and transitions, as at different stages you need to pay attention to different outcomes.

    Perhaps you are in your twenties and have worked a few years but want to take time out to travel. You're still uncertain about your future and want to spend time discovering what you really want to do and which are your most valuable skills. Maybe you are in your thirties and hope to raise a family or switch career paths, having realized you're on the wrong track. In your forties you consider that you've already worked for twenty years, but with thirty more still to go you'd rather retrain for something different.

By your fifties you might need time to look after your parents; by your sixties you can't afford to retire but are ready for a different lifestyle. Maybe you'll get to your seventies and eighties still wanting to work but needing a role with less stress.

It is the evergreen shift of leisure toward years before retirement that creates these multistage careers. Longer lives give us more time and those years can be used across all our life. The passing of time will also force more transitions and change upon us. The combination leads to multistage lives.

2. *Be prepared*: To be prepared for the voluntary and involuntary transitions that a multistage life brings you need to think about your finances, your professional and personal networks and your identity. Crucially you need to give yourself options at a later date and you need to build these options up by conscious investment. Your finances will be needed not just for retirement but to tide you over during times when you may not be working or are earning less. Networks are crucial because you need to be able to discover new pathways and career options as circumstances change. If your networks are too centered on your current role that won't help you transition into another. Similarly, identifying too much with your current role makes later transitions all the harder. Across a longer life your tastes and values will change and you need to give yourself room to accommodate them.

3. *Back to school*: The evergreen imperative to age well means a lifelong focus on health and education. It is probable that you will live for longer and if you are to enjoy the extra time, you need

to keep in step with the future. Education in particular cannot just be abandoned once the first part of your career is underway; it needs to be a lifelong endeavor, either through continual incremental updates or by taking blocks of time to retrain. Already there is an explosion of short courses and longer degree programs emerging as firms and colleges sense the commercial opportunities from this expanding market. Whether in person or online, you need to continually scan what you need next.

4. *Diversifying for the future*: Given the greater length of careers, if you are just setting out it is important to build a good base. That means discovering what you are good at and what you like as well as thinking not just of the skills needed for the current job but what the role is teaching you that could be useful in later transitions.

   Conversely the longer you spend in a specialized role or sector, the more useful your skills are in that role but the danger is they are less useful elsewhere. That's a much greater risk now that you have to work for longer.

   You need to take a self-audit and answer some basic questions such as: Are you working in a declining sector? Is your current job age-friendly so you can comfortably continue in the decades ahead? Can you see yourself getting bored and stale if you continue? Do you have skills that are portable to other occupations or sectors? Can you imagine yourself persuading a prospective employer of that? While longer careers increase the risk of not being able to carry on in your current role, they also give you more time to invest and shift into new roles.

5. *Going beyond a peak*: In a three-stage life there is a lot of focus on career progress and advancement and the notion that the "only way is up." In a longer career with multiple stages that thinking makes less sense. Your motivation for working will shift at different ages and so too will what you seek in a job. It may be that as you get older you will want fewer demands, less pressure and not so much responsibility and more flexible work. That

is likely to come with a lower salary. But this reflects a different form of career progress. Financially the reason we need to work for longer is to earn more. But it is lifetime income that matters, not that your income continues to rise every year.

What Should Firms Do?

There's a flipside to the need for workers to structure their careers differently—employers will need to change their approach too. The obvious question is why on earth should firms bother doing so?

In the United States in 2021, in the aftermath of Covid-19, there were 11.5 million job vacancies but only 6 million people unemployed. In the UK, for the first time ever there were more jobs than unemployed workers to fill them. Employers struggled to recruit but labor markets were tight, putting upward pressure on wages. According to the International Monetary Fund, the most significant contributor to this unforeseen shortage of labor was an exodus of older workers.[32]

It's almost as if the future was trying to send us a message. As older workers become a more significant proportion of the workforce, firms must dedicate policies to support them in order to hold on to them. Currently, too many firms are blissfully unaware of even the age profile of their workforce and the problems that will arise as more of them retire. When older workers were a smaller part of the workforce no special attention to them was required. That is no longer the case. In 2000, only one in six US workers was over fifty-five; by 2050 that number will be one in four. That is why employers need to get serious about age-friendly jobs. Given fertility trends, firms will find themselves competing with one another for fewer younger workers and increasingly turning to older workers. Offering jobs that can be part of a multistage career will help them win that competition. So at both ends of the age distribution firms will be fighting for talent and have an incentive to offer different ways of working and structuring a career.

Yet despite these economic arguments many firms remain hesitant about supporting an aging workforce. Often this reflects simple agism and a tendency to discount the productive potential of older people. The most depressing example of this may well have come from Mark Zuckerberg, co-creator of Facebook and master of the metaverse. "Young people are just smarter," he once told an audience at Stanford University. Zuckerberg turns forty in 2024. It will be interesting to see at what point he decides he is less smart than his younger employees.

As to whether older workers are less productive, you can pick from a host of studies that reach a wide range of conclusions. What is clear is that the firmly held and widespread assumption that productivity declines with age doesn't have such strongly matching empirical support. Too many variable factors make sweeping conclusions unwise. Heterogeneity within age groups, the importance of factors such as education, variations across sectors and in the occupational tasks involved all mean that there is no simple correlation between older workers and productivity.[1]

Probably the most accurate summary is that productivity tends to increase with age but can then plateau—although that is to ignore striking variations across different occupations.[33] In some occupations declining physical strength inevitably means declining productivity. Even Roger Federer had to finally hang up his tennis racket at the age of forty-one. Yet in other occupations productivity may even increase with experience. Warren Buffett is known as one of the most successful investors of all time (and currently ranked the sixth richest person in the world) and is still working at ninety-two. The point here is that blanket assumptions about an aging workforce are likely to be wrong.

The focus on whether productivity declines with age is a natural line of thought given the aging society narrative. But as always there is a different way of presenting the issue that reveals the real challenge. Historically the workforce has had a pyramid structure with a lot of younger people and fewer older people. The workforce of the future will have a much more even spread across the ages. In other words, the real story is one of growing age diversity in the workplace rather than just more older workers.

If older and younger workers were interchangeable, then the age structure of the workforce wouldn't matter. Young and old workers would be the same and perform the same roles. You don't have to resort to Peter Pan outcomes to see that older and younger workers in some ways are more similar now. In 1990, an American worker aged between twenty-five and forty-nine was nearly twice as likely to be a graduate compared to those aged fifty to seventy-four. By 2020, the odds were almost the same.

But older and younger workers differ in ways other than just health and education. For instance, young graduates entering the workforce are likely to know more about current general technology trends. In contrast, older employees will have much greater knowledge about how the firm operates and its customers.

As we age, our skills shift. As he closes in on forty, Zuckerberg may no longer be the brilliant teenaged coder who literally built Facebook line by line. But he seems to have learned other skills to compensate based on his experience of running a multi-billion-dollar company, with numerous mergers and acquisitions and interactions with powerful politicians. Skills shift in other ways. There is, for instance, evidence to suggest that on average older workers are driven less by ego, draw from experience rather than theories and are better at empathizing with teammates and customers.[34]

So if older and younger workers have different sets of skills, firms can exploit this diversity in ways that enhance performance. Clues as to how this might work can be seen from a study of biomedical researchers.[35] As intuition might suggest, newly qualified researchers were far more likely to experiment with new ideas than established ones. But the outcome changed when looking at teams instead of individuals. The most productive combination in terms of generating new ideas mixed younger researchers with more senior staff. The combined forces of innovation and experience proved more effective than age-segregated teams of either younger or older workers.

These intergenerational linkages are going to be an important driver of future innovation. The more diverse the team, the more new ideas are likely to develop and generate technological growth.[36]

SEIZING AN ECONOMIC DIVIDEND

With so many countries experiencing declining populations with fewer working-age individuals, the success of future innovation will depend on the inclusion of older workers. The precise mix will vary according to the nature of the business—a software company has different needs to, say, an accountancy partnership. Yet as the working life of employees extends, businesses will need to adapt. Right now few businesses make a priority of managing the age structure of their workforce. An evergreen society requires it.

Remaining Dynamic

Albert Einstein was twenty-six years old when he published his historic papers on special relativity and mass-energy equivalence and presented us with arguably the best-known equation of all time: $E = mc^2$. James Watson was twenty-four when he co-authored the paper describing the double helix structure of the DNA molecule. Steve Jobs founded Apple when he was twenty-one, Bill Gates taught himself computer programming at thirteen and founded Microsoft six years later. These stunning achievements help explain why we tend to look to the young for dramatic breakthroughs and radical ideas. They may also explain why so many people associate an aging society with a lack of innovation. The phrase "aging society" has a double meaning: on one level it is merely a statistical reference to the rising age of the population. But it also carries an emotional resonance implying decline, decay and a lack of innovation.

But as with productivity, the empirical evidence on innovation isn't as clear-cut as you might think. A study of famous inventors and Nobel laureates shows an increase over the last century in the average age at which notable breakthroughs have occurred.[37] Two of the leading scientists involved in the successful deciphering of the human genome in 2000 were Craig Venter and Francis Collins, then aged fifty-four and fifty respectively. By the end of the twentieth century, notable inventors were on average eight years older than a hundred years earlier. In 2016 the median age of American innovators—based on patent applications and industry awards—was forty-seven years old. The youthful examples of Einstein, Watson, Jobs and their ilk remain eye-catching, but are becoming rarer.

The key to this is recognizing that as knowledge accumulates, becoming expert on a topic requires more years of study as topics develop greater complexity. That makes it harder for younger innovators to come up with great inventions and points to the rising importance of experience compared with pure ability.

While encouraging from the viewpoint of an evergreen economy, the results still sound a note of caution. Can we expect significant breakthroughs from people in their eighties or nineties? This is perhaps the hardest question to answer when considering an evergreen agenda. Our extreme Peter Pan case bestows eternal youth in terms of health and mortality but remains silent on the issue of psychological curiosity and a desire for learning and exploration.

The good news is there's plenty of anecdotal evidence to show that the search for scientific discovery and innovation knows no age limits. At the age of 101 Charles Greeley Abbot, an American astrophysicist and an early director of the Smithsonian Institution, became the oldest person ever to register a patent (it related to solar energy, which he had studied for seventy years). Professor John Goodenough of the University of Texas at Austin shared the Nobel Prize in Chemistry in 2019 for his work on lithium-ion batteries. He was ninety-seven years old at the time and today, aged a hundred, is still searching for breakthroughs in battery technology.

These are all great examples of what is possible but don't necessarily show what is probable. The danger with longer working careers is that an older leadership develops whereby industry and society cater primarily for the old. If the old are conservative and protective of their achievements and working routines, intergenerational teams are less likely to be innovative. As the German theoretical physicist Max Planck pithily remarked "science advances one funeral at a time."

There is certainly evidence of a growing role for older workers. Between 2005 and 2019 the average age of incoming CEOs of 500 large companies listed on the Standard and Poor stock market index rose from forty-five to fifty-nine.[38] The American quarterback

Tom Brady, the basketball player LeBron James and the footballer Cristiano Ronaldo were all still playing at elite levels of their sports at an age that previously wouldn't have been thought feasible. Even Hollywood has experienced a similar phenomenon (at least for male actors). Back in 2000 the average age of male actors in the top-grossing films of the year was twenty (admittedly impacted by the success of the first Harry Potter movie). By 2021 it had risen to nearly forty.[39] Returning to a role he first played thirty-six years ago, Tom Cruise, now aged fifty-nine, scored another huge success in the 2022 hit *Top Gun: Maverick*—much of which revolves around the theme that older pilots are still on top of their game and have a great deal to teach the young.

All of this isn't necessarily a problem. As more people maintain their health and productivity for longer this is exactly what we would expect in an evergreen world. But to ensure that longer working careers are intergenerationally fair and don't stymie innovation changes are needed that embed age diversity into workforce teams. Ensuring that voices of all ages can be heard will become more important. New career paths may also need to incorporate term limits on executive roles, ensuring turnovers at the top and chances of advancement for younger employees. The opportunities that multistage careers offer for new arrivals into an industry also need to be exploited to boost innovation.

The most important challenge, though, will be a personal one. As we age we will individually need to recognize the trade-off between stability and reinvention. The need to remain evergreen is about personal renewal and openness to new ways as much as it is about maintaining health and skills.

6

Money and Your Life

If you don't find a way to make money while you sleep, you will work until you die.

Warren Buffett

Traveling on British roads in the seventeenth and eighteenth centuries was not for the faint-hearted. It was the age of abundant highway robbery. Notorious bandits such as Dick Turpin and Katherine Ferrers—known as the "Wicked Lady"—made a living ambushing travelers on the country roads between towns. They gave birth to an order that rang down the years: "Your money or your life." It is the demand issued in countless novels and films about that period, whenever masked villains point their guns at their terrified victims. Sensible travelers took suitable precautions to ensure they reached the end of their journeys with both money and lives intact.

By now that order should sound familiar. As our lives extend we need to take action to ensure we hang on to our money. Our problem, for the most part, is no longer murderous highwaymen, it's that the journey of our life is getting longer and thereby more expensive. We can't choose either money or life: evergreen living needs both. So how do you make sure you don't run out of money too soon? If the previous chapter was about how you earn the money to support a longer life, this chapter is about how you manage that money and set up your personal finances in response to greater longevity.

One of Aesop's fables tells the tale of the ant and the grass-hopper. During the summer the ant works hard collecting and storing grain for winter. The grasshopper prefers to dance and sing through those sunny months, mocking the ant's industrious labor. Come winter the grasshopper starves and begs the ant for food. The ant refuses and suggests the grasshopper try dancing through the winter while ruing its summer idleness.

This fable has fueled innumerable moral debates over the centuries, veering back and forth between praising the ant's virtues of hard work and forward planning or criticizing its lack of charity and compassion. Today it provides a helpful insight into a less abstract phenomenon—pension planning. If a theme of this book is the tendency to underestimate the potential of later life, that isn't a criticism you can direct at the financial sector. They think living longer is great because it provides an opportunity to tell you that you need to save a lot more money. As life gets longer, as your chance of living into those winter months increases, it would seem we all have to be more ant and less grasshopper. For financial firms that has the happy con-sequence of leading to more funds under management and so more fees earned. Wealth management firms love the idea of a hundred-year life.

It turns out, though, that the evergreen financial agenda is much more complex than a simple exhortation to channel your inner ant and save more. In particular, longer lives require us to answer three key financial questions: How much do we need to save to support a longer life? If a longer life becomes multi-staged when do you save and when do you borrow? And finally how do we cope with the uncertainty around how long we might live? Answering these questions requires shifts in our financial behavior but will also require new financial products and ser-vices. As we shall see, there isn't a single right answer to any of these questions. Dealing with that ambiguity is a key part of the financial challenge of longer lives and the need to retain both your money and your life.

Money (That's What I Want)

In 1959 Barrett Strong released "Money (That's What I Want)," which became the first hit record for Motown. There have since been literally hundreds of cover versions including by luminaries such as Jerry Lee Lewis, Etta James, the Beatles, the Kingsmen, the Rolling Stones and Little Richard. I first heard the song in my teenage years courtesy of the wonderfully eccentric version by the Flying Lizards (a YouTube video of the song features the band's leader, Dave Cunningham, drumming on a teapot with a fork). It is a song to make the heart of any financial advisor soar.

As the song suggests, it isn't just financial advisors armed with brochures competing for our money who focus on the need to save. It is a natural instinct we each have to assume that longer lives mean more savings. But that isn't necessarily the case.

First of all, it depends on how much money you need in retirement. You may for instance be comfortable living on what the state provides. Currently, the average US Social Security payment to a retired worker is $21,408 per year, just over a third of typical (median) earnings.[1] In the UK the maximum state pension is £10,600 per year, also around a third of median earnings. For those people who are earning above average or who can't manage on only a third of what they earn that isn't enough and so additional savings will be required.

The good news, according to the US Federal Reserve, is that three-quarters of the US population have some form of retirement savings.[2] The bad news is that three out of five people feel their retirement savings aren't on track. In the UK, the government estimates 12.5 million individuals are undersaving given their retirement needs.[3] According to one analysis of six major economies, the typical individual is on course to outlive their savings by between eight to twenty years.[4] If you don't have a plan or your plan isn't on track, financial logic suggests you need to save more.

But saving is one of only three ways to find the money you need over a longer life. As emphasized in the last chapter, working for longer is another route. Given these statistics on how insufficient our current savings are, more years of work seems an important way to rise to the challenge. If you turn into Peter Pan, never retire but instead work until you die, then you won't need to save at all. But even if you don't spend all the extra years working it still doesn't mean you have to save more. You may even be able to save less. If you leave the length of your retirement unchanged by retiring later then you can spread the cost of saving for retirement across more years of work and thereby save less each year.

There is also a third way, summarized by Warren Buffett in the quote that begins this chapter. Make your money work for you round the clock. The higher your investment returns the better you'll sleep, knowing you'll wake up a little bit wealthier in the morning. There's a snag, of course. Earning a higher rate of return generally means taking on more risk. If that works out then great, but if you invest in the wrong hot trend today you might instead wake up a lot poorer tomorrow.

If you invested in cryptocurrencies during the past few years you will be only too aware of the risks that come with chasing a higher return. Consider the fate of Terraform Labs, a 2018 crypto start-up that shot to investment prominence with its Luna tokens, a kind of digital coin. Between the beginning of February and the end of April 2022 the price of Terraform's Luna cryptocurrency more than doubled.[5] That kind of rate of return solves most financial problems if it can be sustained. But it rarely can and soon enough Luna was rapidly eclipsed. If you bought it at its peak of $119.18 a coin, you would have arrived just in time for a massive sell-off that turned into a panic, crashing the price to less than a cent.[6] That's the problem with risky investments—get out at the right moment and the problem of financing a long life is solved; guess wrong and your problems have just got larger.

Investing in cryptocurrencies represents the more extreme end of risky assets but this problem of unpredictable returns applies to all investments. As noted in a previous chapter, in 1985 a UK investor earned 4 percent above inflation on their savings. At that rate, your money doubles in terms of purchasing power after eighteen years. Right now in 2022 interest rates are below inflation. That means your money will never double in purchasing power. This variation and unpredictability in rates of return make long-term financial planning difficult.

There is another important uncertainty when managing longer lives. Exactly how long will you live for? The ant strategy of just stockpiling savings is going to require an awful lot of money if you are going to live to a hundred. It is also going to turn out to be a very bad decision if you sadly don't make it past seventy. But there are multiple other risks around too. Will you be healthy and active and able to keep earning? Will you need to pay out for long-term medical care? A successful evergreen agenda is the best way to reduce these risks but in the meantime we need the financial sector to deliver new ways of managing them.

So these are the challenges that longer lives present to us and the financial sector. Meeting them requires some mix of either working for longer, saving more, chasing a higher rate of return, as well as finding ways to insure ourselves against very long lives. As we adapt to longevity we have to decide which combination of these responses is optimal.

At the heart of this planning problem is a fundamental and intractable difficulty. If you want to know for sure how much money you require you need answers to four questions: When will I stop working? How much will I need in retirement? What rate of return will my money earn? How long will I live for? While you may be able to guess at answers to these four questions you cannot know for sure what the truth is. This represents a profound uncertainty that cannot be removed. That tells us that the optimal strategy isn't going to be just saving more but requires a multi-pronged approach, and how to deal with this uncertainty is a major challenge for the financial sector.

In the search for resources to finance a longer life there is, though, another solution: get someone else to pay for it all. From an economic perspective, street protests about raising the retirement age are a political debate about how to pay for longer lives—taxes or working longer. But they are also about who pays. If social security and retirement do not change in response to longer lives then either taxes or government borrowing have to rise. Government borrowing is just a way of deferring tax increases so either way a lack of reform shifts the burden onto taxation, either current or future. There is no magic solution to longer lives; resources need to come from somewhere. Should it come from making people work for longer? From the ordinary taxpayer or from firms and the rich? Or perhaps we should just leave the whole pension mess for future generations to fix.

A similar tug-of-war is happening over who bears the risks that longer lives bring. Many businesses and governments are shifting away from comparatively generous defined benefit pensions that base your entitlement on how many years you've worked and the final salary you were paid and then pays you that amount until you die. Instead they have turned to defined contribution schemes, which depend not on how much you earned but on how much of your salary you saved in a pension fund and how that fund's investments have performed. A defined benefit scheme provides two incredibly valuable forms of certainty to the individual—you know how much you will receive each year and you know you will receive it every year of your life. Under a defined contribution scheme, if your money hasn't grown much then you will have a small pension and if you live a long time you will run out of money. The result is a major shift in the risk of maintaining a standard of living in retirement away from firms and governments and toward you the individual.

Do We Have a Pensions Crisis?

Just as discussions of geroscience quickly shift into debates about immortality, so any discussion of an aging society seems invariably to lead to bleak warnings of an impending pensions crisis. While immortality grabs our attention with its reference to an infinite span of time, talk of a pensions crisis bludgeons our senses with reference to mind-numbing shortfalls of money.

The American physicist Richard Feynman won the Nobel Prize for his work on quantum electrodynamics. He once remarked:

"There are 10^{11} stars in the galaxy. That used to be a huge number. But it's only one hundred billion. It's less than the national deficit! We used to call them astronomical numbers. Now we should call them economical numbers."[7] When you start examining the gaps in pension funding the numbers become very "economical" indeed.

The World Economic Forum estimates that in the United States alone there is a $28 trillion shortfall between funds currently earmarked for future pension payments and how much future pensioners are expecting.[8] That deficit isn't going away; it's getting worse. The Forum projects that without changes to the current system, the gap will grow at more than $3 trillion a year and by 2050 will have reached $137 trillion.

There's a simple reason for this worrying financial outlook and that is a failure to adjust to new demographic realities. It is a problem not just in the US but across the world. The arithmetic is comparatively simple. People living for longer means pensions must be paid for longer. Fewer people being born means fewer people working and less tax to pay for those pensions. The result is these huge gaps in pension funding.

The fact that nations haven't been saving enough means that many government-funded pensions operate like a pyramid scheme, with earlier members taking out more than they contributed. The worry is that like any pyramid scheme eventually the system will collapse. The situation is made even worse if the retiring generation is especially large, as it is with babyboomers. This is why governments want to raise retirement ages, increase contributions and lower benefits.

In addition to government-financed pensions there are also commitments made by employers in the form of defined benefit schemes. If employers haven't put enough money aside to meet these promises then the gap will need to be made good by tapping into future profits.

In the US and the UK many of these defined benefit schemes are public sector pensions paid to government employees (distinct from government pensions such as Social Security that are paid to the wider public). In the UK the total value of these obligations to public sector employee pensions is £2.2 trillion, about the same size as

the overall government debt.[9] In America there are also large obligations at the state level. The California Public Employees' Retirement
System—known as CalPERS—controls assets worth $440 billion in
2022, making it the fifth largest public pension fund worldwide.[10]
That $440 billion however represents only 72 percent of what the
system needs to fund future payouts. California, though, ranks
among the better-performing states; others are in bigger trouble. In
New Jersey, Illinois and Kentucky future public sector pensions are
currently only 52 percent funded.[11] For governments, these shortfalls
in public sector pensions will need to be financed by some combination of higher future taxes or cuts in government expenditure.

As these numbers reveal, there are enormous funding gaps
between what funds are available and what future pension commitments have been made. But there are plenty of other pension gaps
around that make the situation even worse.

The most important gap of all is due to the fact that not everyone
is lucky enough to be able to look forward to a pension. According
to the International Labour Organization only three-quarters of
people of retirement age globally receive some form of later life
financial support.[12] That is because only 106 out of 195 countries
offer a government-financed pension. Extending financial security
to those excluded millions is clearly a priority. This is especially a
challenge in low- and middle-income countries where a large number of older people live. It is a bigger problem to receive nothing at
all in old age than to receive only part of what you expected.

Similarly, if pensions are based on pay and you get paid less
than others then your pension will be less too. In this way social
inequalities create gaps in pension provision that are nothing to
do with how well funded the underlying schemes are. The World
Economic Forum calculates that in Japan there is a near 50 percent
gap between the retirement income of men and women.[13] There are
also growing concerns around "gig economy" workers, such as Uber
drivers and Doordash/Deliveroo deliverers, who don't have access
to work-based pension schemes. A related problem concerns defined
contribution pensions. Unlike defined benefit schemes these never
have a funding gap in the sense that what you take out is limited to

what you put in and how it has grown since. But there is the potential for a much more important gap—between what you need and what you have. If you haven't invested enough or investment returns have been disappointing then a defined contribution pension won't have much in it and you may be in for a shock.

So when it comes to pensions there are gaps all around—gaps in terms of the money behind existing promises, gaps between what we need and what we are likely to receive and enormous gaps in terms of who will receive pensions and who won't.

But it is easy to be overburdened by the scale of Feynman's astronomical/economical numbers. It is important to recognize that while the problem is daunting, it's a long-term issue that will stretch across decades to come. The numbers are so large precisely because they represent the sum of all known future liabilities. There doesn't come a single moment when a $137 trillion invoice is slapped on the table and money has to be found. That means we still have time to avert the problem.

Take the US Social Security fund as an example. This is a government fund into which past taxes have been paid and then invested in low-risk US Treasury securities. Each year the government takes out money to help pay for retirement, disability and other federal benefits. The fund currently has assets of $2.9 trillion. That may sound a lot but under current projections the money will run out in 2035, a date encased in many an alarmist headline. But that doesn't mean that in 2035 the US will have to stop paying Social Security. Right now the fund itself only pays about 20 percent of the overall bill; the rest comes from taxes. If nothing changes between now and 2035 then the US will therefore have two options. Either cut the pension by 20 percent or raise taxes/cut spending to fill the gap. There is a third option. The government can raise more money by issuing more debt. That can't be done indefinitely—the height of the federal debt ceiling is a constant source of party political dispute in Washington, D.C., and there may eventually be a limit to what investors are prepared to lend. But it does enable governments to further postpone a day of reckoning.

Kicking the can down the road may have its attractions but better still is to implement now the changes necessary to close the funding gap. The sooner the pension deficit is tackled the smaller the final bill that will need to be paid.

So how will these funding gaps be eliminated? One possibility is that governments and firms will default on their commitments and you won't receive a pension. Around one in four Americans aged fifty and over think by the time they retire they will receive no benefits, and that rises to nearly one in two for those aged less than fifty.[14]

Rather than outright default, most governments and employers are eliminating funding gaps by reforming their pension schemes to make them more sustainable. The idea is to match the size of your pension income more closely to the size of your lifetime pension contributions. As a result, around one in two Americans aged over fifty think they will receive retirement benefits in a less generous form than is currently paid.

It is hard to argue against policies that make pension schemes sustainable. Who wants to be on an unsustainable path? But a sustainable pension scheme isn't the same as a generous one. What you end up with is going to depend on how much you've paid into your fund. If you don't put much in you won't take much out. A second problem is that the reforms governments make to put pensions on a sustainable path tend to be commitments to future actions and not current changes. They are offering the pensions version of St. Augustine's celebrated prayer: "Lord make me pure—but not yet."

In 1983 the US Social Security Amendment Act announced an increase in the full retirement age from sixty-five to sixty-seven. A brave but sensible reform, only the increase didn't happen in 1983. It hadn't happened by 1993. The process started in 2003 with an increase to sixty-five years and two months and then in further two-month intervals until sixty-six was reached in 2008. It should reach sixty-seven by 2027—forty-four years after the increase was announced. It's always good to take a long view, but that one needed a telescope.

This slow phasing in of change creates a problem of intergenerational fairness. Making pension reform gradual shifts the burden onto the young. They end up with a pension scheme that is actuarially fair for them but they also have to pay for the shortfall of older members. The sooner schemes are made sustainable the smaller the financial burden placed on later generations.

This brings us back once more to the evergreen agenda—to ensure that longer lives are both healthier and productive for longer. The pensions crisis is always couched in terms of money but ultimately it is about resources. How does society produce the goods and services that people need in retirement if there are fewer workers and more people retired? The solutions to this problem at a national level are the same as those we face as individuals. We can save more—which for governments means higher taxes—or spend less—lower social security payments. We can work for longer (governments increase the age at which social security and a pension is paid). Or governments can earn a high return on their investments. Given that future pensions are paid out of future taxes, that means boosting GDP growth.

The last two—working longer and boosting economic growth—are important parts of the evergreen agenda. Finding ways that make us healthier and productive for longer is the only way to generate the resources that a longer life requires. If we don't earn enough over our lifetime to pay for pensions, we will continually steal from younger generations to bridge the gap. If we can produce more over our lifetime, the problem is solved.

So is there a pensions crisis? There is certainly a large bill to be paid because we haven't adapted sufficiently to life expectancy gains. That bill will just get larger and larger if we don't change. But the real crisis is perhaps less in the financing and more in the concept of a pension. Put simply the concept of a pension and retirement reflect three-stage life thinking. As we deal with the implications of longer lives it is far from obvious that we should seek to safeguard pension systems in their current form. Retirement has already changed dramatically in its timing and nature, and that inevitably means pensions have to as well.

Ultimately the pensions crisis is not due to increasingly longer lives but to the form those longer lives are taking. Struldbrugg increases mean more of our years are spent in poor health and being less productive and that makes a decline in our average standard of living inevitable. Solving that problem is the aim of a longevity imperative. We need to create more resources over a longer life.

But the more we age in an evergreen manner the more we have to consider questions broader than pension sustainability. What exactly is the purpose of a government-funded pension? Is it about overcoming our short-term biases to ensure we have money in old age? Is it about targeting poverty in later life to help those who haven't been able to save? Or is it simply a reward for reaching old age? These are very different goals that may well be better addressed with very different systems. We might dig even deeper into the philosophy behind pension payouts. If the system is a form of universal basic income aimed at providing financial security, why is it only paid to those of a certain age? Wouldn't this income also be useful to people during the transitions and shocks that inevitably come with longer lives and longer careers? Why should we have to wait to access pension funds?

In short, there are multiple distinct pensions crises. But the most telling one is not financial but resource-based. It isn't about how much we save or who pays taxes but how we create over our lifetime the income needed to support longer lives. All of these challenges are mitigated by making lives healthier and productive for longer. It is an evergreen agenda that removes a pensions crisis. Making pensions financially solvent doesn't address an evergreen agenda. We need to look at the problem the other way around.

Personal Finances

In addition to introducing government-financed pensions, the twentieth century also saw the growth of an asset management industry enabling individuals to build up their own pensions through a variety of investment products. In the US there are currently 330,000 personal financial advisors, earning a typical (median) salary of nearly $100,000.[15] Globally, pension funds are estimated to have $56 trillion under management.[16] Big business doesn't get much bigger.

This sector is set to get even larger as a result of government efforts to reduce their exposure to a pensions crisis. At the same time as reducing the generosity of social security pensions governments are increasingly emphasizing what are called auto-enrollment schemes. The name describes exactly what they are—anyone working for an employer is automatically enrolled in a pension scheme and each year a certain proportion of their salary is invested in an account with their name. The exact proportions invested and the mix between employee or employer contribution varies from country to country, but auto-enrollment schemes are growing rapidly.

Australia introduced auto-enrollment in 1992 through company superannuation schemes which all employees have to join. Employers make annual contributions calculated as a percentage of salary. The contribution rate started at 3 percent, is now at 10 percent and will eventually reach 12 percent. The total investment in what Australians call "supers" now stands at US $2.3 trillion. In the UK auto-enrollment was introduced in 2012 and requires a minimum contribution of 5 percent from the individual and 3 percent from their employer. In 2022 the US Congress, in a rare bipartisan vote, chose to join the auto-enrollment gang by voting in the SECURE 2.0 Act (SECURE is a laborious acronym for Setting Every Community Up for Retirement Enhancement). Amid a raft of provisions aimed at increasing incentives to invest in a pension was a requirement that employers automatically enroll employees in retirement plans (401(k)s) with minimum contribution rates which will rise over time.

The introduction of auto-enrollment in so many countries means that increasing numbers of people have their own personalized retirement fund. As a result the responsibilities and risks of managing pensions are transferred from companies and governments to individuals. That makes knowing how to manage your money even more important.

Make it Personal

A three-stage life ending in a short retirement period lent itself well to standardized financial products and advice. As lives extend, retirement becomes more varied and careers more multistaged; one-size-fits-all advice won't work anymore. Some people can work for longer and want to. Others can't or don't. Some value money and its purchasing power; others value simpler pleasures. Different people with different preferences and circumstances will seek different options. The clue is in the phrase the industry has devised for itself but not yet wholly embraced—*personal* finance.

The essence of personal financial planning in an evergreen society is deciding how you want to use that extra time and then creating a plan to finance it. Too much current financial advice reverses the priority and instead suggests how you should adjust your life to support financial plans. Along with coining the phrase "There's a sucker born every minute" the great nineteenth-century showman P. T. Barnum also said "Money is a terrible master but an excellent servant." Good financial planning requires making money your servant. Ramping up your savings in the face of longer lives might be what works for you but it may not. If it isn't then you are allowing money to become your master. If you do seek professional financial advice the earlier they ask you what you want to do with your life and the later they bring out the investment brochures the better. You have to support your own preferred mix of ant and grasshopper.

As personal finance plans become more bespoke and as more funds are held in individual schemes there will be a growing need for financial advice. But that brings a problem. Wherever there is a large amount of money there is the risk of financial fraud. The risk of fraud and misselling is made all the greater when products become complex and bespoke. Throw in that as people become older they are more vulnerable to cognitive problems such as dementia and longer lives create the possibility for a whole new chapter in the long-running history of financial fraud.

That is creating a tension. The rising need for individualized financial advice is interacting with regulators keen to ensure that only licensed advisors can give advice. That restricts the number of potential advisors at just the time when more advice is needed. In a world of longevity we have to ensure that financial advice can be provided cheaply and easily to everyone and not just to those with substantial wealth. The great hope in making things more straightforward is "robo advisors" and the smart use of AI as a way of providing easy access and good advice to the many.

Whether you do or don't use an advisor, real or robo, it is hard to avoid the conclusion that it is a good idea to spend time improving your financial literacy. Finance professors Olivia Mitchell and Annamaria Lusardi have investigated both the scale of financial literacy as well as its benefits. They found that financial literacy is poor among most Americans. When asked three basic questions about investments to do with interest rates, inflation and risk, less than half knew the right answers.[17] The problem, though, isn't just confined to Americans but is present in most other countries. It varies with education. Only one in five high school graduates got the right answers compared to two out of five college graduates and three out of five postgraduates. That still leaves an awful lot of people with low levels of financial knowledge. Answers also differed between men and women. In Germany around one in two women got the right answers (one in five in the US) compared to three out of five men (two out of five American men). Intriguingly the evidence points to women being aware they probably didn't know the right answers. Men in contrast were overconfident. Being ill-informed is bad news for your investments but so is being overconfident in your expertise.

Most importantly of all, research shows that financial literacy matters. Financially savvy people are more likely to plan, save and invest and earn higher returns. They are less likely to have credit card debt and more likely to refinance mortgages in cost-effective ways. With changes to the pension environment making individuals more responsible for their own financial future, understanding how your finances work becomes more valuable.

Work, Save or Invest?

To illustrate these two financial features—making your plan personal and the importance of financial literacy—let us take a look at how you can think through the various trade-offs around financing a longer life. What is the relative role of our three different strategies—working longer, saving more or getting a higher return on your investments?

To make things concrete assume you have calculated that on top of the government-provided pension you receive you need an additional $10,000 a year in retirement. What size pot of money do you need to have accumulated by the time you retire to achieve that? And how would that change if your retirement lasts longer than you think and your investment return isn't as attractive as you hoped?

As stressed earlier, this is a difficult question to answer because you cannot know for sure how much money you will need, how long you will live for or what rate of return your investments will earn. Dealing with that uncertainty is an integral part of how you manage your finances over a longer life. But we can get some idea of the basic trade-offs involved if we treat it for the moment not as a financial advice problem but as a mathematical one and make the unrealistic assumption that you know how long you will live for and what your investments will earn.

The results are shown in Figure 5, which lists how much you need to have saved by your retirement age if you want to be able to spend $10,000 each year based on different assumptions about length of life (years of retirement) and investment returns. It assumes that you are not intending to leave an inheritance so plan to have no money left at the time you die.

Obviously, the longer you live in retirement the more money you need. So the sums required increase as you run down the columns. The higher the return your investments earn the less you need to save so the amount goes down as you move across the rows. If you want to know how much you need for $5,000 a year or $100,000 then just multiply everything by 0.5 or 10 respectively.

Length of Retirement (Years)	0% Return (After Inflation)	1% Return (After Inflation)	2% Return (After Inflation)	5% Return (After Inflation)
5	$50k	$49k	$48k	$44k
10	$100k	$95k	$91k	$79k
15	$150k	$139k	$130k	$106k
20	$200k	$181k	$165k	$126k
25	$250k	$221k	$197k	$143k
30	$300k	$259k	$226k	$155k
35	$350k	$295k	$252k	$165k

FIGURE 5: How Much Money Do You Need at Retirement?
(Author's calculation, based on the (unrealistic) assumptions of no inheritance or bequests, no uncertainty over how long you live and guaranteed rates of return.)

For most people the table is a sobering read. They don't have enough savings for anywhere near the length of retirement they'd like. According to the latest numbers from the US Survey of Consumer Finances the typical (median) fifty-five- to sixty-four-year-old American has around $134k in a retirement account.[18] That may sound a lot but based on current US mortality data, a sixty-five-year-old can expect to live another 18.5 years on average. Assuming that $134k manages a yearly return of 2 percent over inflation (more than is currently available), your savings would provide you with $722 a month over those 18.5 years—a modest addition to the average social security payout. The combined amounts would give you an income of $2,506 a month, around half of median earnings for one person. At that rate you would rightly be worried about living longer than average. That would demand you stretched your money out for longer, giving you even less each month.

The calculations also show how important knowing your life expectancy is for financial planning. TIAA (Teachers Insurance and Annuity Association of America) has more than 5 million members drawn mainly from the education sector and over $1 trillion of assets under management. Given that according to the Society of Actuaries teachers have the longest average lifespan of any public employee and are twice as likely to live to a hundred, that makes longevity an important issue for them.[19] TIAA polled their members and found that only around a third of them could select the correct option regarding the expected life expectancy of American sixty-year-olds.[20] One quarter didn't know and another quarter underestimated life expectancy. That means one in two polled have a major problem when planning their retirement finances.

The other feature that stands out from Figure 5 is the importance of the rate of return your investments earn. Financing another $10,000 a year if retirement extends from thirty to thirty-five years requires a full $50,000 if your money earns nothing. But you need only an additional $10,000 if you can find a way to earn an impressive 5 percent on your investments.

So what is the right balance between working longer, saving more or rolling the dice on more risky assets? This is where we come back to the personal nature of personal finance. There isn't a right answer. A lot depends on you and your circumstances. Let's take the case where due to a ten-year increase in life expectancy you can now expect to have not fifteen years in retirement but twenty-five years. Assume that you earn 1 percent on your investments over inflation. Then according to Figure 5 you now need to have $221,000 when you retire, not $139,000. That is a lot of extra saving to do over your working career. It is exactly this failure to save more that explains why so many countries, schemes and individuals face a pensions crisis.

Perhaps instead the more attractive option is to work for an extra five years, so you spend only twenty years in retirement. In that scenario, you need to save $181,000 by the time you retire. That is not trivial but remember you will also have five more years of work to accumulate the extra funds as you are retiring five years later. Or perhaps you feel that fifteen years in retirement is all you need so you will work the whole extra ten years. Under these assumptions you need $139,000 when you retire and you now have ten more years to acquire it. That means you can save less each year, spend more while you work and still have the same in retirement. Which of these scenarios is the right one will depend on your preferences. How much do you value today versus tomorrow? How much more could you save now? How much do you hate work? Can you carry on working? Remember it is your financial plan and it is the answers to these personal questions that should determine what you do with your finances.

A New Approach to W/Health Management

Perhaps all these options are just too bewildering and you can't decide between them. That is understandable. After all, planning a long life isn't going to be easy. But there is another problem with this approach that really limits its usability as an input to financial planning.

That is the uncertainty that you don't know how much you need in retirement, you don't know how long you will live for, you don't know what your investment returns will be and you don't know how long you can carry on working for. It is a financial version of the Yiddish proverb "Der Mensch Tracht, Un Gott Lacht" or "We plan, God laughs." There just isn't a correct answer. You are trying to pin down one thing—how much to save—but there are just too many unknowns. What if you plan to retire at seventy expecting to live to ninety but you live to ninety-five? What if you retire expecting to earn 2 percent on your money but instead only earn 1 percent? What happens when you plan on working to sixty-five but lose your job at fifty-seven?

The former heavyweight world champion boxer Mike Tyson has a related quote that points to a way forward. Tyson was asked before his bout with Evander Holyfield whether he was concerned about the latter's fight plan. He answered: "Everyone has a plan until they get punched in the mouth." In dealing with the financial implications of longevity these profound unknowns around your health, your life expectancy and your career mean that you need to have built-in flexibility to any plan. You have to have the ability to adjust.

In an earlier book, *The 100-Year Life* (co-authored with Lynda Gratton), I noted that any assessment of your wealth should also include what we termed your intangible assets—your skills and knowledge, your health, your friendships, your sense of purpose and your ability to navigate through change. Each year you need to check across this whole portfolio to make sure you are plugging any gaps that are appearing. It is by investing in this broad range of assets and not just your financial assets that you create the capacity to deal with the punches in the mouth that Tyson refers to and that over a long life will happen.

If you are going to adjust your financial plan by working for longer because your investments have done poorly, will you have the skills to do so? If you want to enjoy a long retirement, is your health good or will those years be plagued by ever rising medical costs? Will your family enjoy having you around for longer? You have to avoid warning lights flashing on your dashboard throughout your life.

From a financial perspective that has a number of implications. For instance, it points to the need to integrate your financial planning with health assessments. With twenty years of funding in the bank, you might feel that retiring at eighty will allow you to live safely until a hundred. It would be a shame if you then died aged eighty-one. To help with your financial planning you need to keep updating your likely longevity. That explains why the financial planning industry is becoming even more interested in measures of biological age. Deciding when to stop work, how much money you need and how much you are likely to need for medical care are all decisions improved by better knowledge of your biological age. Just as investors regularly check their financial portfolio, so you will need to regularly check your health portfolio and what you find there will influence your financial planning.

The other key variable to invest in is your skills and knowledge and the various attributes that help you remain productive and employed. Economists refer to this as your "human capital." We have already documented how longer lives require longer careers. Dealing with uncertainties around rates of return and life expectancy also involves being able *if needed* to work for longer. You have to keep investing in your human capital as a source of insurance. In the language of economics, not running out of money over a longer life is going to require investing more in your human capital relative to your financial capital.

Richer and Poorer

It is natural to think that longer lives require more savings. But longer lives also have implications for borrowing. If longer lives lead to longer careers then you have more time ahead of you to earn, which means you can afford to borrow more now. Of course, over a lifetime your finances have to add up so you can't borrow more forever. But if your working career lengthens then you have more time to build up financial assets for retirement as well as pay off debt such as mortgages and loans.

This aspect of longevity will make a substantial difference to wealth across your lifetime. That in turn will mean major shifts in the distribution of wealth across generations. Longer working careers require more education so more people are starting work later and with more debt. With more working years ahead of them they can also take on more debt. The result is at younger ages we should expect people to be worse off financially than past generations. Similarly people in their fifties have longer working careers ahead of them than past cohorts. That means they still have time to pay off debts and build up savings and so compared to past fifty-year-olds may seem to have weaker finances. Conversely, if retirement is now longer then older ages will need more wealth than previous generations in order to finance that additional time. The consequence is a major change in the life cycle dynamics of wealth and a big shift in the distribution of wealth, with more of it in the hands of older people.

This process is already happening. In the US in 1990 19 percent of all wealth was owned by those aged seventy and over and 13 percent by those aged under forty.[21] By 2022 those numbers were 26 percent and 6 percent respectively. Increases in life expectancy are contributing toward growing wealth inequality between older and younger generations. That isn't necessarily a sign that the old are mistreating the young or that the young are destined to be forever poor. Wealth dynamics over a life cycle will change in response to longevity.

Living Insurance

A theme of this chapter is the problem of managing your finances over a longer life given the uncertainty around how long you might live and what return your investments will earn. If we could remove these uncertainties then financial planning would become easier and we could be more confident of achieving a guaranteed income regardless of how long we lived. This is why we turn now from a focus on savings to concentrate on insurance.

Life insurance was created to deal with the risk of you dying young and leaving your family financially insecure. Given increases in life expectancy we need to start thinking about *living insurance*—finding ways to ensure we don't outlive our resources in the event we live to a very old age. Life insurance policies are easy to understand. Every year you pay a premium in return for a specified payout when you die. Around half of Americans have a life insurance policy. It is big business with net premiums paid in the US in 2021 totaling $635.7 billion.[22]

But that wasn't always the case. As you can imagine in an industry that takes your money now and promises to pay out when you die, it has had its fair share of frauds, scandals and missellings. The early days of the industry were hardly auspicious. The first English life insurance policy was issued in 1583 on the life of William Gybbons, a salter of meat and fish, but the underwriter refused to pay out when he died. That was because the insurance company claimed the policy was defined by a lunar year (which is 354 days) and not a calendar year (365 days). That mattered because Mr. Gybbons died in that eleven-day gap. It always pays to read the small print when it comes to insurance. That said, the beneficiaries of the policy took the underwriters to court and won.

But over time, regulation, firm reputation and familiarity have produced a multi-billion-dollar industry. Given the challenge long lives bring to long-term financial planning, shouldn't we expect similar rapid growth in living insurance policies in the decades ahead? To see the need for such a shift, take a look at a very somber chart—the distribution of age at death for adults in France across a variety of different years (Figure 6).

First note that while average life expectancy is a useful statistic it isn't a very reliable guide for your financial planning. In France in 2020 average life expectancy was eighty-two years and eight months. However, only one in forty deaths in 2020 were people aged eighty-two. Most of us aren't, in other words, average. That means there is considerable uncertainty around when you might die. Average life expectancy isn't even the most common age at death—that was eighty-nine. This introduces considerable uncertainty into any life-time planning.

The other remarkable feature is a shift in the timing of when we are likely to die, which changes our insurance needs. Let us assume that if you die before retirement age (pre-Macron reforms that's sixty-two) your surviving family is at risk financially. Your working life has ended abruptly, your financial plans are incomplete and your family vulnerable. That is going to make this age group especially interested in life insurance.

In France in 1813 three out of five adult deaths were before sixty-two (though remember there was no such thing as retirement then, you would have worked until you couldn't). By 1913 it was one out of two, in 1970 one in four and by 2020 it had reached one in eight. None of this is to say that life insurance is no longer important (especially with retirement age increasing and more people at older ages having outstanding mortgages). But it does point to a dramatic shift. The risk is now less of dying before your career is over but of dying after you have stopped working.

This shift has produced a substantial increase in the risk of living for a long time. In 1813 and in 1913 only one in a hundred adult

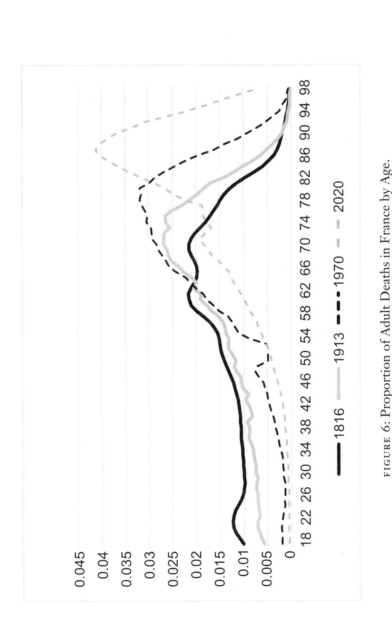

FIGURE 6: Proportion of Adult Deaths in France by Age.

(Source: HMD, Human Mortality Database: Max Planck Institute for Demographic Research (Germany), University of California, Berkeley (USA), and French Institute for Demographic Studies (France). Available at www.mortality.org)

deaths in France were among those aged ninety or older. In 1970 it was one in sixteen and by 2020 more than one in four. That makes living insurance more of an issue. The risk now is not so much about dying before you have accumulated enough savings but of dying after you have spent all the money you accumulated for retirement.

The uncertainty about how long you might live is driven by two components. One is individual uncertainty. Average life expectancy in France is eighty-two but as I remarked earlier most people aren't average so are unlikely to die at that age. So you need insurance to deal with the uncertainty of variation around the mean.

But there is a second form of uncertainty. The average itself may shift. As the data for France shows, the most common age of death has increased substantially—from sixty-three in 1813 to seventy-three in 1913, eighty in 1970 and eighty-nine in 2020. Might it not do so again in the future? If you are aged thirty today you aren't so interested in the data from 2020. You will be much more interested in what you can expect 2070 to look like. That's what you need to know when preparing a lifetime financial plan.

If the next fifty years witnesses the same progress as the last fifty then the most common age of death in 2070 would be ninety-eight. Perhaps it will surge even higher, powered by breakthroughs in geroscience. Or maybe there will be a ceiling, and for unforeseeable demographic, political or health reasons it declines. How do you cope with that uncertainty when it comes to pension planning? The challenge for the financial sector is to come up with products that help reduce that uncertainty so that we can be sure of receiving a guaranteed income each year in retirement for as long as we live.

Before moving on to consider ways to achieve this it is worth taking a more personal look at living insurance. The fact that very few people die at the exact age of average life expectancy has important implications for relationships. If you live with a partner, your financial planning needs to deal with the difficult issue of how long both of you might live. The good news is that due to increases in life expectancy and declines in mid-life mortality couples are much more likely to become old together. But that doesn't mean they are likely to die at around the same age.

The Actuaries Longevity Illustrator is an online tool developed by the American Academy of Actuaries and the Society of Actuaries.[23] By providing some basic information on your general health, it will provide insights into your longevity as partners. For instance, based on information about me and my wife it tells me there is a 50 percent chance that one of us will live to ninety-six years of age, but only a 50 percent chance that we will both live to eighty-six. That is a painful thought. It certainly demands some careful financial planning. But it also requires a number of other painful conversations that fit under the umbrella of "living insurance." Atul Gawande's brilliant book *Being Mortal* talks about the importance of conversations around end of life and the key choices that matter.[24] A longer life doesn't mean there is no end to life just greater certainty you will experience it at an older age. Preparing yourself not just as an individual but in terms of relationships goes way beyond just financial planning.

Income Guarantees

Returning to our financial planning, what we are after is a way of guaranteeing income once we have stopped work regardless of how long we might live. How can we achieve this income guarantee?

There is already one form of living insurance readily available to us in the shape of government-financed pensions such as social security. As long as you live you will receive a payment. Social security pensions are an important way of providing us with income security over longer lives. Similarly, if you are one of the dwindling number of people in receipt of a defined benefit pension—a sum guaranteed for life and calculated from your final salary at retirement.

Alternatively you may belong to a family that has the means and desire to support you however long you live. Do bear in mind, though, the experience of Shakespeare's *King Lear*. He gave his money to his daughters and expected them to support him, only to discover too late: "How sharper than a serpent's tooth it is to have a thankless child." As those extra years of longevity roll past, even the most loving families may start wondering what they've let themselves in for.

If you are one of the lucky ones above, then congratulations are in order: you have devised your own living insurance. But most people aren't so fortunate. If you belong to the worried majority, what should you be doing?

By now you should know that one option is just to keep working or, more generally, make sure there's work you could return to if necessary. In 2022, as the cost of living soared and financial markets fell, there was much talk of the "great unretirement" as older individuals were forced back into the labor market. The best form of longevity insurance, in other words, is your own earning potential—your human capital. Working for longer also helps deal with another risk—rising inflation. Pensions are vulnerable to rising prices; wages offer a better hedge against inflation.

Stockpiling savings is another route but that's a tough challenge if you want to be financially secure and live as long as Jeanne Calment's 122 years. Saving enough to live comfortably that long is beyond the capabilities of most of us. It is also very inefficient. If you follow that path and keep stashing away funds for a sixty-year retirement, you can expect to die with a lot of money left in your bank account. If you don't need the money during your lifetime or you hope to leave a sizable inheritance, dying rich may not matter to you. But few of us have that sort of money to spare.

This is where insurance comes in. Insurance is a way of spreading risk so that you don't have to pay in full yourself for unlikely but expensive outcomes such as living to 122. While each of us may not live exactly as long as average life expectancy collectively by definition we must do. That enables insurance companies to pool risk and remove individual uncertainty.

This pooling of risk is what underpins an annuity, a financial asset that provides an income guarantee. To see how an annuity works consider an imaginary case of twenty seventy-year-olds all worried about running out of money. From hypothetical actuarial tables they know that on average one of them will die each year. As a result they all have a life expectancy of eighty but one of them will die as young as seventy-one and the oldest will die aged ninety. If they each want to make sure they have $10,000 a year to spend in a world where investment returns are zero then they each need at age seventy to have a savings pot of $200,000—twenty years of $10,000. For the person who dies at seventy-one that means they will leave behind $190,000 unspent. The one who dies at seventy-two will leave behind $180,000 and so on.

An annuity provides living insurance and avoids the need for everyone dying with money in the bank. They can take a multiplicity of forms but let us take the case where every one of our twenty seventy-year-olds invests $100,000 in buying an annuity. This annuity then gives each person who is still alive $10,000 a year. That's a bad deal for the person who dies at seventy-one—they only get $10,000 and bought the annuity for $100,000. But it's a great deal for the person who lives to ninety—they paid $100,000 and got back $200,000. But the person who dies at seventy-one still gains relative to when they had to save $200,000. Because of the annuity they only need to have $100,000 in their retirement pot to cover the risk of living to ninety. By pooling risk the annuity provides everyone with a guaranteed income and avoids them having to oversave.

Annuities make a lot of sense but for varying reasons they aren't as popular as finance professors would like. Some investors worry about the liquidity of annuities—the extent to which they can easily be cashed in if you suddenly find yourself needing more money.

Another problem is that annuities are often seen as expensive. In other words, relative to the price of the annuity the annual income you get is low. One reason for this is the risk that the insurance company is taking on. That is especially a problem around the risk of increases in average life expectancy. Annuities can help pool risk across individuals but they cannot protect against increases in average life expectancy.

Imagine what would happen to an annuity if geroscience produced a magic pill enabling those seventy-year-old annuity holders to live for twenty years longer. In other words, now their average life expectancy is a hundred and one dies at ninety-one, one at ninety-two, with the final one dying at a hundred and ten. Everyone bought the annuity for $100,000 but the person who dies earliest at ninety-one now gets paid a cumulative total of $210,000 and the one who dies at a hundred and ten gets a total payout of $400,000. You can see the problem—the insurance companies who issued the annuities would go bust due to the increase in average life expectancy.

To deal with this risk of increases in average life expectancy, insurance companies have to hold back money in the form of capital in case they need to pay out more than expected. That is expensive for them as it ties up money, meaning they earn less on their investments. As a result, some of that cost is passed on to the annuity holder in the form of lower rates making annuities expensive to buy.

But annuities aren't the only way to pool longevity risk. Lately there has been a resurgence of intellectual interest in a financial investment tracing its roots back to the seventeenth century.[25] It is known as a tontine, after the Italian financier Lorenzo di Tonti, who persuaded King Louis XIV of France to try a money-raising scheme he had developed. For somewhat mysterious reasons di Tonti ended up imprisoned in the Bastille, but his financial idea became increasingly used by the French government and was also one of the first forms of government debt issued in the UK.[26]

As with annuities, at the heart of a tontine is the notion of risk pooling. But whereas an annuity provides a guaranteed income while you live, a tontine in its purest form ends up with those who survive seeing their income grow so long as they outlive others. That creates some nasty incentives to bump off other members of the scheme. Highway robbers might have pointed a gun and said: "Your money or your life." With a tontine it is more a case of "Your life and my money." That has made tontines a great dramatic vehicle for a number of books, films and TV series.

It isn't just among scriptwriters that tontines have proved popular. In 1905 there were 9 million insurance policies in the United

States which had a tontine element. But in 1906 the US government declared them illegal. They had become tainted by a spate of embezzlement scandals and complaints of misselling and fraud as well as a general unease at the idea of becoming richer through the death of others.

So how do tontines work and how did they get this bad reputation? Here's a quick example of the basic idea of a tontine. Three savers come together and each pool $20,000 to create a tontine worth $60,000. That sum is duly invested and assume that the pool grows by 2 percent, adding $1,200 in the first year. This $1,200 is split between the three subscribers so each gets $400.

In the second year one of them dies. Her $20,000 stake is split between the other two, whose shares of the pool therefore increase to $30,000 each. At 2 percent interest, each of them now earns $600 at the end of the second year. In the third year a second partner dies, leaving the entire $60,000 fund in the hands of the remaining survivor. The annual dividend shoots up to $1,200 *and* the longest-lived partner gets to keep the entire fund.

If we can get beyond the sensationalism that appeals to scriptwriters, what is the appeal of tontines from a longevity perspective? The first is they provide an answer to the guaranteed income problem. Of course, strictly speaking your income isn't guaranteed with a tontine—if you live longer than other subscribers your income actually increases. But that is surely an easy problem to deal with. Our fear is of not having enough money, not about what to do if we end up with too much. Rising tontine income may even be an advantage if health and care costs rise with age. Private care in the US costs from $20,000 a year for adult day care and $108,000 per annum for a private room in a nursing home—and those are average costs.[27] That is an expense that requires an insurance solution.

The second advantage of tontines is that they reduce the problem of aggregate longevity risk that afflicted annuities. If increases in life expectancy happen so that none of the tontine holders die, everyone just keeps earning $1,200 every year. There is no capital at risk and so tontines should be able to offer better returns than an annuity.

A Financial Solution

So there are a variety of ways we can achieve income stability in the face of longer lives. I outlined a particular version of an annuity and a tontine but there are hundreds of variants, each with different features offering different combinations of risks and trade-offs. As this discussion suggests, no one way is perfect. Annuities help against individual risk but the level of risk around average life expectancy makes them expensive. Tontines aren't exposed to aggregate risk but you need to invest a lot more money to get the same level of income.

What is likely to emerge is a range of schemes offering different types of insurance. They won't be able to offer complete guarantees forever but they will help reduce worries about how long you might live and what your money will earn.

We started this chapter asking the question of what combination of working longer, saving more and chasing higher returns would be needed to finance a longer life. The answer is the usual "it depends and it's a mix." But we can say more than that. Saving more will be important but is unlikely to be the best way to secure financial security. You also need to invest in your human capital—your skills and health. Remaining fit, healthy, productive and engaged is the best way of ensuring you maintain your money and your life. That and using the power of insurance to pool risk is how to deal with longevity risk.

There is another way that the insurance sector can help us. But in this case it's not about helping us avoid outliving our finances but rather helping us avoid outliving our health.

Life insurance companies like it when we live for longer. If tontine holders have an incentive to kill one another, your life insurance company has an incentive to keep you alive. The more years you live the more premiums you pay and the further in the future any payout is. That gives insurance companies more chance of earning profits when they invest your premiums. Exploiting this, some companies have already begun to offer gym memberships, free health monitoring devices, discounts on health foods and other incentives to keep you fit and well. The more you take advantage of these offers, the better your health and the lower your premiums.

While discounted gym memberships and fitness watches are relatively small financial incentives, there's plenty of room to incorporate more expensive health care benefits. This may be a route to finance any emerging medical treatments that help extend life expectancy. A quick internet search gives me a quote of a $5,000 annual premium for a seventy-year-old American woman buying $250,000 of life cover for the next twenty years. Every extra year they are alive is $5,000 to the insurance company and postpones paying out $250,000 for longer. If they can support her living beyond the twenty years then there is no payout. That is a big incentive for life insurance products to incorporate coverage for life-extending treatments and potential future gerotherapeutics—a mutually beneficial marriage of money and health.

The Business of Longevity

One of the three ways you can find the resources a longer life requires that I have suggested is by being lucky with your investments. That brings us to our final look at money and longevity.

Investors are always on the lookout for the next "big thing" and things don't get much bigger than longevity. Put together our two main results—billions of people are living longer and aging well is worth hundreds of thousands of dollars to each of them—and you get an enormous business opportunity. At London Business School I run a course called "The Business of Longevity." Speakers drawn from a wide range of sectors speak to my students of the enormous commercial potential offered by this dramatic change to our lives.

Throughout these pages I have outlined numerous factors that have to change if we are to rise to the challenge of a longevity imperative. I have stressed what that means for you and governments but business has an equally important role to play in bringing about that change. As we have seen with the finance sector, it is they who produce and distribute the new goods and services that a longevity imperative requires.

If you are excited about the potential of geroscience but concerned about how to finance a radically longer life then investing in biotech start-ups might be a form of living insurance. If geroscience companies make breakthroughs that extend your life expectancy then their share price should surge, providing you with the money to buy their products and fund that longer life.

But when it comes to risky investments be warned that things don't get much riskier than early stage biotech. There are many more examples of biotech companies which go bust than that achieve fantastic growth, and for all the optimism of longevity pioneers there isn't yet a single treatment that has been shown to be as effective as a drug.

There are, though, many other ways to invest in longevity and they aren't all as risky as biotech. The EU defines the silver economy as "the sum of all economic activity that serves the needs of people aged fifty and over, including the products and services they purchase directly and the further economic activity this spending generates." Organizations such as the AARP (founded in 1958 and originally known as the American Association of Retired Persons) or the International Longevity Centre emphasize that this silver economy represents an enormous business opportunity. The logic is simple. There is a rising number of older people. Older people tend to earn more than the young, have more wealth and spend more. The fifty-plus generation already accounts for a large slice of the economy and it will only get larger in the decades ahead. So begins the investor slide pack for a host of start-ups aimed at this older population.

As is always the case with demographics, it is easy to throw around huge numbers to make the case. According to the AARP, spending by the over fifties contributes $45 trillion to global GDP.[28] In the United States, fifty-six cents of every dollar spent is by those aged over fifty. If by some magic trick you could form a new economy comprised only of American spenders aged over fifty, it would be the third largest in the world with an annual GDP of $8.3 trillion. There are similar trends in other countries. In the UK, 54 percent of consumer spending is by the over fifties (£319 billion) and that is expected to rise to £550 billion (63 percent) by 2040.[29]

According to this welter of statistics, far from being a burden this older population is the world's largest and fastest-growing "emerging market." The sectors that are predicted to benefit are those involved with companionship, care, mobility and dealing with disabling illnesses such as dementia.

Viewing older customers this way provides a welcome corrective to the doom and gloom so often associated with an aging society. The capacity of older people to contribute positively to economic growth should not be underestimated. But there are—as usual—a couple of caveats to this view of older workers as an economic engine. Some of this silver economy analysis slips into a perverse way of finding advantages. For instance, one much trailed statistic is that since 2011 Japan has sold more adult diapers than baby diapers.[30] That is certainly a major business opportunity but it seems more a case of "doom and boom" and making profits from poor health than through promoting an evergreen future. Is that really how we want to see the over-fifty market in a longevity society?

One major problem with trying to identify the silver economy is simply defining what it is to be old. Does old age start at fifty? Sixty-five? Eighty? Does it even depend on chronological age?

It is perhaps understandable why the AARP would use the cut-off point of fifty years as a measure of who is "old." The AARP was founded in 1958 and was originally known as the American Association of Retired Persons. Initially it provided insurance cover and support to retired teachers over fifty. It has since evolved to become a 38-million-member organization that through government lobbying, information provision and negotiating deals for its members tries to meet the needs of those aged over fifty. The commercial potential of this age group is apparent in the fact that the AARP (a nonprofit) has accumulated net assets of $3 billion and in 2021 achieved annual revenues of $1.8 billion. Defining older people as aged fifty and over is consistent with AARP's historical remit and its membership base.

However, the diversity with which people age and the gains in life expectancy that have occurred since 1958 lead to problems in identifying this single age group as either "old" or sharing much in the way of common interests. Defining old age as starting at fifty inevitably captures an enormous number of people and phenomenal spending power but at the same time it isn't clear it usefully defines a single market. Just as there isn't a single unified under-fifty market, it is doubtful there is a single over-fifty market.

The idea that there is leads firms into exactly the sort of agist prejudices that the AARP is keen for you to avoid. As a result the silver economy is often focused on frailty and needs (eldercare robots, pillboxes, fall alarms, etc.) rather than wants (fun, entertainment, travel, company, etc.). As MIT's Professor Joseph Coughlin says, the attitude of many firms to older consumers is akin to assuming that the only product teenagers would be interested in is acne cream. If that is your attitude toward teenagers you won't sell much. Similarly with older people.

I confess to being nervous about the concept of a silver economy. Although it attempts to describe a positive version of an aging society it is prey to the same issues of stereotyping and pandering to a supposed homogeneity that may not exist and disguises the point that in many ways the big change is older and younger people becoming more similar.

There is another reason to go beyond the "silver economy" characterization. We need to encourage an evergreen society not an aging society, but the silver economy is simply the flipside of an aging society narrative dressed up as a positive for firms.

An evergreen economy is about supporting changes in how we age rather than meeting the traditional needs of older people. It is concerned with new financial products that combine health and wealth, food and beverages that help us maintain our health for longer, an education system that supports lifelong learning, pharma that is skewed more to geroscience, health care focused on screening, monitoring and digital health, and a leisure sector supporting exercise and fitness, of social entrepreneurship supporting greater engagement over longer lives. By focusing on all of life rather than the end of life the evergreen sector will be spread across many different investor themes.

Both the silver and evergreen sectors are important and both matter, but I cannot help feeling that it is the evergreen economy that will represent the largest and most valuable growth sector.

I am prepared to spend a lot to be well looked after if I were to get dementia. I would however be prepared to spend an awful lot more if I thought there was a way to avoid experiencing dementia in the first place. That is why I believe an evergreen economy is more important and more valuable than a silver economy.

PART III

Delivering an Evergreen Society

7

The Meaning of Life

People are often advised to "prepare" for old age. But if this merely applies to setting aside money, choosing the place for retirement and laying on hobbies, we shall not be much the better for it when the day comes.

Simone de Beauvoir

Something important has been missing so far from our discussion of longer lives. We have examined the "how" of living longer—the scientific and medical shifts required, the necessary changes in behavior, how to adapt work and careers and how to prepare financially. But we haven't touched upon the "whys"—why are these extra years valuable and why is it important to extend them?

The fable of the ant and the grasshopper emphasized the importance of preparing for our future, but a different Aesop fable warns of the dangers of mindless accumulation. It tells of a miser who buries gold in a secret place in his garden. Each day the miser digs it up and counts it to make sure it is all there. One day he is observed by a thief who sneaks into the garden at night, digs up the gold and makes off with it. The miser is distraught but is given harsh advice by an unsympathetic neighbor. What's the point of hiding your wealth and never spending it?, the neighbor asks. He gives the miser a stone and tells him to bury it instead. The moral of the tale: gold is worthless unless you use it.

Similar criticism is often leveled at those who pursue a textbook longevity regimen with joyless determination. Each day, their quest for a longer life compels them to go hungry through fasting, to sweat through hours of high-intensity training and to obsess over their daily intake of supplements while monitoring their body's responses on elaborate digital devices. They are no different from the hoarding miser. His gold is measured in ounces or ingots; their gold is measured in added time alive (probably to be spent in yet more fasting, training and obsessing). They may be delighted at the lifespan they attain but, really, what use does that additional time serve? What additional fulfillment do they derive from it? There is an Italian saying *a tavola, non s'invecchia*—"at the table, one does not grow old." If food, conversation and good company are what give life meaning and keep you young, fasting may add years to life but won't meet John F. Kennedy's challenge to add life to years. You rarely hear of fasting with friends.

A similar dynamic is happening in broader society. Gains in life expectancy are increasingly accumulating in later years, when agism and a lack of supportive institutions restrict options and reduce opportunities. What is the point of accumulating additional years of life if there's no way of utilizing them to the full?

That is why we worry about outliving our purpose and our relationships, of becoming bored and irrelevant. Perhaps that is also why in a 2022 IPSOS Mori poll of the British public only one in three hoped to live to be a hundred.[1] How do we change how we age in a way that preserves meaning and fulfillment in our longer lives?

The challenge of doing so is the theme of a celebrated short story, "The Immortal," by the Argentine author Jorge Luis Borges. It is written as the autobiography of a Roman soldier, Marcus Flaminius Rufus, who becomes immortal after drinking water from a stream. Rufus spends centuries pondering his condition and eventually hears of a distant river whose waters restore mortality. He gloomily wanders the world in search of the river so he can drink its waters and bring an end to his life.

Jonathan Swift used his Struldbruggs to demonstrate the disadvantages of living a longer life in failing health. Borges goes a step further suggesting that even a healthy life can eventually become a crushing burden. Borges's immortals are sullen, lonely and unmotivated creatures. One of them who follows Rufus is revealed as Homer, the Greek poet widely although not universally credited as

the author of the *Iliad* and the *Odyssey*. Homer and his fellow immortals—referred to by Borges as Troglodytes—become desperate not
because life is short but because it is endless. Immortality renders
their lives unbearably dull and devalues their achievements.

The British philosopher, mathematician and Nobel Prize winner Bertrand Russell famously suggested that given enough time a
chimpanzee would eventually type out the works of Shakespeare as
a random sequence. In Borges's story Homer takes the argument
further and says that with infinite time available "it is impossible that
the *Odyssey* should not be composed at least once" by every immortal
person. All achievements are possible in an immortal life, everyone
has time to try everything, so everyone ends up the same: "No-one
is someone, a single immortal [person] is all [people]."[2] That is a
different take on a multistage life.

For the Troglodytes, there are no new experiences to be had, no
new challenges to face, no new things to do, nothing and no one to
learn from and no new jokes to hear. Were I to experience immortality, I would not only live long enough to see my beloved football team
Tottenham Hotspur finally win the Premier League; I would also live
long enough to get bored when they win it ten times in a row.

Borges's story is striking and at twenty pages brief enough that
you don't need to be immortal to read it. But as so often with discussions of longer life, the question of eternity distracts us from more
pressing issues. Whatever conclusions academics reach about who
really wrote the *Odyssey*, Homer is known to have lived around three
thousand years ago. Had he enjoyed the immortality conferred on
him by Borges, he would not only be alive today, he would still be
around 5 billion years from when the sun finally runs out of fuel and
humanity, or what's left of it, is destroyed. If you and I had 5 billion
years to look forward to, we might be forgiven for feeling bored,
stale and unmotivated unless we were blessed with an imperfect
memory. The real question is will we also feel bored and apathetic
if we live to a hundred or a hundred and twenty?

Sir Winston Churchill thought so. Near the end of his life he
remarked: "I don't mind dying. I've seen everything there is to see."
He was ninety when he died in 1965 and his dying words were "I'm

bored with it all." If someone like Churchill—with all his wealth, achievements and connections—can tire of living then perhaps there's a lesson for us all.

The French intellectual and feminist Simone de Beauvoir had similarly striking thoughts on aging. In her 1970 book *La Vieillesse* (Old Age) she wrote with anger and frustration about how society fails and oppresses the old. It is a dark and disturbing book about not just physical and mental decline but also exclusion, marginalization and discrimination. The book amounts to a forceful condemnation of the ways society underestimates and limits the capacity of its older citizens.

Part of the problem for de Beauvoir was capitalism, which she saw as providing no useful role for older people, thereby hastening their solitude and decline. De Beauvoir was a lifelong socialist with Marxist tendencies but there's more to her theory than ideology. It's a curious paradox that as life expectancy increases so we have become more negative about aging and the old. In a society where death has become increasingly taboo and more concentrated at older ages and where our social role and identity is frequently determined by our work, we struggle to understand the value of these later years and exclude them from our thinking and institutions. It is precisely that thinking that leads to the aging society narrative's favorite concept—the "old-age dependency ratio," the proportion of the population aged over sixty-five. Is that the best we can do in thinking about later life? Define it purely in terms of dependency?

For de Beauvoir old age reveals a fundamental problem. If society has no use for us anymore and our own activities are restricted by agist exclusion then the lack of purpose we fear when old is not a natural component of old age itself, but a reflection of the agism embedded in our culture and institutions. In that case, there is little point in extending life. De Beauvoir concludes that

> once we have understood what the state of the aged really is, we cannot satisfy ourselves with calling for a more generous "old-age policy," higher pensions, decent housing and organized leisure. It is the whole system that is at issue and our claim cannot be otherwise than radical—change life itself.[3]

That is quite the clarion call for an evergreen agenda, issued more than half a century ago.

What Borges and de Beauvoir remind us of is that we cannot look to geroscience and technology to ensure a long life becomes a good life. How we age also depends on both our individual psychology and the external perception of aging reflected in our culture. If an evergreen agenda is about changing how we age, our psychology and culture need to change too. We need to escape the limits we place on ourselves and dismantle the institutional agism that de Beauvoir angrily targeted.

The fact that we are still debating what de Beauvoir saw so clearly in 1970 demonstrates the scale of the challenge. Current patterns of cultural and psychological belief have been formed by millennia of human experience, centuries of social conditioning and decades of personal experience. That is a problem in a new evergreen era where we need to change how we age. So deep-rooted are these existing mindsets that I wonder if the more miraculous achievement would not be geroscience-induced reversals of aging but changes in society's attitudes and prejudices toward aging.

It is to these more human aspects of longevity that I now turn. What are the fundamental human opportunities that longer lives bring? What does aging differently mean psychologically at different stages of life? In what ways do we need to change our cultural attitudes toward aging? While we search for radical new treatments that can help us age biologically better we have already at our disposal a powerful force – our mind. Individuals who have positive self-perceptions of their future aging live longer—by 7.5 years—than those who are less positive.[4]

Time to Grow

There is a reason why discussions of longevity and geroscience turn so often to immortality. Human existence is structured around two basic and contradictory views. The first is that we are hardwired to want to survive. In evolutionary biology terms we are "survival machines," geared to staying alive in order to reproduce and secure the survival of our species. At a psychological level it goes even deeper. The thing we are most conscious of is our own existence. But it is precisely because our conscious thought starts with awareness of our own existence that we cannot fully comprehend what it means for us not to exist. Johann Wolfgang von Goethe, the great eighteenth-century German writer, summarized this tension between our consciousness and the idea of oblivion. "It is quite impossible for a thinking being to imagine nonbeing, a cessation of thought and life," he argued. "In this sense, everyone carries the proof of (their) own immortality within (themselves)."[5]

But at the same time we are only too aware of our own mortality. Even though mortality rates are declining at every age, lifetime mortality remains stubbornly fixed at 100 percent. We know our lives come to an end even if we don't know when or how. This sets up what Stephen Cave, director of the Leverhulme Centre for the Future of Intelligence at Cambridge University, calls the "paradox of mortality"—we know we are mortal but we cannot know what it is like not to exist.[6] That is why we have been drawn to a search for immortality throughout history. From the pyramids of Giza and the Epic of Gilgamesh right up to modern efforts of pounding the treadmill or billionaires investing in geroscience, we seek ways to deny the grim reaper.

Classical philosophy, however, offered a resolution to this paradox. For the Roman statesman Seneca, "learning how to live takes a whole life and . . . it takes a whole life to learn how to die." For the French Renaissance philosopher Michel de Montaigne, the very definition of his subject was reflected in the title of one of his essays: "To Study Philosophy is to Learn How to Die."

The emphasis here is on how a longer life offers the opportunity to accumulate wisdom and knowledge. Even as the body changes and its impermanence becomes clear, the mind discovers something fundamental and constant which transcends our individual selves. From this perspective, it is a mistake to see aging as something biological. Neither is it about the simple passing of chronological time but rather arriving at a greater understanding of ourselves and the meaning of time and our place in it.

The inspiring insight here is that the ultimate advantage of living for longer is the prospect it offers for personal growth or "adult development." What form this development should take has different advocates. Bertrand Russell, who wrote of chimpanzees and typewriters, also produced an essay called "How to Grow Old." He was well qualified for the task—he wrote it aged eighty-one (and went on to live until ninety-seven). In it he suggested:

> An individual human existence should be like a river—small at first, narrowly contained within its banks, and rushing passionately past rocks and over waterfalls. Gradually the river grows wider, the banks recede, the waters flow more quietly, and in the end, without any visible break, they become merged in the sea, and painlessly lose their individual being.[7]

This idea of wisdom as rising above our individual needs and perspectives is still with us today. It is why in some judiciaries, including the case of the United States Supreme Court, there is no age limit on being a judge. This perspective mocks Mark Zuckerberg's claim that young people are just smarter. While knowledge of most recent technological advances is greatest in the young, there are other important forms of knowledge which increase with time.

An alternative view is to see adult development and personal growth in terms of acquiring self-knowledge. For a man whose career was marked by a succession of distinct personas—from Ziggy Stardust to Aladdin Sane and the Thin White Duke—it is perhaps not surprising that David Bowie, the master chameleon of rock, viewed aging as a series of transitions. For Bowie the purpose of these transitions was to arrive at a fixed point, making aging "an extraordinary process whereby you become the person you always should have been." As with so much of Bowie's wonderful work the message isn't entirely original but echoes the insight of the sixth-century BCE Greek poet Pindar: "Become such as you are, having learned what that is."

Here the focus is not on waking up old one day and finding you've lost your ego or your sense of individuality, it's about a journey of discovery toward your true life, then living it to the full. It's about a longer life blessing you with greater self-knowledge and self-expression and ensuring you realize your full potential however old you become.

In the 1970s the German psychologist Paul Baltes developed this idea into a lifespan view of human development. He argued that as individuals age, they face different challenges, setbacks and opportunities that "give direction, force and substance to their development." But this notion of continued development is at odds with our cultural assumptions. Instead we tend to think that our character and beliefs are shaped by our earlier years, and become locked in place with age. This perceived inflexibility encourages the belief that old age is a path to irrelevance and boredom. If we define old age solely by decline, it becomes logically impossible to associate it with development and growth.

This difficulty reflects an inevitable asymmetry. Older people know what it is like to be young but it is hard for the young to imagine being old. There is an echo of Goethe's point here. When I am young I know who I am, so it is hard to conceive of me being a different person when older. I cannot comprehend the future non-existence of the character that currently defines "me," or its replacement by a new form of "me." Perhaps this is why so many of us think that aging is something that won't happen to us.

But the difficulty also reflects the fact that throughout human history the young did not expect to become old, nor did most of them reach old age. When reaching into old age was an experience for a minority a focus on finishing adult development early made sense. But that has the consequence of making old age an appendage lacking coherence with the rest of our life and plans. The development of retirement in the twentieth century was partly a solution to this problem, but as life expectancy increases retirement is proving ill-equipped to cope with the demands made on it.

If our later years are to be evergreen and enjoyed, we need to recognize them as an integral part of our overall development. We should understand that our desires and our potential evolve continually over time, and construct new avenues of development that enable us to flourish at every age. Achieving this requires changes in attitudes and individual practices to prolong our adult development. Whether those avenues involve seeking wisdom, self-expression, continuing to work, changing careers, community building, family support or pursuing individual interests will vary from person to person. But the key to rethinking longer lives is recognizing that adult development doesn't stop at the age of twenty-one or even at sixty-five. It is an ongoing process. Recognizing it as such will go a long way to reversing past tendencies to underestimate older people and the potential of our own later years.

Déjà Vu All Over Again

Reshaping the arc of our lives sounds daunting but it has been done before. For all the excitement at the potential of geroscience to change the way we think about aging, humans have been there and done that—repeatedly.

According to the French historian Philippe Ariès, the notion of childhood as a clearly distinct emotional stage of our development did not emerge in western Europe until the seventeenth century.[8] Before then children were essentially seen as little adults. Similarly, for most of human history, individuals crossed swiftly and often brutally from childhood to adulthood. But in 1905 the American psychologist G. Stanley Hall published his seminal work *Adolescence* providing a coherent definition and analysis of the phase.

The phrase "teenager" is also a twentieth-century invention, becoming commonly used from the late 1930s as extended education became the norm postponing adulthood. In this sense, my parents were never really "teenagers" as they were both fourteen when they started the decidedly adult pursuits of working and paying rent. Today, age-related behaviors are still changing as formal education extends later into life and marriage and raising a family are postponed, and sociologists have identified a new period of "emerging adulthood."[9] Just as I experienced the teenage years in a way my parents never did, my three children are experiencing their twenties and early thirties in a markedly different way from mine.

Later life has been similarly transformed. The modern view of old age and retirement was heavily shaped by the introduction of pensions in the early twentieth century—most notably the doctrine that old age began at sixty-five. With this redefinition of old age came the need to define and characterize "middle age."[10] As fertility rates declined, our "middle" years became less about nurturing families and saw a greater focus on individual needs. Reflecting this, the phrase "midlife crisis" was coined in 1965 by Elliott Jaques, a forty-eight-year-old Canadian psychoanalyst and management consultant. Like other age-based stereotypes, the term "midlife crisis" became more popular with film directors and magazines than academics, many of whom questioned the evidence for its existence.[11]

In this broader historical context, the evergreen agenda is merely the latest in a long line of revisions to the life course. It demands that we redefine stages of life to support adult development throughout an extended second half of life. But in changing this second half it also demands and enables changes earlier on. An evergreen agenda points to the need at younger ages to invest more in our future but by also providing us with more future time it provides more options and possibilities to pursue now.

Health and biology will inevitably influence the shape of our new, multistage lives and what we do and at what age we can do it. It was of course ever thus. In Shakespeare's play *As You Like It*, the relentless pessimist and court jester Jaques delivers what has become known as his "seven ages of man" speech, beginning with one of the best-known lines in theatre history: "All the world's a stage . . ."

In this gloomiest of surveys of the human lifespan, Jaques describes "the infant, mewling and puking in the nurse's arms"; the "whining" schoolboy; the lover with "a woeful ballad"; the soldier "full of strange oaths"; the justice, "in fair round belly"; the sixth age "with spectacles on nose and pouch on side." And then Jaques reaches the seventh and final age, an agony of absence: "sans teeth, sans eyes, sans taste, sans everything."

Let's start by looking at this from Dorian Gray's perspective. If the dream of a Dorian-like life is achieved then we would reach our seventh age in good health. We would still have our teeth, still have our eyes, still taste our wine, be lacking for nothing. We would need to find another way to define our later years.

Rather than define old age by "sans" or the lack of something, we need to define it in terms of a presence and a purpose. We need a richer appreciation of our older years, what we want from them, and what this extended adult development might involve. Right now we focus too much on health in defining the needs of older people, to the detriment of any broader notion of development. As more people live into older ages we need to think differently about this common experience.

Of course we need to keep a sense of proportion. In advocating a move from focusing only on decline we shouldn't overcompensate and elevate our later years to an exalted status. In seeking a positive role for old age and longer lives there is a tendency to focus on the teleological—to see life as aiming at some goal or purpose which gives our life a sense of meaning and direction. The danger is seeing adult development as a progression toward *something*—whether that is wisdom or self-knowledge.

This goal-oriented notion is a heavy burden to place on old age and not one we demand of other life stages. Ultimately the advantage of a longer life is having more time to use in any way you value. It is not a competition; there should be no stress or fear of failure. Discovering as you proceed through each stage of life what success means to you given your circumstances is what extended adult development is for.

Changing How We Age Individually

In 1969, in an interview with the *Washington Post* journalist Carl Bernstein (later of Watergate fame), the psychiatrist Robert Butler coined the phrase "agism." Butler defined agism as "a systematic stereotyping of and discrimination against people because they are old." Agism remains a major obstacle to extending adult development over a lifetime. It is the core component of how we underestimate capacity in later life.

Whether it is the allocation of health resources in a hospital emergency ward, discrimination in hiring and firing, the images of wrinkled hands and tired older people the media uses for stories about aging or everyday interactions in the shopping mall—"What a sweet old lady/miserable old so-and-so"—it is easy to find examples of agism. As the number of older people increases, agism is on the rise, and with the new reality of the young destined to become old it is something most of us can expect to experience. What makes it all worse is that agism intersects with and amplifies other forms of prejudice, such as racism and sexism.

Agism affects behavior in two limiting ways—an external way that is embedded in our culture and an internal way reflected in our individual psychology. Agism in our culture shapes our collective behavior, policies and institutions and limits the options available to the old. Discrimination about hiring older workers robs them of job opportunities that go to younger candidates, restricting their ability to extend their working lives.[12] At the same time, individuals internalize this agism, which further disadvantages them. If you believe that your later years will be less productive, you won't bother to invest in them. You then create a self-fulfilling prophecy that risks leaving you jobless or underemployed.

Criticism of agism comes in three forms. The first is that age-based stereotypes have never been relevant. Old age is in general just misunderstood. The young struggle to imagine being old and therefore fail to identify with older people. The old are then regarded as "not like us," leading to discrimination, exclusion, prejudice and stereotypes. If for most of human history the young were unlikely to become the old, this sense of the "otherness" of old age was understandable. In an evergreen world it isn't. Agism is a prejudice against your future self, an act of future self-harm which life expectancy trends are making ever more likely.

The second criticism of age-based stereotypes is they fail to reflect the diversity with which people age. It is easy to find inspirational examples of spectacular achievements by older people. Take Lester Wright, a Second World War veteran and a centenarian who in May 2022 set a new world record for the hundred-plus age group in the

100-meter sprint: 26.3 seconds. Yuichiro Miura reached the summit of Everest aged eighty. Or consider Iris Apfel, an American entrepreneur and fashion icon who at the age of ninety-seven was signed up by IMG as a model. We've already mentioned Mick Jagger, still rocking and rolling at the age of seventy-nine.

At the same time, we all know of many others who haven't aged as well, whether due to genetic inheritance, circumstances, bad luck or a combination of these. This diversity of activity and achievement at older ages makes a mockery of stereotypes, especially when they tend to focus all too often on the worst outcomes.

The third criticism is that even if age-based stereotypes used to have some accuracy they no longer do. Let's return again to Zuckerberg's quote that young people are just smarter. Over the past century, the time we devote to our education has steadily increased. Both my parents left school aged fourteen and my grandparents aged twelve. In England now you cannot finish your education until you are eighteen. When education increases across the generations it is natural to think that the young are smarter, if education is indeed what makes you smart. But that increase in education has been leveling off. The result is that young and old now have much more similar levels of education. In 1950 only one in twenty-five of the US population aged over sixty-five had been to college (university) whereas today it is nearly three out of five.[13] Today one in four of those aged twenty-five to sixty-four are graduates, not too dissimilar to the one in five of those aged over sixty-five. The result is that older and younger workers have become much more likely to have similar levels of education.

That agism exists and has damaging consequences is readily apparent. The AARP estimates that age discrimination in employment costs the US around $850 billion annually.[14] But there is an irony that at the same time as agism is increasingly becoming a social issue we live in a society where the old have never had so much political power or financial muscle. When the president of the United States is aged eighty and running for office again, when the majority of employment growth in high-income countries is explained by those aged over fifty and the same group accounts for fifty-six cents out of every dollar spent in the US,[15] agism is clearly more nuanced than a simple blanket prejudice.

Agism abounds because we have a deep instinct that there are significant differences between the young and the old. Even those who argue against common negative stereotypes often do so by trying to supplant them with positive ones—older people are wiser, better at making teams work more efficiently, more punctual, etc. We may fail to properly acknowledge the diversity with which we age but we do think that differences in chronological age (years lived), biological age (the state of your health) and thanatological age (years until death) lead to differences in behaviors and attitudes. That is why we trade so readily in age-based stereotypes.

In an evergreen world the relationship between these three concepts of aging will lead to changes in the behavior of older people. Evergreen lives don't dispense with aging but will alter how we age. To understand how aging is likely to be modified, where our agist stereotypes are likely to mislead and how you must act differently we need to unravel the separate roles of these three distinct concepts of age.

It is too easy to think of aging only in terms of health. But we know aging is much more than that. That is why, even if geroscience could deliver the extreme Peter Pan case where a ninety-year-old and a twenty-year-old have the same health and mortality risk, they would still be different because of their chronological age. Being ninety in this case is not the new twenty just a new ninety. But what set of behaviors would make it new? Would we expect a ninety-year-old to go clubbing as much as their twenty-year-old biological twin? How would that extra seventy years of life experience influence them? How would a ninety-year-old with thirty more years of life ahead of them differ in their behavior from a ninety-year-old expecting just five more years of life?

Becoming More Open to Risk

As we age we tend to become more risk averse.[16] The older we get the less inclined we are to try out new things, seek new friendships or invest financially in equities. Is this an intrinsic feature of becoming old or something that will change in an evergreen world?

Aristotle is a towering influence in philosophy. Even so, some of his views on older people win few supporters among contemporary gerontologists and reveal just how long-lasting agism is. He thought them cowardly, bitter, jaundiced and with a tendency to talk too much. He believed them to be cynical because they had the misfortune of living long enough to see their hopes disappointed. By contrast, he felt that the young are driven more by hope than experience and are more optimistic. By his account, the passage of time and the disappointments of life make older people more risk averse.

An alternative view of rising risk aversion links to shrinking thanatological age. When you expect to live for many more years you can afford to gamble with your investments. If they turn out badly you have time to recover and still come out ahead. When you start to run out of time, you get nervous about betting the farm.

It is possible, of course, that both explanations are true so that increasing risk aversion in those who are older is a product of both learning over time and a shortening of time horizons. But so long as the role of thanatological age is important the implication is clear. In an evergreen world, as you age you should be more open to risk than past generations. That may show itself in being more interested in new roles at work, seeking new life challenges or friendships or holding your investments in equity for longer.

Be More Wolverine

Another age-based stereotype is that we become more conservative and less open to change as we age, more fixed in our habits. Yet again the widespread conviction of this age-based stereotype isn't matched unequivocally by academic research. While through illness and retirement older people may have more fixed behaviors due to limited options, there is evidence they are often more open to new ideas than younger people.[17]

But there is a logic to this stereotype. Even if a sixty-year-old has the same level of intelligence and cognitive functioning as a twenty-year-old, they have a different incentive to adapt to new ideas and habits. A sixty-year-old has not just to learn something new but also to forget what they know. The twenty-year-old by contrast has a different choice. Their sole decision is whether to invest in a skill—new or old. They also have a longer time ahead of them in which to benefit from learning the new.

The point of this description is not to prove that all older people are conservative and reluctant to change. If you are someone who loves learning then whether you are sixty or twenty you will eagerly seek something new. The point is instead to show that how we age is not fixed but depends on the mix of cognitive, biological and thanatological age.

As life expectancy increases so at every age you have more years ahead of you than previously. Longer lives mean you are younger for longer, at least in a thanatological sense. That means it makes more sense to invest in the future and learn those new skills, to leave old knowledge and habits behind. Psychologically you need to be like Wolverine, regrowing and recharging your values, skills and relationships.

Forward Versus Present

But the gloomy specter of the Troglodytes conjured up by Jorge Luis Borges still looms over us. At what point does an evergreen life go on too long? I have moments when I am bored but I have a long and still expanding list of things I want to do. As each year goes by the list doesn't get any shorter and it will take me more than a good part of infinity to achieve a small part of what Churchill did. Is boredom really inevitable and is it so unbearable? But that is the trouble with writing about aging when you are fifty-seven. I cannot know what the future will bring. As the American comedian Steven Wright said—"I intend to live forever. So far, so good."

In this context, I take great comfort from the work of my friend and colleague Professor Laura Carstensen, the founder of Stanford

University's Center on Longevity and creator of the concept of a New Map of Life, a project I am delighted to be involved with.

For all our fears of old age, researchers have consistently shown that it is the years in midlife that are the unhappiest.[18] While happiness does eventually decline in old age, it still remains higher than its midlife nadir. That always comes as a surprise to middle-aged people, who often fear getting old. To explain this apparent paradox, Carstensen looked at changes in adult behavior over time and concluded that as we move through life we reprioritize our goals. As a result she developed what she called her "socioemotional selectivity theory" (SST), a neat modern take on the notion of becoming wiser with age grounded in awareness of our own mortality.

When we are young and time stretches far ahead, we emphasize future-orientated goals such as education and learning, finding new friends and experiencing different ways of life. As we get older and the time remaining to us shrinks we put greater weight on present-focused goals such as spending time on familiar things that reliably bring us meaning and pleasure. We become, for example, more interested in existing relationships than making new friends.

The consequence is that the young engage more in knowledge-building and exploration even though these may be emotionally challenging. Whereas the older we get, the more we focus on more immediate emotionally meaningful goals. That is why older people are happier. Carstensen conducted further studies to be sure that this was a feature of shortened time horizons, rather than an intrinsic consequence of age: she found similar behaviors in younger people who for varying reasons believed they faced a limited future.

Another feature of SST is the way that diminishing time horizons affect our mental outlook. As we start running out of years, our minds shift toward seeking more emotionally satisfying stimuli. The result is a "positivity bias" whereby older people remember past events more favorably than the young and are less negative about daily events. Carstensen even found support for this during the early days of the Covid-19 pandemic, when older people displayed lower levels of psychological stress despite their greater mortality risk in the midst of a global pandemic.[19]

Carstensen is not suggesting that older people force themselves to be cheery. Rather, the impact of time and the changing context of life brings about a shift in what they choose to do, directing them toward more emotionally satisfying experiences.

There is much to like in Carstensen's theory. It offers both a reminder and an explanation of why on average older people report higher levels of psychological well-being than those in middle age. Given the negativity attached to later years, that is an important fact to emphasize. It also provides a sense of adult development and adaptation in later years without being prescriptive. Older people are better at being in the moment, at focusing on the things that matter and protecting their emotional state. But it isn't that they have developed an elevated level of consciousness and superior wisdom. They are instead simply adapting and developing in response to the passing of time.

Carstensen's theory also sheds light on how behavior will change as we live longer. It takes a while to make an "old friend" but it's harder still when you're eighty with a life expectancy of eighty-five. As one of Carstensen's older interviewees remarks: "You can't make new 'old friends' when you are eighty years old. The numbers simply do not work." But if life expectancy extends to a hundred then the calculus changes and whole new friendship options open. The need to invest in new relationships will extend into later years as life expectancy increases.

There's a familiar message here: renewal and future investment are keys to an evergreen life as time horizons expand. It also suggests a new valuable skill—accepting the need to be uncomfortable as you get older in searching out the new and not always focusing on the more immediately emotionally rewarding.

Age Gaps

Carstensen's research also provides insight into why intergenerational friendships should become more important in an evergreen world. Despite improvements in life expectancy, mortality rates still rise with age. Friendships among people of similar age become "risky" at older years because of the higher chance that one of the friends will die. In America today an eighty-year-old has a two in five chance of living to be ninety but that means the chances of two eighty-year-old friends both making it to ninety are one in six. Losing lifelong friends at older ages can be a bitter and lonely experience. Investing in friendships with those younger than you will minimize this risk. That could be through bonds within the family, with a neighbor, a work colleague or through a broader social network. As with all evergreen initiatives, the earlier you bear this in mind the better.

In case "investment" and "risk" in friendships sounds more like bleak economic analysis than human sensitivity, it is worth emphasizing that cross-generation relationships have a special human warmth in them with benefits flowing in both directions. Experiments introducing older people living in care homes to visiting young children show benefits for both. Students who lodge for free in homes with older residents report the same. Positive intergenerational relationships have long been a Hollywood staple, featuring in films as diverse as *The Karate Kid*, *Grandma* and *Up*.

Age-gap friendships are particularly valuable in an evergreen world. In families with fewer children, more relationships will be cross-generational. The bonds between younger and older friends are, for the older generation, the psychological equivalent of Wolverine regeneration. In a world of longer lives and lower fertility they need to be encouraged, not just from an individual perspective but for social cohesion too.

Changing How We Age Culturally

It's up to each of us to work on our individual needs and avoid internalizing agism. But we also need a reset in society's cultural assumptions. Without a radical shift in attitudes toward the old and aging we will be unable to seize the advantages that longer lives offer us.

Throughout history two contrasting views of old people have competed to shape our thinking. One sees old age as a dark place, as exemplified in de Beauvoir's *Old Age*. Declining physical and cognitive capacity, a loss of independence, social exclusion and approaching mortality all combine to present it as a bad experience. For de Beauvoir "It is old age, rather than death, that is to be contrasted with life. Old age is life's parody."

The alternative view of old age is more optimistic and most famously articulated in Cicero's dialogue *On Old Age*. Cicero creates a conversation between an older Roman senator, Cato, and two young men in their thirties, Laelius and Scipio. He cleverly inverts the negatives normally attributed to old age and presents them as advantages: "It is not by muscle, speed, or physical dexterity that great things are achieved," he writes, "but by reflection, force of character, and judgment; in these qualities old age is usually not . . . poorer, but is even richer."

Cicero's point is that aging doesn't mean things get worse. There are plenty of ways to enjoy life. What you need and what you want change with age. To the young this may sound like a process of loss, but Cicero argues it is one of gain. This is an account of personal growth, accepting physical decline but recognizing that with age other things will improve. His advice is to focus on the internal and see age as a process of increasing maturity, not decline.

The balance between these two contrasting views of old age has changed continuously over time and also varies across cultures.[20] It is argued that with the advent of the Industrial Revolution came a greater emphasis on work as a way of measuring an individual's contribution and a move to more negative concepts of old age. Western cultures with their greater attention to individual self-expression are often assumed to have more negative perceptions of aging compared to societies more centered on the collective. Societies based on Confucian ideas, with its stress on filial piety and ancestral worship, in particular are thought to hold more positive values toward older people.

As with so many neat grand theories, these assumed cultural differences don't hold up in their entirety when exposed to empirical scrutiny. One study of twenty-six countries found that while cross-country differences exist, they are not as stark as you might expect.[21] In particular there is little evidence for simple-minded East/West or rich/poor country dichotomies. Intriguingly, one strong finding was that the greater the proportion of people aged over sixty-five in a country the more negative were views toward older people. This helps explain why Japan, despite its Confucian influence, is nestled among Western countries in terms of its attitudes toward the old. The Japanese have seen a new word, *rogai*—written with the characters for "old" and "damage"—emerge to cover the negative impact of the old on society—from the depressing effect on economic growth right through to everyday irritations such as the inconvenience of being held up by slower-moving older people. This is a reminder that our attitudes toward becoming old aren't fixed but can change.

Wanted—A New Culture of Aging

An evergreen agenda requires more than just zigzagging back and forth between these two contrasting narratives. It also requires moving away from overly positive or overly negative conceptions of later life.

Clearly the negative perspective summarized so angrily by de Beauvoir needs to be jettisoned in an evergreen era. A pessimistic outlook can't possibly help us recognize the potential of our later years. With its more positive outlook, Cicero's view has much that appeals. There is an emphasis on continued adult development and enhancing existing qualities. There are evergreen elements in its key message to not underestimate our later years and a stress on the quality of later life.

But there are also discordant notes. Cicero's senator, Cato, is a wealthy old man with land and resources at his disposal. He can afford to be contemplative and focus on inner peace. If you were an older slave in ancient Rome, inner peace was presumably hard to come by.

Cicero's work also has a prescriptive tone with its idea of aging as developing moral character. This is a shared problem with many attempts at painting a positive picture of old age and any definition of what "aging better" means. The contemporary concept of "successful aging" (defined as high physical, psychological, and social functioning in old age without major diseases) is often criticized for implying that "unsuccessful" forms of aging exist.[22] Shouldn't all forms of aging be considered successful given the alternative is dying?

There is also a flavor in Cicero's account of what the Cambridge philosopher G. E. Moore dubbed the "naturalistic fallacy." The fallacy is to assume that because something is natural it is also good. Just because something "is" doesn't mean it is what it "ought" to be. If a second longevity revolution is about changing how we age then we need to avoid falling for this fallacy. If geroscience leads to substantial improvements in biological age then how we age does not need to conform to Cicero's acceptance of physical decline and finding comfort in what is gained. But even without scientific breakthroughs, we should be prepared to grow old disgracefully and energetically rather than philosophically and stoically, if that is our preference.

Mind Your Language

Another Cambridge philosopher, Ludwig Wittgenstein, once remarked that "the limits of my language mean the limits of my world." When it comes to debates about aging and the need to move toward a more evergreen culture our current use of language is a problem. It's all too easy to get into a linguistic tangle over the related but separate concepts of aging, old age, end of life and death. A good example here is the tendency to think of longevity and longer lives as meaning more years at the end of life rather than more time across our life. Similarly, everyone is "aging" but an aging society is always interpreted as about old people.

This conflation can be explained as a consequence of the first longevity revolution, with its reduction in infant and midlife mortality, so that most people now die in old age. Dying and being old have become statistically more closely associated than ever before. Paradoxically, at the same time, the gap between old age and end of life is widening. If we stick with the bureaucratic definition of "old" as sixty-five years of age and above (which we shouldn't) then in 1851 it was certainly true that the end of life followed closely behind becoming old. At that time only around one in four Swedish sixty-five-year-olds could expect to live to eighty and only one in fifty to ninety.[23] Now it's three-quarters and one in three.

One obvious response to this is simply to redefine what it means to be old. Rather than define old age chronologically (sixty-five years or more) we could do so in terms of remaining life expectancy. Old age might be redefined in thanatological terms as less than ten years left to live. Using that definition Swedish old age would have begun at age eighty in 2022, compared to seventy-two in 1951 and sixty-six in 1851. This is the approach that the United Nations has adopted, based on research by Warren Sanderson from Stony Brook University and Sergei Scherbov of the Vienna-based Wittgenstein Centre for Demography. The two researchers proposed a new concept of "prospective age" based on remaining life expectancy.[24] With this redefinition of who is old there is much less statistical support for an "aging society" and a rising proportion of older people.

What becomes apparent from this discussion is that the meaning of "aging" and "old" vary according to context and we have an insufficiently rich vocabulary to deal with this. These linguistic limits fuel confusion. That is why the phrase "aging society" slides barely noticeably from "aging" to "old" to "end of life" in public discourse.

The American linguist Benjamin Lee Whorf is often remembered for promoting the claim that Arctic Inuit and Yupik peoples had an extensive range of different words for "snow" reflecting its importance in their lives. Over time, Whorf's example of what he called linguistic relativity became something of an urban myth—or what one critic described as the "great eskimo vocabulary hoax." While there appear to be many different-sounding words used in snowy conditions, other researchers—among them the Harvard linguist Steven Pinker—believe that few are applied to the actual frosty white substance that is snow.[25] Whether the Inuit do or do not have an extensive vocabulary for snow, in an evergreen world we need a richer vocabulary to deal with aging and the issues of old age.

However, I am not sure that creating new definitions of "old" and "aging" is the best way to clear up the confusion. Perhaps chronological, biological and thanatological age and their ilk can be used to build a new evergreen vocabulary. But the reasons we want to define "old" are so varied and so dependent on context that greater precision is a technical rather than a cultural exercise. If instead we view aging as a malleable process that will take us along different individual routes at different paces, we can start to create an evergreen culture around aging. A culture that helps us focus on the lifetime aim of aging better and recognizes aging as a process we are all embarked on. One that doesn't rely on simple stereotypes and which supports the notion of lifelong development. The key is to see aging as a state of flux involving us all and not an event or a state that segregates one group from another.

Life Is Just One Thing After Another

As life lengthens the number of transitions from one stage to the next will increase. Sometimes these may be abrupt (you lose your job, you get divorced, you suddenly fall ill). At other times they will appear more extended and cumulative (you develop new interests and habits and become interested in new things, you become bored or restless, you gradually find certain things physically more challenging).

This revised view of aging helps to reframe notions of decline. The evergreen view is that not everything declines as you age and not everything that does decline matters. There will be different moments when we hit our peak physical capacity, our top earning potential, maximum social reach or happiness highs. From this perspective we will frequently be passing one peak or another. Linguistically that requires a move away from agist language such as "over the hill" or "past it." What does matter as we navigate different life stages is that we are in good enough shape to meet the demands of whatever the next stage requires. Like relay runners passing on the baton, we need to make sure the next stage gets the best possible start.

In ancient Egypt, the dead were buried with their organs and food in the belief that they would be needed in the afterlife. That was about immortality but we need to think of similar gifts to help progressions across an evergreen life in order for our future self to thrive. As each stage of our life unfolds, we should consider how we'll get through what comes next. The longer our futures extend, the more help we'll need from our younger selves.

But what will your future self want and need? And why should you care? It's a fair question and the Norwegian philosopher Jon Elster neatly summarizes the problem. "The absolute priority of the present is somewhat like my absolute priority over all other persons," says Elster. "I am I—while they are all 'out there.'"[26] As life gets longer so we need to tackle two related problems: our tendency to focus on now and not the future; and how we form a link between who we are today and our future selves.

With a longer life we have a duty of care to our increasing number of future selves. The sixty-year-old me will be different from the seventy-year-old, and now perhaps I have to consider the eighty-year-old me and maybe the ninety-year-old too. How do we exercise that responsibility? A clue emerges in the work of the late British philosopher Derek Parfit. Derek spent most of his career at All Souls College in Oxford where in 1990 I was awarded what is known as a Prize Fellowship. That presented me with many opportunities to talk with him over various meals in the august surroundings of the college dining hall and buttery. My fifty-seven-year-old self today wishes my twenty-seven-year-old self had spent less time answering his kind questions about my research and more time asking about his groundbreaking work on moral philosophy.

I always found Derek charming and kind but colorful stories about him abound.[27] He is said to have hated wasting time and would wear the same clothes and eat the same food each day in order to minimize time spent making decisions. His enthusiasm for efficient time management meant he would also read philosophy papers while brushing his teeth. He got through startling numbers of toothbrushes as the papers grew longer and he kept brushing as he read.[28]

Derek's work focused on establishing a solid foundation for moral actions that extend beyond just self-interested behavior. Through a series of clever thought experiments variously involving teletransportation to Mars, having duplicates made of your brain and various other science-fiction-inspired scenarios, he argued that our concept of "self" is much weaker than we might imagine. In particular, he disputed the view that our sense of identity is defined by the person occupying our body traveling continuously through time and accumulating experience. For Parfit what mattered most for our identity is not physical but psychological continuity. By that he meant the links between our past beliefs, desires, values and actions and those we now hold or undertake today.

There is, for example, a psychological continuity between me writing this book today and the me in the past who became interested in longevity. In that earlier time I was bored and frustrated with my previous macroeconomic interests and found this new topic fascinating. I started to learn more, to think and write about and discuss the subject with others. As a result my views evolved and altered, my skills, interests and friendships were different. This led me to change my mind about my future, what was important to me, and how society should think about longevity. That prompted me to write this book, to organize my own thoughts with the hope of changing the views of others. Much is different now. My body has aged and most of my bodily cells have been replaced so I am quite literally not the person I physically used to be. What I value and focus on has also shifted, my friends and work relationships have changed. I have moved house and city, separated and married. What makes this *my* path and *my* identity is not that it has all been experienced by my physical body. Rather, the psychological continuity of experiences makes it mine and defines me.

This sense of continuity as the core to our identity is attractive as a foundation for an evergreen culture of old age and aging. By focusing on the psychological rather than the physical it makes clear that aging isn't necessarily about decay. If a Wolverine-like treatment becomes available that restores my body to its twenty-seven-year-old state, that would of course be a major change to my appearance and future prospects. But suddenly possessing an abdominal six-pack and a slimmer waistline won't change my psychological history. I will still be a fifty-seven-year-old and not a twenty-seven-year-old. My identity hinges on psychological continuity, not physical regeneration. This idea fits well with the notion of aging as a process rather than an event or a state. It also involves no sense of one path being better or worse than another. It is about evolution and adaptation rather than prescribing a particular path. The path you follow is literally what defines you.

Yet Parfit's insights also present a problem for longevity; as we have already seen, it is hard to identify with your future self. The longer life extends, the greater the number of cumulative transitions and changes in our identity and the tougher the task to connect with our future selves. Our future selves become more and more distant from us in time and effectively become more and more of a stranger to us. Why should we go out of our way to look after someone we don't know?

This is where Parfit's theory takes an interesting turn. If our identity comes from psychological continuity, it is defined by a much broader range of interactions and connections. We are in part those we meet and spend time with. Because my sense of self is not bound up so much with me as a physical individual, I should act morally and kindly to those with whom I connect and that also includes my own future self: all in some way are part of me.

By loosening our sense of identity from a firm sense of space and time Parfit's theory helps reduce the sense of "otherness" of old age. It also offers a way that prevents us from seeing our early years purely as a vehicle for investing with joyless urgency in our later years. My future self also has obligations to me today. Parfit's theory has a sense of timelessness that allows for the recognition of today but enmeshes it within a broader web of obligations and connections that define me.

This approach echoes Buddhist thought, which explains why one monastery in northern India incorporated passages from Parfit's 1984 book *Reasons and Persons* into their chants. That is a form of psychological continuity of which Parfit, who died in 2017, might well have approved.

For Parfit, these weren't just philosophical thoughts but led to changes in how he saw his own life.

When I believed [that physical identity is what matters], I seemed imprisoned in myself. My life seemed like a glass tunnel, through which I was moving faster every year, and at the end of which there was darkness. When I changed my view, the walls of my glass tunnel disappeared. I now live in the open air. There is still a difference between my life and the lives of other people. But the difference is less. Other people are closer. I am less concerned about the rest of my own life, and more concerned about the lives of others.

In this way Parfit sees identity very differently from the Troglodytes dreamed up by Borges. In the Borges story immortality leads to a loss of identity as everyone becomes indistinct from one another. For Parfit our identity is constructed more broadly. In its focus on connectivity with others it also resonates with Carstensen's socioemotional selectivity theory. Parfit's approach further suggests a softening or even a resolution of the paradox of mortality as it makes death a very different type of transition.

When I believed [that physical identity is what matters], I also cared more about my inevitable death. After my death, there will be no one living who will be me. I can now redescribe this fact. Though there will later be many experiences, none of these experiences will be connected to my present experiences by chains of such direct connections as those involved in experience-memory, or in the carrying out of an earlier intention. Some of these future experiences may be related to my present experiences in less direct ways. There will later be some memories about my life. And there may later be thoughts that are influenced by mine, or things done as the result of my advice.

My death will break the more direct relations between my present experiences and future experiences, but it will not break various other relations. This is all there is to the fact that there will be no one living who will be me. Now that I have seen this, my death seems to me less bad.[29]

This notion of our psychological continuity extending past our lifetime goes back to reaffirming the value of friendships across the generations. If your friends live on far beyond you, your psychological continuity is extended.

Building Blocks for a New Culture

So what are the ingredients of a reimagined culture of aging that are fit for an evergreen life?

First is a greater sense of individual agency. We need to make fewer assumptions about what older people are like and what they need. We should aim instead to provide more options and easier platforms for them to make their own decisions. Dismantling agism would be a good start. Reorientating our health systems away from intervention to a focus on quality of life would also help us to increase individual choice. As people age so medical care needs to be directed at what is most important for them in terms of the life they want to lead.

Cicero's emphasis on the internal acceptance of aging is important but should be supplemented by outward action, social engagement and purpose driven by the individual themselves. People need to be able to construct the future life they want.

We need assessments of aging that are neither prescriptive nor judgmental. We don't give people prizes for winning middle age or beating adolescence and it isn't obvious what criteria we would use if we did. Old age should be no more of a competition than any other age and the individuals concerned are the best judges of how it's going. David Bowie's notion of aging as a series of progressions toward the real you is inspiring. As a university professor I find Cicero's emphasis on reflection appealing. But the real point of an evergreen agenda is to make every age, including old age, whatever you want it to be.

Above all we need to move away from seeing aging as an event and old age as a state. Marcel Proust's famous seven-volume novel *À la recherche du temps perdu* (In Search of Lost Time) is about life and the passing of time. Perhaps befittingly *The Guinness Book of*

Records hails it as the longest novel ever written—it is twice as long as Tolstoy's epic *War and Peace*. In Proust's final volume, *Le Temps retrouvé* (Time Regained—a suitably Wolverine title) he writes: "And now I began to understand what old age was—old age, which perhaps of all the realities is the one of which we preserve for longest in our life a purely abstract conception."

We struggle to identify with old age because it is about a future person who is different from whom we are today. As a result we see old age as an abstraction. We understand that at some point we will cease to be our youthful or middle-aged selves and become someone else—an older version of the original. But it's hard to see that person from here, so we assume there must be an event— "aging"—whereupon we shed abstraction and enter an identifiable state of being "old." The most obvious example of this event/state process is the bureaucratic notion that we become old at sixty-five. That has become the boundary that effectively separates the young and the old.

There are multiple problems with this blinkered view of aging and old age. The first is that aging occurs continuously throughout our life. There is no single year when aging happens, and no set age when it stops and your state becomes immune to change. One of the biggest challenges of an evergreen agenda is to persuade the young that aging is not just for old people. The young need to think about it too. It may not be the most pressing problem of their early years but they need to be aware that aging doesn't start at sixty-five.

In a similar vein, aging occurs at different speeds for different people. That biological reality renders the task of defining being "old" well-nigh impossible. Aging is too diverse a process to be squeezed into stereotypes or convenient pigeonholes. Bertrand Russell's analogy of human existence as a river also holds for biological aging. We are all floating in the same direction, but currents and rapids will sweep some along faster while others might travel more serenely. The time you start doesn't determine how far you will get. Look around—you'll see some people paddling frantically, others letting the river do the work. Eventually, we'll all end up at the same destination—but we won't all arrive at the same time.

The notion of old age as a separate state also reinforces the stigma of "otherness" that feeds into agism and our fear of becoming old. It breaks the link between ourselves today and ourselves in the future. That is disastrous for an evergreen agenda.

If, instead, we see aging as a continual process, we can understand better how today is linked to tomorrow and how to exploit the malleability of age. Aging is about moving continually through time, not about crossing the threshold of a door marked "old." In an era when the young can expect to become old and potentially very old, the focus must be on aging as a process, not an event or a destination.

8

The Generational Challenge

The failure to invest in youth reflects a lack of compassion and a colossal failure of common sense.

Coretta Scott King

On his twentieth birthday in February 1945, my father was serving on a Royal Navy minesweeper. In that same month, Churchill, Roosevelt and Stalin met in the Black Sea resort of Yalta to decide the postwar fate of Germany. The end of the war in Europe was only three months away. Within a year my father would be out of the navy and rejoining civilian life.

I celebrated my own twentieth birthday forty years later. Unlike my father, the closest I had come to war was listening to protest songs. Top of the UK music charts at that time was "19," a song by Paul Hardcastle lamenting the loss of so many young soldiers in Vietnam whose average age was nineteen. Within a year I was thinking about where to apply for graduate school, worrying about the Chernobyl nuclear explosion and mourning England's exit from the World Cup at the hands of Argentina or more precisely Diego Maradona's "hand of God" goal.

In 2019, it was my youngest son's turn to reach twenty. Amid growing debate about climate change, the UK recorded its then hottest-ever August bank holiday with temperatures in west London reaching 33.3°C (91.9°F)—that is high for this rainy island. Microsoft invested $1 billion in OpenAI, which had just launched Chat GPT-2 with its revolutionary potential to change employment prospects. Within the next year, my son would be finishing university in the midst of a global pandemic and trying to find a job in an increasingly competitive labor market.

Three generations, three very different twentieth birthdays. Each of us was dealt a different hand in terms of how the world was treating us and what our future looked like. We each faced different daily concerns and had important short-term obstacles to overcome.

While individually each of us is having to adapt to the reality of longer lives, we are all having to do so at different points in the life cycle and in different contexts. That leads to a number of generational challenges that will be played out at the economic, social and political level as well as within families.

In particular, younger generations such as my son's face two distinctive challenges that past cohorts didn't. They are the first cohort growing up with not just the possibility but the expectation of living into their ninth or tenth decade, if not beyond. The longevity imperative is most important for them. But there is a second distinctive feature that defines them. Because of past longevity gains, they are the first cohort growing old while the majority of their parent's generation is still alive. If each age group changes how they age in response to longevity it has consequences for the groups following on behind them.

We can look to Buckingham Palace for an example of what we might call the traffic-jam effect of increased longevity. The late Queen Elizabeth II was the oldest monarch in English history when she died in 2022 aged ninety-six years. One consequence of her striking longevity was that her son, King Charles III, is also a royal record holder. No heir to the throne has ever waited so long to reign. By the time Charles finally succeeded his mother he had waited seventy years to be king.

When an older generation lives for longer it has an impact on younger generations—not only for privileged royals but for ordinary family businesses, finances, homes and lifestyles. It forces the young and the middle-aged to age differently. It affects their employment, pensions, taxation and voting power.

A key aspect of the longevity imperative is this generational challenge. How do we get the young to realize they need to age differently in order to make the most of longer healthier lives? Linked to this is the need to alter the focus of governments away from the idea that aging is a challenge only for the current old. That brings us to the greatest generational challenge of all—how do we factor intergenerational fairness into our evergreen calculations, avoid generational conflict and harness the potential of generational diversity?

Once in a Generation

Within my own family the concept of "generations" is straightforwardly sequential. My son is the next generation after me just as I followed my father. In this context, the word "generation" is emphasizing the tiers of a family tree and the genetic hierarchy between different generations. But there is another sense of "generation" that provides a different perspective. As developed in the 1920s by the Hungarian sociologist Karl Mannheim, this alternative concept looks beyond family trees to a social concept of generations defined by a thicket of interconnections and shared and distinct experiences.[1]

Each of us travels through time in two dimensions. Chronologically we all age, one calendar year at a time. My father, myself and my son were all twenty at some point. But we also experience time as history unfolding, which makes the context of our aging different. My father was twenty at a time of world war while my son turned twenty as AI began to show its power and potential. If the world is different in significant ways then the way we age is different too. Being twenty in 1945 is a very different experience from being twenty in 2019. Using this insight, for Mannheim a generation consists of a cohort born at approximately the same time experiencing the same historical realities at the same life cycle stage.

Mannheim's concept of generations is therefore the product of the interaction between three distinct factors—cohort (the group born at the same time as you), period (the time during which you are alive) and life cycle (the progression from youth to old age). For a particular generation to be distinctive there has to be a shared experience that separates it from what went before. An obvious example here is the baby-boom generation born between 1946 and 1964 (or 1965—definitions vary). This postwar cohort was born into a world of peace, prosperity, reconstruction and general optimism. Millennials (born between 1981 and 1996) are the children of boomers and are primarily associated with the rapid spread of personal computers, cellphones and the internet. It is these historical contexts that mark generations as distinctive in ways other than just being young or old.

Of the three components in Mannheim's theory, life cycle influences are the easiest to understand. As we age we tend to change in different ways. Many people have a tendency to put on weight. Those lucky enough to own property find themselves wealthier as house prices rise over time and mortgages are slowly paid off. As far as my family was concerned, we were all slim aged twenty and none of us owned any property. Today I have more pounds (both £s and lbs) than my twenty-year-old son but from a Mannheim generational point of view that alone isn't enough to make me a different generation from my son. That is just a life cycle effect.

This is why period effects also play an important role in defining this social concept of generations. My father's twentieth birthday celebrations must have been muted on a wartime minesweeper. Faded black-and-white photos show that food rationing meant he wasn't just slim—he was skinny. Fast forward to my son at the same age, and he faced a very different regime: his last year at college and first year at work were shaped by Covid lockdowns, making his advance on adulthood very different from mine in terms of what he could and couldn't do.

Finally, there is the cohort factor. My son is a "digital native" born when the internet was ubiquitous. He was eight years old when the first iPhone was released. A world of screens and apps is natural to him and those of his age. He has never had to stand in a phone box, searching his pockets for coins, or indeed look for a phone box that hasn't been vandalized. I, on the other hand, can recall the changes from landline to cellphone and from cellphone to smartphone. My father was born in a house with no telephone at all. Our different exposure to changing technology distinguishes us as different cohorts and influences how we communicate, interact, gather information and spend our time.

This sociological concept of generations makes my son's youth very different from my own and similarly makes my future old age very different from my father's. While all three of us were once twenty, viewed from this generational perspective we were never twenty in the same way. The evergreen agenda requires that we won't all experience seventy the same way either.

Mannheim's concept of generations is one of those academic concepts that is eagerly picked up and used by everyone. Mainstream media loves to divide and subdivide past and present generations and pin upon them particular values, features or foibles. My father was born in 1925 so was part of the "Silent Generation" who are apparently thrifty, loyal and determined. I was born in 1965 so depending on which chronological definition you use I am either a babyboomer (self-assured, competitive, goal-orientated) or I belong to "Generation X" (born 1965–1981; resourceful, independent, good at work–life balance). My younger son is "Generation Z" (born 1997–2012). This apparently makes him highly collaborative, self-reliant and pragmatic.

As the above suggests, generational labels risk descending into nonsense. They resemble a form of demographic astrology whereby the period in which you were born is randomly associated with qualities you might like to share. It seems a priori obvious to me that the range of characteristics displayed among say Gen Zers is much broader than any differences between the average Gen Zer or average babyboomer. That is a massive problem when relying upon generational stereotypes in any social analysis. When thinking of the different characteristics of my children it never occurs to me to base it around the fact that two of them are Millennials and one is Gen Z. Similarly, in my professional bio I never feel the need to describe myself by any generational label. It just isn't very informative or useful.

But while much of what is written about generations is misleading and unscientific that doesn't mean the concept is uninformative. Bobby Duffy, director of the Policy Institute at King's College

London, covers this demographic terrain in his excellent book *The Generation Myth*, which is subtitled *Why When You're Born Matters Less Than You Think*. He documents in numerous ways how the generations differ from one another. For instance, younger generations in the US and UK tend to be less religious and more inclusive around issues of sexuality and ethnicity. But that doesn't mean that different generations are polar opposites to one another.

Indeed, it is striking that on nearly every significant cultural issue there are rarely signs of sharp breaks across the generations. Social trends tend to be most pronounced in the young but spread rapidly through the broader population. Think of these trends as an escalator carrying society from one set of values to another. Younger generations tend to be social innovators because they don't have existing values that require revising or changing. In other words, they jump on the escalator first, but others soon follow. A good example is internet usage, which is rising across all ages. It is just taking older people longer to catch up, mainly because they weren't reared on a diet of portable screens and social media in the same way as more recent generations. For other elements, such as the decline in religion, it is as if the generations are a human tower with the youngest generations showing the highest levels but building on changes that occurred in past generations. The important point is that differences between generations don't mean they are implacably opposed to one another. However tempting it may be to think of the young being on an up escalator while the old are going down, the reality is this: we're all heading in the same direction but from different starting points.

That's important because in an evergreen world intergenerational connectivity matters more than ever. Declining fertility and mortality rates mean the population is becoming spread more equally between young and old, which leads to a much greater chance of random interactions between people of different age groups. A three-stage life is implicitly based on age segregation and explicitly so with creations such as retirement communities. A multistage life breaks up that pattern, especially if people work longer. Furthermore, the more interactions occur across the generations the more positive are the attitudes of the young toward the old.[2] This makes Duffy's finding that generations are different but not in opposition so important. We don't start from a natural position of antagonism.

Engaging the Young

For all the differences in our lives as twenty-year-olds, my father, my son and myself shared one characteristic. None of us were thinking at that age about how best to prepare for a long life. My father has the best excuse. When you're a twenty-year-old caught up in fighting a world war, you tend not to worry too much about what your life will be like when you're eighty. Mostly you're praying you can make it to twenty-one. But it's also a challenge in more peaceful times. When you're twenty years old, being eighty isn't just an abstract concept but a faraway land. In your twenties you have other priorities and worrying about how you age is unlikely to be one of them.

But this is where the sense of different cohorts of twenty-year-olds becomes important. One of the things that makes my son at twenty so different from my father at the same age is his probability of living into older age. Based on 1945 data, my father had a less than one in four chance of making it to eighty. He died at seventy-seven, consistent with that grim statistical assessment.

My youngest son, on the other hand, is estimated to have a one in four chance of making it to ninety-nine. According to 2019 data from the UK government statistics agency, my son at twenty had a three in four chance of reaching eighty and a one in ten chance of making it to 104.[3] That is a very different future from my father's or mine.

Dick Van Dyke, the ninety-seven-year-old star of stage and screen, summarized the implication of these statistics when he said: "If I'd known I was going to live this long, I'd have taken better care of myself." But how do we get the current young and middle-aged to think that far ahead? This is a new challenge because they are the first generation with a greater than 50 percent chance of living into their nineties. Our existing social norms are not enough to keep them evergreen to the end.

In F. Scott Fitzgerald's short story "The Curious Case of Benjamin Button" the unlucky Button ages in reverse. He is born with the physical appearance of a seventy-year-old but the older he gets the younger he looks. For Button, chronological and biological are inversely related. Aged twenty he is kicked out of Yale because he is seen as a deranged fifty-year-old. When he reaches fifty he looks like a twenty-year-old and succeeds brilliantly in his first year at Harvard. But by his senior year he is fifty-four with a biological age of sixteen and is struggling academically and athletically as his mental and physical abilities deteriorate. As he ages, he ends up in kindergarten with no memory of his past. In the world of Benjamin Button, whichever way you look at it, the young know what it is like to be old. But in reality we age in the opposite direction, making identifying with our future older self beyond our imagination. That makes coming to grips with the notion that an evergreen agenda is as much or even more about the young than the old a challenge for our non-evergreen thinking.

One part of the solution might be longevity literacy—raising awareness about the length of life and the different possibilities that brings. My previous book *The 100-Year Life* was published in Japan with the translated title "Life Shift." It is now being produced there in a version aimed at schoolchildren. It has also been used in primary schools in New Zealand and in the UK during career discussions with school leavers. Career and financial planning, a focus on healthy behaviors and an emphasis on time and how best to use it are all key components of greater longevity literacy.

Literacy is one thing; experience is quite another. That is why the MIT AgeLab has developed AGNES—Age Gain Now Empathy System. It's an aging suit that attempts to approximate the motor and visual skills, the flexibility, dexterity and strength of the old. Its aim is to help firms design products that are simple and easy to use for older people. When younger people try on AGNES it gives them a much greater appreciation of aging as a physical process. It provides an opportunity to briefly experience being Benjamin Button—old when young.

One problem, though, with longevity literacy is our deeply ingrained tendency to short-term thinking. We find it difficult to think too far ahead and take steps today that have benefits far into the future. But this is where we have to be careful with how we convey the evergreen message. The benefits of an evergreen life are far from being future orientated. The evergreen agenda is not about sacrificing your earlier years in return for healthy more prosperous later years.

The longevity imperative is to increase the number of healthy and productive years you can expect. The more that is achieved then the more that longer lives really are about extra time that can be used at any age. Want to take time off now to travel? That is fine if you can work for another year later on. Want to take time out now to raise a family or look after older parents? Again, that won't hurt your lifetime income if you can be more flexible later in when you work. But if your later years are spent in Struldbrugg health then those earlier decisions have greater consequences in terms of your standard of living—less money and in poorer health. If longer lives are to be about greater options when you are twenty, and fifty as well as eighty then it has to be because of an evergreen agenda. Supporting a longevity imperative is something that requires action at all ages but also brings benefits across a whole life. It isn't short-term loss for long-term gain.

So what are the themes that will persuade the young to start thinking evergreen? I strongly doubt it will be the issues of retirement, pensions and life insurance that tend to consume the lives of older people as they wake up to the financial reality of longer lives. That isn't because those initiatives aren't important or interesting for the young. The earlier you start saving the more compounding of interest does the work for you. It just doesn't seem the most obvious place to begin a discussion with the young around longevity. I think that perhaps the best theme to raise awareness around is issues of health, fitness and making the most of extra time.

Television programs focused on geroscience and tips and short-cuts to "hacking" aging tend to make me nervous. It is not that I don't believe in the potential of geroscience, but right now there is a significant gap between what we know is possible and what we might achieve. But Hollywood has many virtues, and a good film about the effects of age is a great way to grab the attention of younger age groups. Take the Australian actor Chris Hemsworth, famous for his role as the Norse God Thor in the *Avengers* films. In *Avengers: Infinity War*, Thor is revealed to be over 1,500 years old and undeniably looking good for his age. It's a Peter Pan outcome with chiseled abs.

Hemsworth also explored real-life paths to a longer life in *Limitless*, a National Geographic television documentary series. He swims across an Arctic fjord, fasts for four days, walks along a skyscraper crane and undertakes several daunting physical tasks. He also tries on AGNES—"this suit sucks" was his response as Thor finds himself utterly exhausted after an aerobics class. As well as the physical the series looks at the spiritual as well as the geroscientific. As someone who studies longevity, I have to admit that Hemsworth's film got more younger people talking to me about my subject than anything else. It wasn't about pensions. It wasn't about the end of life. Instead, it was firmly based around the idea of the malleability of age, of aging as a process and how we might fight back in what Hemsworth described as "the battle against what time can do to us." It was, in other words, a positive longevity narrative rather than a negative account of an aging society.

Taking Care of the Future

As well as getting the young to understand the importance of the longevity imperative, we also have to get governments to realize that aging isn't only about the old. Again, the aging society narrative performs a disservice. Its focus on aging as an event and old age as a state combined with short-termism in government thinking leads to a focus on the current rather than the future old.

This problem runs the risk of becoming even more challenging in the years ahead due to a political bias. The sheer size of the baby-boomer generation and the fact that older people are more likely to vote means democratic governments need to tread carefully around older voters.[4] We are already seeing this in practice. Pensioners in

Britain long counted among the poorer sections of society. Today, after taking into account housing costs, the average UK pensioner has more money to spend than many adult working households.[5]

As a result of governments' slow shift toward sustainable pensions, a financial burden is being put on younger generations whose taxes will have to fill gaps in past pension commitments. But what do the young receive in return? We need to ensure that paying to support their elders does not leave one generation better off at the expense of another.

This can be done in two ways. The first is by ensuring that the young and the middle-aged are more productive over their lifetime than previous generations. This will help maximize their chances of having a higher standard of living than their forebears even after paying for the past generations' social security bill.

The second way is to try to ensure that our current cohort of young people becomes the healthiest older generation in history. The value of aging well is enormous. If our scientific, medical and managerial skills can help the current young become the healthy future old, that would be a perfect payoff for any financial services rendered. These two components—making longer lives more productive and healthier lives—are of course what defines a three-dimensional longevity dividend, but they also are what delivers intergenerational fairness.

So just as we need to get the young on board with the longevity challenge we need governments to wake up to demographic realities. An aging society agenda begins when you have lots of people aged over sixty-five. An evergreen agenda begins when you have lots of people expected to live beyond sixty-five.

Generational Conflict

The static nature of the aging society narrative, with its focus on the needs of the current old, also runs the risk of stoking the flames of intergenerational conflict. Phrases like "old-age dependency ratio" encourage the notion of the old as a burden depriving the young of much-needed resources.

Those flames are further fanned by the widespread use of generational labels. The main insight of an evergreen agenda is that the young have never been more likely to become the old. That should mean the young would have a greater interest in ensuring that society looks after the old. But generational labels break that connection. Instead the different generations become like the boarding houses at J. K. Rowling's Hogwarts: once the Sorting Hat has selected you as a member of Slytherin, you'll never be a member of Gryffindor. By the same token, you can't escape your Generation Z or babyboomer label. It pits you and those like you against the "others." For some commentators, this generational division will eventually take over from class war as defining modern politics.[6]

In late 2019, these tensions surfaced in a row over the use of "OK boomer." The phrase had been coined a decade earlier, but it resurfaced on TikTok and quickly went viral as a catchphrase and internet meme used by Millennials and Gen Zers to mock their babyboomer elders. It turned up in the US Supreme Court and as an answer to a question on *Jeopardy!*, America's most popular television gameshow.

With its dismissive, sarcastic tone, the phrase took aim at an older generation considered selfish and out of touch. It promptly made a lot of people a lot of money from merchandise sales, including OK boomer T-shirts and hoodies. As one eighteen-year-old remarked:

> The reason we make the OK boomer merch is because there's not a lot that I can personally do to reduce the price of college, for example, which was much cheaper for older generations who then made it more expensive . . . There's not much I can personally do to restore the environment, which was harmed due to the corporate greed of older generations. There's not much I can personally do to undo political corruption, or fix Congress so it's not mostly old white men boomers who don't represent the majority of generations.[7]

There is nothing new in the young criticizing the old. Indeed, given their record as social innovators it is to be both expected and encouraged. Nor is there anything new in older generations lamenting the failings of youth. In the eighth century BCE, the Greek poet Hesiod wrote that there was "no hope for the future of our people if they are dependent on the frivolous youth of today, for certainly all youth are reckless beyond words." A modern echo of Hesiod's dismissive tone can be found in the derisive "snowflake" label used to lampoon a younger generation criticized as overly emotional and easily offended with an inflated sense of their own importance.

Such generational back and forth is a historic constant. As George Orwell described: "Each generation imagines itself to be more intelligent than the one before it, and wiser than the one that comes after it."[8] But there is something that is different this time. With a falling birth rate and longer lives, the need for intergenerational harmony and cooperation has never been greater. But that means the cost of generational conflict has never been higher.

There is a further important difference that goes back to Mannheim's definition of a generation. So much of the focus on how we define generations assumes that the major change that distinguishes them is their exposure to technologies. The Millennials grew up with the internet, Gen Z with the iPhone, and Generation Alpha (born after 2012) with technology such as Alexa that talks to them. But that is to ignore another critical distinguishing feature about the context of their lives. These are the first generations to grow up in the shadow of a large older cohort who maintain their presence in the commanding heights of business and politics.

When part of the defining nature of a generation is changes in longevity and the age structure of the population, we can expect generational tussles to reach a level beyond historical cliché. The prospect this engenders for intergenerational dispute is explored in *The Pinch*, a 2010 book written by David Willetts, a former UK minister for universities and science. The "pinch" refers to a common event that all aging societies will experience at some time. In the UK, Willetts dates 2035 as a key pinch point when babyboomers enter their eighties in large numbers. It is then that the cost of pensions, health treatments and care will have maximum effect on the standard of living of younger generations. Willetts aptly subtitles his book: *How the Baby Boomers Took Their Children's Future—And Why They Should Give It Back.* The impression he gives of the babyboomers is a plague of locusts devouring resources as they pass through life leaving those following in their footsteps surveying a barren landscape. A short summary of the book would be the oft-quoted first lines of Philip Larkin's poem "This Be the Verse"—"They fuck you up, your mum and dad. They may not mean to, but they do."

As the large babyboomer cohort reaches into retirement and old age, the inadequacy of preparations for their extended longevity is being revealed. The problem is that the system is only being patched up to deal with the unexpected longevity of the babyboomers. It isn't being changed to support an evergreen agenda. As a result, younger generations sense a stalling of economic progress and an uncertain future as the world grapples with climate change and the employment consequences of AI. But the older generations above them paint a very different picture. The babyboomer generation has entered into older age with levels of financial wealth as well as health and life expectancy greater than any previous generation and in larger numbers. Of course this resort to generational labels hides enormous problems. Not all babyboomers are aging well in terms of either health or finances. But still the contrast is striking—an older generation clearly better off than their predecessors and a younger generation sensing a stalling of progress.

All the ingredients are then in place to warrant concern about generational conflict. In an interview with a Japanese website in 2021, Professor Yusuke Narita, an economist at Yale University, grabbed attention with his deliberately provocative suggestion: "I feel like the only solution is pretty clear. In the end, isn't it mass suicide and mass seppuku [ritual disemboweling] of the elderly?"[9] Narita, thirty-seven, was far from alone in offering outlandish proposals for Japan's demographic crisis. The plot of the Japanese film *Plan 75* revolves around salespeople signing up older citizens for a government voluntary euthanasia scheme. In a world characterized by Struldbrugg outcomes the need for broader discussions around euthanasia is clear. But enforced mass suicide is a step beyond that, as Narita himself notes. Remarking that he now uses different language to make his point, he stresses that he was not really advocating mass seppuku but trying to make a less dramatic point about the need to end the dominance of senior people in leadership roles in Japanese government and business.

When public debate turns to mention of senicide it is clear we need to take into account the most important generational challenge of all—achieving equity across different cohorts. How do we transform our approach to aging in a way that supports both the current and future old, that is fair and inclusive for all generations?

There May Be Troubles Ahead

From a longevity perspective there are emerging signs in several countries, especially the US and the UK, that the young and middle-aged are not reaching the milestones required for an evergreen life.

Some of the most alarming statistics involve health. While in general more recent cohorts have been aging better than past ones, there are signs that these trend improvements are slowing and on some measurements even reversing.[10] Particularly concerning is the rise in obesity. Between 1988 and 1994 around one in five twenty- to thirty-nine-year-olds in America was obese. That proportion has since doubled. There is a similar trend among forty- to fifty-nine-year-olds.[11] Most worrying of all is that the same figures apply to children—one in ten used to be obese; now it is one in five.[12] The numbers are increasing faster than our waistlines. As obesity is a major risk factor for noncommunicable diseases and multi-morbidities, these trends bode ill for future aging. It helps only partly that younger generations on average both smoke and drink less than their parents and grandparents.

Mental health is also a concern. Over the last ten years the proportion of teenagers with depression and undergraduates with mental illness has more than doubled in the United States. Suicide rates and hospital admissions for nonfatal self-harm have also increased.[13] These are worrying trends in their own right as well as casting an ominous shadow on longevity prospects.

It isn't just at the youngest ages where problems are showing up. In the United States, 32.6 million adults are estimated to be impacted by alcohol use disorder, defined by the National Institute for Health as "a medical condition characterized by an impaired ability to stop or control alcohol use despite adverse social, occupational, or health consequences."[14] That contributes to the previously discussed "deaths of despair" that are increasing midlife mortality in the US and which led to more than 1 million deaths.[15] This is a major current public health crisis as well as boding badly for future of aging.

Stalling Income Growth

Economic and financial statistics also give cause for concern. Partly this is due to a general slowdown in productivity growth in high-income countries. Over a lifetime, individual wages increase either because they rise in line with average pay or they benefit from faster growth due to promotion or seniority bonuses. The result is that wages at the end of a career are usually substantially higher than at the beginning.

The average babyboomer was born in 1955. Assuming that they remained in work for forty-five years between 1975 and 2020, they would have experienced an increase in GDP per capita of 2 percent per annum in the US and 1.5 percent in the UK. In contrast, a Millennial born in 1980 who started work in 2000 would only have benefited from a per annum growth over the next twenty years of 1 percent in the US and 0.4 percent in the UK. Those differences across generations may sound small, but they really stack up over a forty-five-year career. Those rates imply average incomes for US babyboomers increased by two and a half times in that period while they doubled for British babyboomers. Assuming the same lower growth rates for Millennials over the rest of their careers predicts that US Millennials will see their incomes increase by only a half and in the UK by a paltry fifth. Those are small gains compared to what their parents saw.

Part of this slowdown is due to a leveling off in educational improvements. A lot more babyboomers and their Gen X successors made it to college than past generations. That led to their income being much higher than their parents or grandparents. But the education curve is leveling off. Older workers are now almost as likely to have college degrees as Gen Zers. That doesn't make the young necessarily poorer than their parents but it does make it more likely they will earn the same as them, bringing to an end decades of progress whereby children could expect to be better off than their parents.

That is a problem if the older generation expects its young to pay higher taxes to meet their pension and health care costs. That is before factoring in the considerable uncertainty younger generations face about the impact of forthcoming technological progress in AI. The issue of whether AI will ride to our rescue and boost productivity, wages and our standard of living or replace jobs and leave us financially insecure is a question that even ChatGPT cannot answer.

In addition to concerns over income there are also worries about wealth accumulation. Many young people carry a far greater burden of student debt than their forebears. No sooner will they have paid for their educations than they will run into trouble saving for their retirement. The move toward defined contribution schemes (based on the amount paid into occupational pension funds) means that younger generations won't experience the generosity of past defined benefit schemes (based on years of employment and final incomes). They will also face greater risks as with defined benefit schemes the individual is insured against insufficient savings or returns but under defined contribution schemes the risk falls on the individual. If the young face the prospect of the longest lives they also face the greatest exposure to failing to adapt to longer lives.

Generation Rent

One of the greatest areas of strain for the young is housing. House prices have risen more rapidly than income for several decades in many countries, especially in the UK. For much of the second half of the twentieth century, the average house was worth around four times average earnings. By the end of 2022 that had risen to nine times average earnings.[16] That's great news if you own a house but bad news if you're buying your first home. To put down a 10 percent deposit on a house you used to need around 40 percent of your annual income. Now you need 90 percent. That requires a lot more saving and puts owning a home out of reach for many young people. Someone born in 1965 in the UK could on average afford to buy a house at the age of twenty-one. My son born in 1999 is predicted to have to wait until he is thirty-five.

Unsurprisingly, this sustained surge in UK house prices has reduced home ownership in the twenty-five to thirty-four age group from 50 percent to 30 percent.[17] That means a large increase in people either renting or still living with their parents. There has been a similar decline in the thirty-five to forty-four age group, which is now three times more likely to rent than twenty years ago. Older home owners have been a whole lot luckier. In 1961 only one in three of those aged over sixty-five owned their home; today it is three out of four.

This shift in patterns of home ownership has major consequences. Older generations now account for a much larger proportion of housing wealth than previously, not just because of rising prices but also because of the sheer number of babyboomers. This latter effect is important. Because there are so many babyboomers they do hold a large amount of wealth compared to past generations. However, when expressed in per capita terms their advantage is much less. Due to their cohort size, babyboomers being in possession of a lot of wealth doesn't mean that each babyboomer is necessarily richer.

The implications for the longer term if these trends continue are worrying. As a result of delayed access to the housing market the young are on track to have lower levels of housing wealth when they reach older age. That means they are going to have to work for longer or save more if their financial wealth is to reach the same level as those who are now old. People who never manage to buy a house will enter retirement with higher housing costs as they have to pay rent and so will have less money to spend.

These are sobering trends. If we are to transition to a longevity society in which the young and middle-aged prosper through a long life and do not see their standard of living impacted by the need to fund an aging society, there is much to do.

The Rise of a Gerontocracy

Intergenerational tensions can arise as society adapts to longer lives but does so in an uncoordinated way. If older people work longer and younger generations start later then financial inequality between the young and old will increase. But that doesn't have to be a generational problem if it just reflects changes in the life cycle. When the young become old then they too will eventually benefit from the greater financial power of being old and so over their lifetime will not be disadvantaged. Comparisons between thirty-year-olds today and thirty-year-olds forty years ago are unhelpful when the life cycle shifts. In financial terms, thirty could be the new twenty.

But what if the inequality between young and old reflects not a change in a life course but one generation exploiting the system to their own benefit? What if the problems are caused by the rise of a "gerontocracy"—government based on the rule of old people. How do the young advance if the old won't yield the levers of power, but wield them instead to protect their own interests?

There are concerns that this is already a problem as US Senators and members of the House of Representatives routinely remain in office for decades (seven of them have currently served for more than fifty years). The 2020 election was between candidates Joe Biden (seventy-seven) and Donald Trump (seventy-four) and occurred when the Speaker of the House was eighty-two-year-old Nancy Pelosi.

As a consequence, there is growing discussion in America on introducing age restrictions on political service. The concept is far from unheard of—the US Constitution stipulates that no one under thirty-five can be elected president; senators must be at least thirty and members of Congress at least twenty-five. If rules apply to the young, why shouldn't they apply to the old? One opinion poll found that nearly three out of five Americans supported age limits on public service; the most popular age for compulsory retirement was seventy.[18]

As with all opinion polls, it isn't immediately obvious what the main reasons are for wanting age limits. Digging deeper reveals that many people feel age limits are unnecessary so long as people are in good health. On that basis age limits are really a form of agism based on the assumption that older people aren't physically or mentally capable of doing the job. So rather than age limits, Nikki Haley, former governor of South Carolina and fifty-one years of age at the time, proposed "mental competency" tests for all candidates over the age of seventy-five. Why seventy-five? No specific reason is given for that threshold but it is noteworthy that she was expected to be competing with a then seventy-six-year-old Donald Trump for the nomination. Perhaps requiring a mental competency test for presidential candidates is a good idea. But if so, surely it would hold for all ages, not just those over seventy-five?

But there's more to age limits than concern about mental or physical well-being. They are also due to a fear of stagnation and resistance to structural change. Here's Nikki Haley again. "We're ready. Ready to move past the stale ideas and faded names of the past, and we are more than ready for a new generation to lead us into the future. America is not past our prime. It's just that our politicians are past theirs."[19] That is an explicit statement about intergenerational conflicts and the need to avoid a gerontocracy.

Reasons to Be Cheerful

While this analysis outlines a fertile breeding ground for intergenerational conflict there are multiple reasons to be more optimistic. The rhetoric is ahead of reality. While the idea of generational conflict captures the imagination for multiple reasons it doesn't seem likely to replace class conflict as a central driving force in politics. There is for instance little evidence of generational warfare beyond the norm within families. Children still tend to value and appreciate their parents and grandparents and vice versa. Opinion polls show that the young are generally supportive of the idea of financial assistance to the old.[20] Whether this reflects altruism or an awareness that they too will one day be old remains unknown. For now, intergenerational ties still bind.

Another reason for the relatively tepid nature of generational wars to date is the tendency of generational labels such as babyboomers and Millennials to draw starker distinctions between different ages than exist in reality. As Bobby Duffy remarks, "phoney generational labels promote phoney generational wars."[21] Economic circumstances and social beliefs tend to be subject to continuous processes, not sharply punctuated change. Add that to the inevitable diversity within each cohort and it becomes clear that there isn't a single Team Boomer lined up against Team Millennial.

Myths spring from generational labels. There is a widespread belief, for example, that older people do not care about the environment. In an address to the New Zealand Parliament, Chlöe Swarbrick, a then twenty-five-year-old MP, talked about how for her generation climate change was a very real problem that they would experience and not a remote possibility. The more life you have left to live the more you will be impacted by climate change. She was promptly heckled by Todd Muller, then an opposition MP aged fifty-two, and she responded with a swift "OK boomer" putdown.

But although they may be less concerned, older generations aren't entirely resistant to the dangers of a warming world. We are after all traveling along the same escalator. A 2021 Pew Research Center analysis found that 67 percent of Gen Zers and 71 percent of Millennials felt that "climate should be top priority to ensure a sustainable planet for future generations." That compared to 63 percent of Gen Xers and 57 percent of babyboomers. So the majority of all ages agree with prioritizing climate issues. There were only minor proportional differences between Millennials and babyboomers who described climate change as their top personal concern: 33 percent vs. 30 percent.[22]

Based on these statistics, Swarbrick is one of seven out of ten Millennials who believe the climate is a top priority. Muller is Gen X (not a boomer). Six out of ten Gen Xers make climate a top priority. Muller's disagreement therefore says more about him than Gen

Xers as a whole. While differences exist across the generations, we aren't talking about rival blocs with diametrically opposed views.

A consensus direction of travel doesn't remove entirely the risk of conflict. If younger generations are keener for radical change then the longevity of those above them will be a constant source of frustration, especially with a widespread sense of time running out. But once again we need to be careful of slipping into simple age-related stereotypes. There will be plenty of people in the older generations who think urgent change is required just as there will be plenty in the younger generations who don't. Perhaps those with least time left in their life are the ones who are most keen to see change happen in their lifetime and so support more urgent measures. The point is made effectively by the distinguished environmentalist Sir David Attenborough, who believes "we cannot be radical enough" when it comes to climate change. Attenborough is ninety-six years old. Those are words that could just as easily be spoken by twenty-year-old Greta Thunberg.

Passing it On

Another reason for optimism is that part of the reason why younger generations on some financial measures are tracking behind older generations is due to changes in the life cycle arising from longevity gains. For instance, the huge housing wealth currently in the hands of the babyboomers will eventually be passed down to younger generations by inheritance. Falls in the fertility rate also mean that younger generations will have to share this inheritance with fewer relatives. But thanks to increased life expectancy prospective heirs may have to wait—their parents are likely to live longer. That means younger generations may be currently tracking financially below older generations but as they age they will benefit from larger windfalls than past cohorts. The money will just come later.

For all the talk of intergenerational conflict at a social level, families find ways to deal with these tensions. Professor James Sefton of Imperial College London calculates that in the UK each year around £100 billion is passed on in the form of bequests.[23] That's around 4 percent of

GDP. A further £11 billion is handed down in the form of gifts while parents are still alive. Parental help with house deposits has become so common it has led to the creation of a new acronym—BOMAD, for "Bank of Mum and Dad." As Sefton remarks, rather than intergenerational callousness the size of these numbers shows that "The older generation do care and they are passing down a significant amount."

The older generation in the UK is estimated to provide the equivalent of around £132 billion worth of childcare and a further £37 billion of care toward the old. Totaling all this together, that's nearly £300 billion provided by the older generation.[24] That's a bigger safety net than the entire amount the UK government spends on pensions and social security. It's an enormous contribution that is too often ignored when the intergenerational conflict story is wheeled out. So there is far more evidence of intergenerational cohesion than discord but the former goes more unnoticed.

The problem, though, is that not everyone benefits from this largesse. Not every babyboomer owns a house and not everyone will benefit from a valuable inheritance, so the danger is that longevity creates more intergenerational inequality. It will help a great deal to have wealthy parents, but if you don't, you will have to make your own financial way in the world. This is perhaps not so much of a conflict between generations but a problem of intergenerational mobility—of your economic circumstances being pinned down by those of your parents. We need to make sure that longer lives don't lead to initial inequalities compounding even more. That is why a focus on access to opportunities at younger ages becomes an ever more important leveling policy in an evergreen era.

Flattening the Curve

As for concern about a gerontocracy, there is a different way of looking at that shift. Older people have historically been a small minority with the young dominating voting. That is no longer the case. The issue is whether or not that change is bad for a country and if so who suffers. That treads on some interesting democratic issues.

The logic of arguing that a rising number of older voters skews political debate implies that in the past when older voters were fewer in number, things skewed the other way. It was the needs of younger voters that dominated. From this perspective, it's hard to make the case that the rising number of older voters is "unfair." It may instead be correcting a previous problem where the needs of older people were ignored (assuming older politicians are more attuned to the needs of older voters than younger politicians). Currently, 5 US senators and 13 representatives are over eighty. That's out of a total of 100 senators and 435 representatives. In other words, 3.3 percent of Congressional politicians are over eighty compared with 3.8 percent of the population. Is that disproportionate? Is it bad for society? If society has a tendency to underestimate the capacity of older people, the rising number of older people involved in decision-making may be a necessary corrective.

The discussion of gerontocracy in politics is the equivalent of the aging society debate in economics. It is built on a sense of an impending "silver tsunami" that is an obstacle to innovation and change; that it is creating a body politic both physically and metaphorically arthritic, slow to move and presaging decline.

But what is most striking about demographic trends is how they are generating age equality rather than age dominance. Figure 7 shows that between 1933 and 2100 the UN is projecting a massive shift in the US population from being a majority of young people and a minority of older persons to a population much more uniformly spread across the ages. Yes, the numbers of older people are increasing dramatically, especially in their seventies and eighties. That's the effect of longer life expectancy. But Figure 7 shows how these aging trends have flattened the curve. The population is becoming more age diverse and with each age band more equally represented. The young may be losing their numerical advantage but it looks less like an age-related disenfranchisement and more about an equalizing effect. It is better described as a movement away from an ephebocracy (a rarely used word meaning government by young people), not as a shift toward a gerontocracy.

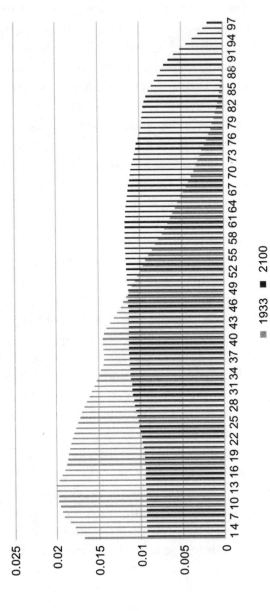

FIGURE 7: Distribution of US Population by Age, 1933 and 2100.

(Source: Author's calculations based on Human Mortality Database (1933) and UN Projections (2100))

Only if we think young votes should count more than old votes does this move toward age equality become a problem. One argument is that because the young have more future to look forward to they may therefore be better at dealing with long-term issues. For this reason William MacAskill, co-founder of the Centre for Effective Altruism, argues that we should weight votes by age—the older you are the lower the weight your vote would get.[25]

Yet as we saw with reference to environmental issues, it is far from clear that older voters are more short-termist than younger ones. If the argument is true, it also has other implications. For instance, it indicates that we should lower the age at which people can vote. It also suggests that democracy is improved by increases in longevity and associated rises in thanatological age making a change of policy less necessary. The average Brit has never been so old but never had so many years left to live. That would point to British democracy becoming less not more short-termist as life expectancy has increased.

Yet it is better not to go down this rabbit hole of some voters are more valuable than others. The notion of counting votes different-ly appears incompatible with conventional "one person, one vote" views of democracy. Putting larger weight on the votes of the young smacks unmistakably of agism and underestimating the capacity of older people.

But perhaps the problem is a completely different one. Perhaps the challenge is not that the young are long-term voters but instead that everyone is selfish and votes for what they are most interested in. The issue then is that if the old receive pensions and health care and only the young work then a gerontocracy votes for higher taxes and more benefits. The unproductive are feared to gang up on the productive and the result will be damaging for the economy.

This is the same argument that was made to restrict the right to vote to only property owners in earlier democracies and persuaded the drafters of the US Constitution to permit individual states to decide which of their citizens should be entitled to vote. That was in the first instance white land-owning men. But even if one were to accept the dubious democratic argument for restricting the voting rights of older people, note two other features that undermine this argument. The first is that while older people do tend to like governments which spend more on pensions and health the impact is relatively small on their vote.[26] People vote on the basis of a much broader range of topics. The second is that in an evergreen world many more older people will be working for longer and paying taxes, which helps to redress this concern of a rising proportion of people happy to tax productive economic activity.

None of this means that all is for the best—we shouldn't fall foul of a naturalistic fallacy in politics. The whole point of an evergreen agenda is that it represents a profound change for humanity and so arrangements and institutions that worked previously when there weren't so many older people may need to adapt. Politically we have to be careful that our institutions never come under the control of only a select group and we need to guard against a gerontocracy. It is curious, though, that when it comes to gerontocracy the United States is an outlier. In Japan, despite an aging population, prime ministers are not becoming older. In Europe in the early 1980s, the average age of political leaders was sixty-seven. Today it is fifty-three. Sanna Marin was elected prime minister of Finland in 2019 at the age of thirty-four—that wouldn't have been constitutionally possible if she were American. The current UK prime minister, Rishi Sunak, is forty-two, the youngest since the 2nd Earl of Liverpool in 1812. European populations may be aging but their leaders are getting younger.

What makes the United States particularly susceptible to fears of gerontocracy? Is it the two-party system combined with the spiraling cost of election campaigns, favoring candidates with carefully cultivated connections and loyal donors? If older politicians benefit from the growing proportion of older voters then would compulsory voting work as a way of boosting the youth vote? Would shifting the time and method of voting help raise the level of engagement of younger voters? Would term limits rather than age limits help reduce the problem and encourage more turnover?

As these examples show, age diversity and intergenerational fairness do not need to depend on ritual disemboweling or mass suicide. An evergreen world demands that we drop simple assumptions about the limits of older people and simple agism. But it also requires much greater thought about the representation of the generations. Agism can work in both directions—it can discriminate against the young (why shouldn't a thirty-four-year-old become US president? Do all jobs demand experience?) as well as demean the old. In politics success requires ensuring a diversity of views are heard and represented. If policymakers are to be conscious of how their actions affect different generations then our political machinery has to find new ways to blend together the generations. Given that society is less aging but becoming more age neutral, we should find institutional forms that leverage this age diversity to our mutual advantage.

From an evergreen perspective that seems appropriate. Having all ages more equally represented in voting patterns is a key component and a means to intergenerational fairness.

An Evergreen To-Do List

So how do we tackle these generational challenges? The first and most obvious task is to find ways to increase productivity. If younger generations can be made richer, they can pay for the current aging society and still be better off. But suggesting higher productivity is a policy solution that applies to nearly every problem. There is a German phrase, *es ist alles in Butter*. It means "everything is fine" or "all OK," but a more literal translation might be that everything tastes good when covered in butter. Politicians feel the same way about economic growth. The faster economies grow, the more resources are available to tackle different issues and the fewer problems threaten the re-election of politicians. Everything is easy when the economy grows fast.

The evergreen agenda might be dismissed as just another challenge easily resolved by higher productivity. But there's a distinction to be drawn here. The evergreen agenda itself serves to raise productivity growth. The challenge is part of the solution. If we invest in the health and skills of the young, middle-aged and old then we can make them all productive for longer and create the additional resources required. That in turn will solve the problem of fairness.

Next on the list is support for the young and middle-aged in achieving Dorian Gray outcomes and matching health with lifespan. That means a focus on preventative measures to preserve physical and mental health with an emphasis on tackling social inequalities. Mental illness is both a problem that requires immediate attention and an ominous longer-term harbinger of future aging setbacks. Even if better health doesn't lead to more GDP it will certainly lead to a higher level of welfare.

In many countries, especially the UK, tackling a broken housing market must also be a priority. Housing should be affordable for the young and not just an asset for the old. Governments need to increase supply rather than offer schemes that boost demand thereby fueling further increases in house prices.

All this requires new resources that have to come from somewhere. The main obstacle to serious reform is that governments continue to focus on aging issues in terms of pension and health care costs. In America, social security and Medicare insurance currently accounts for around 25 percent of federal spending. On the basis of current policies, that proportion is expected to increase to 40 percent by 2052.[27] How will governments in this position contain rising expenditure? The danger is they will squeeze investment in the young and middle-aged. That's a sure way to stifle the evergreen agenda and fuel intergenerational inequities.

To prevent that we need a shift in how we see aging and how we view government policies. For much of history older citizens have been the most financially vulnerable. That's why a state pension was introduced. But as pension provision has improved, as more people live longer, work for longer and enjoy healthier lives, we see great diversity in how people are aging. Some older people are frail; many others aren't. Some are in need of financial support; others are doing very nicely, thank you.

In an evergreen world, no one should underestimate the capacity of older people—including the tax authorities. Tax breaks and other benefits should not be distributed simply because people reach a certain age. In London anyone over sixty gets free travel on trains and buses. That's a marvelous perk, but many of the sixty-year-olds I know travel to work on expensive bikes. Failing to recognize the diversity of health, wealth and capability in older age groups doesn't make sense in an evergreen world. It isn't age that should trigger benefits, but income and needs. In an evergreen world age is simply less informative of need than previously and our policies need to adjust accordingly. That requires revisiting many simple age-based policies.

Governments should consider how their policies impact different generations through their lives. Are they consistently fair to all age groups in terms of income and health? What about the balance of taxes and benefits an individual will pay and receive over their lifetime? Governments routinely publish data on the gap between their current tax revenue and expenditure and future projections of debt. They also need to show what those projections mean for different generations over their lifetime—how much they will pay and how much they will receive.[28]

Reporting on the intergenerational implications of current policies helps achieve two important evergreen objectives. The first is that it helps promote a focus on intergenerational fairness. The second is that it fosters a more long-term approach to how we deal not just with challenges around longevity but with a broader range of issues, including the environment.

9

Pitfalls and Progress

We can only see a short distance ahead, but we can see plenty
there that needs to be done.

Alan Turing

The French poet Paul Valéry was a master of pithy *bon mots*. "The
best way to make your dreams come true," he wrote, "is to wake up."
I have tried to show in these pages how important it is to wake up to
the new reality of longer lives and to try to make our evergreen dreams
come true. We live in a world where the young can expect to become
the very old and that requires rethinking life, what we do at each age,
and finding ways to invest more in our longer futures. Depending on
how far the virtuous evergreen circle can go, these changes may even
push back the limits of how long humans can live for.

But however attractive an evergreen agenda is, it requires deep-
seated changes in our individual behavior, our economic institutions
and our social customs that previous chapters have detailed. The
fact that an evergreen era has emerged indicates only that change is
required, not that it will be quick or easy. "A dream doesn't become
reality through magic," observed the American soldier-statesman
Colin Powell. "It takes sweat, determination and hard work."

It is precisely because this is such a novel challenge that there will
be resistance and many pitfalls to avoid. It is to some of these issues
that we now turn. Convincing governments of the need to build
their policymaking around an evergreen future is sure to stir suspi-
cion, cynicism and doubt. How we overcome short-termism at both
an individual and government level to seize the longevity imperative

will be especially challenging. The stereotypes of aging will be hard to shift and represent a substantial barrier to change. Change will also be required across every aspect of society—that amounts to an awful lot of change. Perhaps that explains the surprising resistance among people not just to the potential of aging better but taking steps to achieve it. There is much here that is common to a climate change agenda, which has taken decades to reach its current level of influence, but still requires so much to be done.

But change does happen. Centuries of change have pushed up our life expectancy, improved our health and created new stages of life. Be in no doubt: we live already in an era of increased longevity. That means an evergreen shift is on the way. The sooner we can make it happen, the better.

Revising Our Expectations

An early problem has already arisen in a few countries, notably the United States and Britain. Far from pressing ahead with evergreen agendas, we are seeing past progress threatened. Yet the affected governments are doing little to turn things around. The health of nations in these countries is not being taken seriously enough.

Rather than longevity, a significant part of both the US and UK population is drifting toward "shortgevity" and there are declines in absolute life expectancy as well as substantial shortfalls relative to expected length of life in other countries. The UK is now five years behind best practice life expectancy and the US more than eight. It is remarkable how little outcry there is over this trend, given that advancing life expectancy elsewhere shows that such declines are not the norm. The lack of protest is even more striking in the aftermath of the Covid pandemic, when governments resorted to extreme steps at enormous economic cost to protect health and life expectancy.

An additional problem is that any trend toward lower life expectancy may encourage the idea that an evergreen agenda is no longer so urgent. We are already way past the point where we can afford to ignore the impact of longer lives. Past gains in life expectancy have already created challenges that have gone unaddressed. The fact that those gains have stalled in certain countries is hardly a case for pretending the problem no longer exists. The truth is that some of these problems might not have emerged had we adopted an evergreen approach much sooner.

This lack of concern at declining or stalling life expectancy links to a general sense that health and life expectancy at later years are of less importance than at earlier ages, as most clearly embodied in the WHO concept of "premature" deaths. Currently in Japan a seventy-year-old woman has a remaining life expectancy of over twenty years. The gains from preserving health over such a long horizon are substantial. At the end of the first longevity revolution, seventy really isn't that old. We need to adjust our expectations to the new reality of longer lives.

So how do we get governments to pursue policies necessary to reverse shortgevity? How do we remove this bias against placing equal weight on these later years? Or the tendency to lump geroscience in with science fiction rather than identify it as the next stage of medicine's progress?

The late Austrian-American management consultant Peter Drucker, often referred to as the "founder of modern management," remarked that "what gets measured gets managed." If we want to deliver an evergreen agenda then governments need to establish a measure of healthy life expectancy. Naturally there are issues about how this should be done. But if we can define a system of national accounts that measures something as abstract and complex as GDP, we can surely arrive at a reliable way of measuring healthy life expectancy.

Adopting a healthy longevity target would help resolve all the pitfalls listed above. Given the changing age structure of the population and the overwhelming preference for Dorian Gray outcomes, it is a natural measure of welfare in a society. It would also require governments to tackle health inequalities. If you want to improve average healthy life expectancy then it should be easier to do so by bringing up those who are below average rather than seeking improvements for those already above average. A focus on healthy life expectancy would mean that avoiding "premature" deaths remains important but it would also put a much greater emphasis on healthy aging from seventy years and up. Such a target would also make apparent the role that gerotherapeutics has in promoting health improvements rather than immortality.

Above all, adopting such a target would demand that we don't just follow a Struldbrugg path. We need to take the lessons learned from Covid seriously and demand we act consistently with them. Our health matters. Age-related diseases are now our biggest health challenge. Setting a target for healthy life expectancy would be the first step to directing our health system to healthy outcomes in an evergreen manner.

Timing is Everything

For most of the 200,000 years or so of human history we lived in a world where Samuel Beckett's gloomy vision of life—"They give birth astride a grave, the light gleams an instant, then it's night once more"—was more reportage than poetry. In the early Bronze Age, life expectancy at birth is estimated to have been eighteen years. By around two thousand years ago, during the Roman Empire's heyday, it had risen to twenty-two. During the thirteenth and fourteenth centuries in England it reached thirty-three. In the early American state of Massachusetts just after the 1776 Declaration of Independence it was thirty-six.[1] By 2021, despite a global pandemic, average global life expectancy was just over seventy-one.

So commences an evergreen era in which the value of aging well has never been greater. The rapid improvements in life expectancy that constitute the first longevity revolution are a relatively recent event in our human history. No wonder our cultural and social views around old age are struggling to adapt. Given this, how rapidly can we realistically expect progress to be in creating a second longevity revolution focused on changing how we age?

Niels Bohr, the Danish physicist who won the Nobel Prize in 1922, once remarked that "prediction is very difficult, especially if it's about the future." If it has taken us 200,000 years to achieve the first longevity revolution, perhaps we should be cautious in predicting the speed of achievement in the second.

When it comes to geroscience breakthroughs the only thing it seems safe to assume is that our knowledge will increase faster than any increase in the complexity of human biology. We will in other words track down more of the mysteries of how we age. That means we can expect progress to be made in understanding the biology of aging and developing helpful therapeutics. But progress takes time with false starts and misdirections. That's why I tend to follow a short-term-pessimist/long-term-optimist combination about the contributions geroscience can make to an evergreen agenda.

But as the opening quote to this chapter from Alan Turing suggests, an inability to see far ahead doesn't mean we can't take action today. While science may contribute in the long run, it is changes in behavior, institutions and the environment that will drive improvement most in the short run. It is precisely because for most of human history the majority didn't live long enough to reach old age that we have never experimented to see how much we can change how we age.

But once we begin the process of change, of rethinking what it is to age and exploit its malleability, future change will be easier. That is because the mechanism behind achieving a longevity dividend— longer, healthier, more productive lives—is the same regardless of whether life expectancy is eighty, a hundred or a hundred and twenty years. It is all about extending health, work and purpose across more time.

That is why I worry less about how we cope with any potential further gains to life expectancy and more about the gap that exists today between where we are and where we need to be. We need to wake up urgently for an evergreen agenda to happen and to make a substantive change with our past. Once in that new era future changes will build and amplify on any initial change. But we need to make the first change now.

Above all scale, urgency and direction is required. In the United States the government has recently enacted the Inflation Reduction Act. This is a massive $740 billion bill with a raft of measures aimed at achieving a green economy using tax credits and industrial policy. It also contains measures aimed at reducing health costs but a similar grand vision is needed to reorientate our economy to make the products and organize the services that keep us healthy. We need concerted government action aimed at tackling health, caring, skills and agism so that more people can work from fifty to sixty-five. There is no point in achieving success in geroscience if the rest of society lags behind.

Evergreen Incentives

Much ongoing debate around health expenditure isn't about achieving better health outcomes. It's about reducing or containing expenditure. Given that US health spending is currently around 20 percent of GDP, it's not hard to see why that is the case. But this is another pitfall that needs avoiding if we are to succeed with an evergreen agenda. If we consider better health outcomes a matter of national importance, we should be prepared to pay the cost. What we should not accept is spending so much money but not achieving good health outcomes. Rather than aiming at cutting costs there needs to be a focus on achieving healthy aging. That will require a major realignment of incentives.

The late Nobel Prize-winning economic historian Robert Fogel viewed spending on health care as a victory, not a problem. Throughout human history we have been preoccupied with surviving to the end of the day and acquiring the essentials such as food, clothing, heat and shelter. As we become richer we are able to spend more on health care. But spending large amounts of money keeping us in poor health is clearly not a good deal compared to spending money but remaining in good health.

In the early twentieth century the American Pulitzer Prize writer and muckraker Upton Sinclair wrote a series of novels exposing corporate malpractice, the perils of unregulated markets and associated skullduggery. His most famous work was *The Jungle*, which outlined appalling labor conditions in the Chicago meat market. In his characteristically trenchant manner Sinclair skewered a key problem with any reform agenda—"It is difficult to get a man to understand something, when his salary depends upon his not understanding it." That is a major obstacle to health reform.

Our current health system is financed by a large amount of money and has achieved considerable past success. But the future needs to shift from intervention to prevention, from disease to health. How do we get those who run our health system to reduce their reliance on the knowledge and policies that made them so successful and so well rewarded financially? How do we get a surgeon whose success has been based on intervention to measure success by her performing fewer operations? How does a preventative health sector that accounts for only 1 percent of all medical expenditure get the political power to grow much more rapidly?

This isn't entirely about naked financial self-interest, although that may play a role. It is about getting administrators and medical staff to understand the need for radical change in an era of longer lives. It means accepting that their hard-earned experience and skills, however valuable in saving lives, do little to help patients to avoid needing care in the first place. The danger is that, like the generals at the Battle of the Somme, the guardians of our health will treat the future the way they treated the past: by calling up reinforcements for an outdated plan. Spending more money but without achieving better health.

Misaligned incentives are also a problem in the pharmaceutical sector. There are enormous amounts of money to be made in developing successful drugs. But the current patent system may not correctly incentivize research into preventative medicines. It was after all developed in a world with a very different outlook on disease.

Drug patents are usually valid for twenty years. In other words, once a company registers a patent it has a twenty-year window in which to research a drug, see if it works, gain regulatory approval and then manufacture and sell it. After twenty years the patent expires and anyone can manufacture the drug. At that point the price falls sharply and its use becomes more widespread. The original developers will make most of their profits when the drug is still under patent protection.

The problem is that it typically takes around ten to fifteen years between registering a patent and receiving full approval to produce a drug.[2] That leaves a window of only around five to ten years for the pharma company to make a profit and it is this that may bias the direction of innovation.

Why should that be the case? First, a drug that extends life—even by a comparatively short time—might be sold at a much higher price. Studies show that when we know we are dying, we are prepared to spend large amounts of money for a little extra time.[3] When we are healthy, we tend to spend much less on preventative medicines each year.

Preventative drugs also tend to require a longer trial length. It takes longer to see if someone doesn't develop a disease than it does to assess whether an intervention helps treat one. That leads to a smaller window between drug approval and the expiry of the patent. Similarly, revenues from a patient for a preventative treatment are spread out over a lifetime and last far beyond the patent window. For a late-stage treatment it is concentrated in a few years.

These biases point pharmaceutical companies to developing drugs aimed at late-stage treatments rather than prevention, toward tackling acute rather than chronic noncommunicable diseases.[4] Take the case of lung cancer where a number of drugs have been approved that target patients at a late stage but no drugs have ever been approved aimed at early-stage treatments or even prevention. The drug Avastin is estimated to extend the life expectancy of people with late-stage lung cancer from 10.3 to 12.3 months at a cost of $42,800 to $55,000. For someone with that condition no doubt that is a cost worth paying. But far better would be a drug that reduced the chances of getting lung cancer in the first place. We need pharmaceutical innovations that promote Dorian Gray not Struldbrugg outcomes and that may require extending patent length or other changes to the current system.

Ultimately all these problems are ones where incentives need to be better aligned. We need governments targeting good health outcomes rather than reducing health costs, a health system focused on healthy life expectancy and a pharma sector incentivized to concentrate on R&D in maintaining health rather than late-stage disease treatments.

The Ultimate Luxury

Economists categorize health as a "luxury good." That means that as our income rises we don't just spend more money on health care but a rising proportion of our income. Back to Nobel Prize winner Robert Fogel. He argued that the future of the economy would increasingly be in what he referred to as "spiritual" commodities. By spiritual he didn't necessarily mean religion or "otherworldly" but rather immaterial commodities that lack physical form.[5]

But if health and longevity are a luxury good then seeking radical changes in how we age will be a particular obsession for the most wealthy. No wonder then that a roll call of billionaires such as Jeff Bezos, Sergey Brin, Larry Ellison, Yuri Milner and Peter Thiel have all invested in geroscience research.[6]

If longevity is the ultimate luxury good and you have surplus funds at your disposal, why not gamble on achieving success in increasing your lifespan? Christian Angermayer is a forty-four-year-old billionaire entrepreneur and investor who started his first biotech company aged nineteen. As both an investor and a consumer of longevity products, he pinpoints their appeal. "If you buy a yacht, you can always get a bigger yacht; if you buy a plane, you can always get a bigger plane. But the [extent to which] your life is changing with more money is actually very minimal."[7] Surely it's better to spend your money not on a bigger yacht but on a healthier and longer life? A modern version of Pascal's wager comes to mind. If I spend the money and it works, what a great return! If I spend the money and it doesn't work then that isn't a problem as over a normal length of life I wouldn't be able to spend all my money anyway.

Success would also bring unimaginable financial rewards. The billions earned through internet search engines or online shopping will be more than matched by those who figure out how to help us live evergreen lives. This association of billionaires with research into longevity is catnip for journalists and readers alike. The vaulting ambition on display, the steely dedication toward peculiar daily routines, the vanity and hubris involved given millennia of failure and the surreal nature of the lifestyle all make for a great opinion piece. Invariably they are seasoned with mockery, judgment and often condemnation.

A good example occurred in January 2023 when the daily routine of Bryan Johnson, a forty-five-year-old biotech CEO and a centi-millionaire, went viral.[8] He is estimated to spend around $2 million a year on his efforts to reverse aging under the supervision of thirty doctors and scientists. His routine is about as radical as human self-denial gets. It involves waking at 5 a.m., not eating after 11 a.m., consuming exactly 1,977 calories a day while eating 70 lbs of vegetables a month. On top of that he takes more than a hundred pills a day, with five or six daily medical interventions including occasional fat injections and a host of regular checks. For two hours each night he wears goggles that block out blue light. His motivation seems a mix of personal interest and challenge, a desire to be a guinea pig for frontier science as well as presumably potential commercial benefits.

If we go beyond the mockery, what should we make of these extraordinary experiments and investments? In a world where governments tend to shrink from betting the ranch on risky projects which won't deliver before the next election, and so prefer to spend money on hip replacements, should we just be grateful for this private money flowing into evergreen research?

The answer is probably no. If this is the only way society seeks to develop geroscience then we have a problem. We cannot rely on billionaires and venture capitalists to arrive at socially optimal evergreen treatments. Just because the market is a powerful force at driving innovation doesn't mean it gets the direction of innovation correct from a social perspective.

We want innovations that give a few extra years of healthy life to the many, not many extra years of healthy life to a few. Billionaires already have access to the resources that help them achieve the current upper level in terms of life expectancy. That makes it more likely they will have a greater preference for research aimed at radical life extension. If it can be delivered cheaply that may be fine, but if not then it will be a problem for national health budgets.

Already pharma companies have a bias toward high-priced drugs. As discussed earlier, the gene therapy medicine Zolgensma is a wonderful one-time treatment for infants suffering from spinal muscular atrophy (SMA). But it comes with a list price of over $2 million. Given the devastating impact SMA has on a small number of people this is manageable. Taking a little bit of money from millions so as to fund treatments needed for a few who have been dealt a cruel genetic fate is socially acceptable. But that doesn't work for conditions that affect everyone—such as aging. When drug breakthroughs require millions of dollars being spent on billions of people then difficult choices need to be made. Unless you are a billionaire, in which case you can afford the treatment.

Consider again Nir Barzilai and the TAME trial, discussed in chapter 4, aimed at testing if the diabetic drug metformin has anti-aging properties. It will cost an estimated $30 to $50 million. The FDA has given approval so all that is required is the funding. But the funding is still not complete so the trial still hasn't started. There are myriad reasons why. For Barzilai an important problem is that "Those big billionaires, they want moonshots, they want a scientific achievement that will make people say 'Wow.'" According to Barzilai: "TAME is not a moonshot. It's not even about scientific achievement really, it's more about political achievement. Metformin is a tool to get aging as an indication."[9]

This isn't an argument to ban billionaires from investing in biotech companies. But it does point to two policy implications. The first is the need for private geroscience research to be open to independent ethical scrutiny by a mix of scientific and health experts as well as the wider public. Technology shapes our lives in important ways and that holds all the more for geroscience, and so the direction it takes needs to be monitored and directed.

This argument also strengthens the case for governments engaging on a scale that can drive research in the direction of accessible Dorian Gray outcomes. Governments do after all have established track records in this area. When Barzilai mentions moonshots he is making implicit reference to X Development, Google's R&D lab. According to X Development, a moonshot is the intersection of a big problem, a radical solution and breakthrough technology. One of its moonshots is the California Life Company (known as Calico), which is aimed at tackling aging and age-related disease.

The irony is that the phrase "moonshot" derives from the government-funded 1969 *Apollo 11* spaceflight, which saw Neil Armstrong become the first human to step on the moon. The government spent $25.8 billion on Project Apollo between 1960 and 1973, which according to the Planetary Society is worth an extraordinary $280 billion at today's prices.[10] The US government also spent freely on the Manhattan Project, which resulted in the development of the nuclear weapons that ended the Second World War. These are both examples of projects that pulled together teams of scientists and researchers aimed at speeding up delivery of a specific goal. Similarly, another profound technological advance—the communication protocols that produced the internet—traces its origins to an academic research network funded by the US Advanced Research Projects Agency. In all these cases broad-based research goals were delivered by collaborative long-range government thinking largely free of pure profit motives.

We need governments to start developing some moonshot thinking around aging and longevity. Rather than sit and bemoan the costs of an aging society and the rising costs of pensions and health care, what are the moonshots that could hasten our evergreen futures?

Increasing funding for research into the biology of aging is an obvious place to start. Cancer and dementia both rightly benefit from huge amounts of private and government research spending but the same cannot be said for geroscience. Funding should be aimed at general research and at creating the foundational knowledge that the private sector could exploit. But it should also be channeled into key areas that offer the greatest prospect for improvements at scale but at low cost. As with commitments around Covid vaccines, the government should make clear to pharmaceutical companies that money will be found for treatments that cost-effectively tackle the most common age-related diseases.

All the Young Dudes

The young of today can expect to live longer lives but will there be enough of them? We are entering an era of unprecedentedly low fertility rates such that many countries will experience declining populations. If sustained, these represent no less than an existential crisis for humanity.

The English author P. D. James imagined a population apocalypse in her 1992 novel *The Children of Men*. Set in a future England, the country is on a path to oblivion because twenty-seven years earlier the male sperm count abruptly fell to zero. With no babies being born the population is declining, and the last cohort of children (the Omegas) are revered and given special treatment. But they become spoilt and dismissive of their elders. In the absence of children, people turn to pets for companionship, dressing them in clothes and pushing them in prams. A society with no children is one with no future and the politics of this imagined England are suitably dystopian as the ultimate aging society heads toward extinction.

Reality is less dramatic but still striking—over the last fifty years the male sperm count is estimated to have fallen by more than 50 percent.[11] How much of a role this has played in lowering the fertility rate is unclear, because the main reason fewer babies are born is people choosing to have fewer children. An increasing number of double-occupation households, the rise of single-person households as marriage isn't just postponed but avoided, the extended time over which children are dependents, and the growing cost of housing in cities all combine to make the cost of raising children ever higher. In countries where firms don't support flexible working practices and childcare is unequally spread between men and women, the fertility rate falls even lower. None of these trends appears likely to be reversed in a hurry.

For many economists, declining fertility isn't necessarily a problem.[12] In fact, in the face of an aging population it can even help maintain living standards. Less money needs to be spent supporting childhood and fewer resources are required to maintain infrastructure and housing. That all helps to finance longer lives. A declining population also means less pressure on the environment.

Yet declining populations do bring social problems. Care for older relatives may suffer if families shrink in size. If you are childless and need care in old age, that is a problem. Resolving that involves either evergreen success or raising the fertility rate.

With fewer people fewer homes will be needed. If high house prices are a problem, that may be good news, but it creates difficulties. In Japan the number of empty homes is expected to reach 10 million in 2023. Most of those homes are in rural areas where villages and towns are dying. In response, the government is offering cash grants of $8,000 per child to young families if they relocate from Tokyo to areas in decline.

There may be direct links between living longer and having fewer children. Certainly rising income levels are a shared driver behind both. Biologically, that seems to be the case too, with studies showing that long-lived animals have fewer offspring—short-lived animals focus on growth and reproduction while long-lived animals put a greater focus on maintenance and repair.

But an inverse link between longevity and fertility goes beyond biology and reflects behavioral change. As lives extend, a greater proportion of our life is spent after our reproductive years. Raising children therefore occupies a relatively smaller role. In response our life cycle is changing. Longer careers demand more education so that the age we start work is increasing. So too is the age of marriage and the arrival of a first child. The window in which fertility decisions tend to be made is therefore shrinking.

The motivation for having children is also changing. Historically children were seen as a way of providing support during your old age. State pensions have reduced this incentive.[13] If having children also interrupts your career and education they also affect your ability to finance a longer life. The combined effect of these factors is that among Americans aged over fifty-five years, one in six are childless. Their number is increasing. The evergreen need to develop cross-generational relationships is getting harder to achieve within families.

There has been plenty of debate about the burdens of an aging society but expect to see a growing alarm about the dearth of babies. Already a number of countries are providing financial incentives to boost fertility. In Hungary couples are given interest-free loans which are canceled when they have a third child. Women are given a lifetime exemption from income tax if they have four or more children. These pro-natal policies work—they boost the fertility rate—but their impact tends to be small. Given the costs of having children, the financial incentives needed to make a lasting difference will be more than most governments can afford.

The best way of raising the fertility rate is to reduce the costs and pressures of raising children. Expect to see more government support for childcare as a consequence. Our lengthening life expectancy can also help in this regard. Achieving a higher fertility rate requires making working life more flexible and ensuring that both men and women can take time to support work and family in equal measure. If longer, healthier, more productive lives give us more time then greater flexibility with that time will help ease pressures on parenting. The concept of "parental" leave is itself likely to undergo substantial change in the years ahead. Individuals will find flexible working invaluable not just in helping to raise children but also with taking care of older parents. Finding ways to make caring easier and less costly will be key to achieving higher fertility rates.

More radical solutions to increase fertility rates may emerge from geroscience. If the aim of geroscience is to slow down aging then one potential area of research is reproduction. Reproductive ability declines in men at the same pace as overall biological aging but for women it happens a lot faster because of menopause. Because of this and the fact that humans are one of only a handful of animals which experience menopause, the topic is of growing interest in the geroscience community. The motivation is twofold—can menopause be postponed to give more options around having children and can delaying menopause help boost female health later in life?

An evergreen agenda with its emphasis on how we age will lead to frequent clashes with long-held cultural assumptions about what we should do at different ages. These clashes are likely to be especially controversial around any success geroscience has in postponing or even preventing menopause.

Because of behavioral changes there is already a trend toward having children later in life. In the UK, more women aged over forty give birth than those under twenty—that is a historical first. But delaying menopause would create a very different balance between reproductive and nonreproductive years. If this was combined with Dorian Gray-like outcomes—healthspan matching lifespan—the result would be dramatically more options regarding the timing of when to raise a family. If more flexible working helps provide more time to raise a family then geroscience aims to provide more flexibility over a lifetime through providing more reproductive years.

For many, raising fertility rates in this way is undesirable. Once more we need to unwind the several different concepts of aging to think through these issues. If we remain healthy for longer then we have more time to raise children even if mothers are much older when children are born. That is why Dorian Gray outcomes are important. But there is also concern around thanatological age. If we postpone childbirth to our later years, we have fewer years of life left to live and perhaps not enough time to raise children. These concerns would only be eased if life expectancy increased à la Peter Pan rather than Dorian Gray.

For others, it isn't moral repugnance about children being orphaned that is the problem. They just don't want to think about having children in their sixties or seventies even if it were biologically possible. That is something for another time of life. Perhaps as life extends, providing more possibilities, the answer may be even to have children earlier rather than later.

Overpopulation

More recently another reason for not having children has emerged: Concern about the impact of overpopulation on the environment. One study estimates that having one fewer child reduces

CO_2-equivalent emissions by 58.6 tonnes per year.[14] That compares with going car-free (2.4 tonnes), a plant-based diet (0.82) and recycling (0.21). Comparisons of this ilk have spawned an increasingly popular BirthStrike movement that advocates childlessness as an important step toward sustainability. This is a contemporary version of the Malthusian theory that an overly large population will overwhelm resources.

The same environmental concerns are also aimed at gains in life expectancy. If people live for longer, the global population increases, placing yet more pressure on scarce resources. Taken to extremes this line of argument can be used for all manner of controversial steps, such as scrapping research into cancer prevention or road safety measures. While no one currently advocates such radical measures, geroscience is often criticized for the risk it brings of overpopulation if people live for longer.

By how much would longer lives contribute to overpopulation? To gauge the impact let's do some demographic sums. Imagine a world where the population is stable—every year a certain number of babies are born and every year the same number of people die. Also, for simplicity, assume everyone dies at exactly the same age. In other words, the first longevity revolution is complete. In this case, if life expectancy is eighty years and 2 million babies are born each year, the population will be 160 million. Think of the population as the number of bricks in a wall. The population increases either by adding more height (more babies are born each year) or by making the wall longer (living longer).

If life expectancy increases to a hundred, the population will eventually reach 200 million in our imaginary world—a rise of 25 percent. But it will take time to get there as it will take a while before those eighty-year-olds reach a hundred. In terms of the metaphor, it takes time to fully extend the length of the wall. Instead the population increases by 2 million each year for twenty years until it reaches its new level of 200 million. That's a little over 1 percent each year.

The actual increase is likely to be less. Firstly, in our example a 25 percent increase in life expectancy leads to an eventual 25 percent increase in population. That is because we assume everyone lives for the same length of time. Allowing for the fact some people die earlier than others will reduce the increase in population size. In other words not everyone makes it to a hundred. Secondly, if people live longer, they tend to have children later, reducing the fertility rate and limiting the population's increase.[15] If the births fell to 1.6 million a year then the population would remain unchanged—1.6 million people living to a hundred is a population of 160 million. This of course is exactly what is happening in so many countries around the world—growing life expectancy, declining fertility and static or even falling populations.

So the tendency for fertility rates to fall with longer lives limits the increase in population that comes from extending life expectancy. But if life expectancy were to jump radically to 500 then the calculations would be very different. Over 420 years the population would increase and reach 1 billion in our example. The rate of increase would be slow but the cumulative effect enormous. The fertility rate would have to plummet if the population were not to explode. So radical life extension would have serious implications for the world population size, more modest improvements much less so.

Considering this issue of future population size and how many children we should have catapults us into many complex ethical issues. If longevity leads to a lower fertility rate and fewer children, is it better that existing people live longer even though it means fewer people will be born and will never exist? If we lower the fertility rate then fewer people will be alive in the future but those who are will benefit from a better environment. But is that better than having more people existing even if they live in a world badly affected by climate change? The moral philosopher Derek Parfit wrestled with these issues in creating the field of population ethics. He struggled with what he called the Repugnant Conclusion—that is the idea that it is better to see a larger number of people existing even if they have lives that are barely worth living than seeing a smaller population with a higher quality of life. Parfit didn't want to accept this conclusion—that is why he dubbed it repugnant—but finding logical and ethical reasons to reject it is not straightforward.

271

The first longevity revolution, whereby the vast majority can now expect to live to seventy or eighty, has contributed to a substantial increase in the world's population. While many express concern over the resulting overpopulation they do not complain that interventions have supported longer lives. It is the number of people, not the length of life, that is concerning. There is once again this enduring sense that seventy or eighty is a natural lifespan.

The second longevity revolution, though, is leading to further increases in life expectancy which go beyond this threshold of conventional lifespan. Because of that geroscience gets criticized for the risk of overpopulation in a way that increasing life expectancy by lowering infant mortality didn't, or research into cancer treatments doesn't. But why do we prefer a world with more people living shorter lives to one where fewer people live longer lives but the world population remains the same? Isn't that to accept the Repugnant Conclusion with respect to life expectancy but not income or the environment?

The only reason that would make sense is if the additional years of life after seventy are in some way seen as not valuable or unnatural. But this seems to be another example of G. E. Moore's "naturalistic fallacy" of assuming there is something natural about living threescore years and ten but living beyond that is somehow different. That the extra years are somehow discretionary. Yet again we need to renormalize what the human lifespan is given the past achievements of the first longevity revolution.

So what should we make of this conflict between environmental pressures and the population impact of longevity? Given waning population growth, the pressures from this direction are abating even if climate issues themselves are becoming more urgent. Further, keeping people healthy in a Dorian Gray manner leads to no increase in population, in which case there is no conflict. That isn't the case for any rapid developments in radical life extension which would reignite upward pressure on population growth. Once again, though, we are back to the issue of whether immediate radical life extension is the most likely outcome. In general, the welfare gains of longer healthier lives are so large and their likely impact on population sufficiently modest that both agendas should be pursued urgently.

Further, in one important dimension the agendas do not conflict but overlap. Air pollution, extreme heat, volatile and dangerous weather are all material risks to our health and life expectancy. Tackling climate change is therefore an important part of the longevity imperative. The health gains from averting climate change only add to the arguments for moving toward sustainability. Similarly, the hope has to be that our own longer individual lives will encourage us to take a more long-term perspective around our impact on the environment. There is also another point to make. If we live sustainably, it doesn't matter if the world's population is 8 or 10 billion. If we live unsustainably, we will eventually reach a tipping point however many children we do or don't have. That's a good argument for making sure we arrive at a sustainable lifestyle as soon as possible.

What Can I Do?

Our futures seem to be changing in profound ways. Technology is hurtling forward and we wonder if we will become enslaved to the power of AI. We watch the weather change, and we worry. For me, dealing with aging and specifically longevity is just as important as technology and climate change in shaping our future. But what makes longevity so fascinating is the way it combines the profound with the deeply personal, the philosophical with the practical. It raises questions about what it means to be human as well as whether or not it is a good idea to eat breakfast.

It is easy when thinking about the scale of necessary changes to be overwhelmed. But if humanity is entering a new era, fundamental change is to be expected and that change will take time. Each of us has significant power over how we age. While in the future we may find more dramatic ways to age better, there are already plenty of things that we know work. It is our incentive to adopt these behaviors that has changed, not the knowledge of what needs to be done. It may be hard to know exactly what you will need when you become older but betting that health, relationships, purpose, skills and money are useful at all ages seems an eminently sensible strategy.

Above all, we should not be pessimistic about living longer lives but we need to be realistic about our prospects. Most of us still have time to prepare. We are, after all, the first generation to be able to contemplate the possibility of evergreen lives. Past generations would surely envy us this evergreen opportunity. Hopefully future generations will thank us for the progress we make.

As the references throughout this book to various ancient philosophers, medieval scientists and contemporary writers and thinkers have shown, the questions of how best to use our time and preserve our health are not novel. The length of life has changed but not our human motivation. Some of the evergreen puzzle is revolutionary, but since it is about what makes for a good life it is a tale as old as history.

So with an eye on the personal here are six broad principles distilled from an evergreen agenda:

1. *Be longevity literate*: All of us have the expectation of more time ahead of us than our forebears. Be aware of how much time you have, think how to make best use of it and keep track of progress.

2. *Make a friend of your future self*: It is crucial that you don't outlive your health, finances, relationships, purpose or skills. You need to invest more in your future self. Remember too that aging doesn't happen when you are old, it is a process that happens continuously. You need to take steps now to support a longer life.

3. *Age differently*: At the heart of the evergreen agenda are the changes in how we age. That has the simple implication that you need to behave differently from past generations and create new ways of aging better.

4. *Use what works now and keep informed*: New insights may be on their way but already we have access to a range of tried and

tested methods. Keep an eye out too for new health break-throughs and treatments. Both lifelong learning and learning about a long life are important.

5. *Don't underestimate the capacity of your later years*: Aging should not be feared. That isn't just because of the sentiment under-lying the Irish proverb "Do not resent growing old, many are denied the privilege." According to the data, old age is not as bad as you fear and because it is malleable it can be improved. Be positive.

6. *Pay it forward/Pay it back*: You have more years ahead of you. But the longer you remain in good health and able to earn later in life, the more options you have today. An evergreen life pro-vides more options at all ages. It isn't all short-term sacrifice for longer-term gain.

Above all, it is important that you take the lead in adapting to a new evergreen era. Society will adapt to a new reality but not as fast as you can. You can act differently today. That makes us all pioneers moving forward. We are unlikely to live long enough to see the full implications that develop, but how humans age and even potentially how long we live are set to change radically in the times to come. It can start with you.

Epilogue: The Power of Love

The evergreen agenda is far-reaching and presents a host of challenges that demand technocratic solutions. I have discussed at length—using economic tools, demographic data, scientific research and philosophical arguments—the case that now, more than ever, we need to age well and invest in our futures. But there's a human dimension the importance of which should not be overlooked—Fogel's "spiritual" commodities. The human activities that give us value, purpose and happiness.

The Harvard Study of Development is an extraordinary research project that is now in its eighty-fifth year. It began in 1938 tracking the lives of two separate groups of people with the aim of understanding how well-being develops; what factors contribute to happy outcomes; and why some people's lives go wrong. The first group comprised 268 white male Harvard College sophomores (an uncommonly elite sample that grew up to include four candidates for the US Senate, a bestselling novelist, an editor of the *Washington Post* and one US president—John F. Kennedy). The second group numbered 465 less socially privileged men from mostly inner-city areas of Boston. As the subjects of the study acquired growing families, the project stretched to cover more than two thousand people from three generations (grandparents, parents and children). The male bias changed steadily.

The dataset is incredibly rich and varied, including quantative detail around health but also a mass of biographical material about feelings, emotions and relationships. As a dataset aimed at revealing what makes for a good life it is fascinating in its detail and breadth. The main message that the architects of the study draw is simple: "If you're going to make that one choice, that single decision that could best ensure your own health and happiness, science tells us that your choice should be to cultivate warm relationships. Of all kinds."[1]

Relationships nurture us and keep us happy and healthy. In a study of more than 600,000 individuals covering a fifty-year period, mortality rates rose by around 15 percent for those who were unmarried (rising more for men than women).[2] Good relationships help us live longer but they are also the stuff of life and death. Among older couples, when one partner died there was an increased risk of the other dying within the next three months. The widow/widower effect could increase the risk of dying by up to two-thirds.[3]

Good relationships are key not just in promoting happiness but in dealing with the uneven, unpredictable nature of life. A longer life will see more twists and turns, more ups and downs. Good relationships hopefully bring about a greater number of ups but they also help us deal with the downs.

The eighteenth-century English poet William Blake, in his poem "Auguries of Innocence," captured the complexity this adds to the texture of human life with the words:

> Man was made for Joy and Woe
> And when this we rightly know
> Thro the World we safely go
> Joy and Woe are woven fine

We are social creatures. Connection and relationships make us happy and give our lives meaning. Family, partnerships and friendships help us deal with both joy and woe. They also supply them. There's no escaping the pain of loss should you outlive a loved one. But if you are lucky, you will by then have had many happy years.

As I reach the last pages of the book I am finally coming to the end of a two-year process of writing a manuscript. Writing about longer lives has given me much to think about. I am as a result looking forward all the more to spending time with those whom during these past two years I have seen less than I should.

I look forward to celebrating finishing the manuscript with my wife Diane. We will be able to spend time discussing so much more than just how the book is coming along and what I am writing about. I will be figuring out how to see more of my daughter, now living in Australia as she embarks on a challenging career as a psychiatrist amid the excitement of a young marriage. Of seeing more of my two sons and taking pride and care watching them grow and navigate their adult lives.

I look forward with relish to the simple yet complex pleasure of going to see the football team I support, Tottenham Hotspur, in action. Regardless of the match result, I get to meet up with my longest-standing friend, Richard, whom I have known since I was seven. We'll be there with his son and both of mine and I'll recall all the times I used to cheer on Spurs with my own father, uncles, cousins and friends. I'm eager to spend more time with the many friends who have entertained, diverted or generously offered comments and advice on my writing. All those who have been there through good and bad times, both past and future.

Yet I won't be able to see everyone I care for. My father would now be ninety-seven had he lived and my mother ninety-five. It is years since I have been able to have a conversation with them. I would give much to be able to do so. And of course also missing is a twin brother David who died days after our birth. He would now be fifty-seven and would have shared my life in a way that no one else could have. If relationships are what matters, here lies the true value of an evergreen agenda, that alternative demographic reality.

The American poet Robert Frost is famous for his poem "The Road Not Taken" that ends:

> Two roads diverged in a wood, and I—
> I took the one less traveled by,
> And that has made all the difference.

Frost's was a long life as he died at eighty-eight in 1963. As was not unusual for someone born in 1874, he experienced much loss in that long life. His father died when he was only eleven. His wife died when he was sixty-three. He had six children and saw four of them die in his lifetime: one after only one day, another aged four from cholera, one who died of puerperal fever after giving birth aged twenty-nine and a son who died by suicide at thirty-eight.

When Frost was eighty-five he was asked what wisdom he had gained over his long life. He replied: "In three words, I can sum up everything I've learned about life. It goes on."

The new evergreen imperative agrees with Frost but provides a major twist. Life goes on, but today it goes on for longer. It also goes on for longer for all those that we know. This creates new challenges. But it also creates new opportunities. More time to spend with those we love and more time to find those whom we cherish.

Acknowledgments

Given how solitary an activity book writing is, it is remarkable how many people I am indebted to for helping shape these pages. A range of people covering a variety of perspectives were kind enough to take the time to offer comments on chapters and earlier drafts of the book. To them I offer much thanks for helping sharpen the draft throughout and for both their encouragement and criticisms. So my deepest thanks to Daron Acemoglu, Laura Carstensen, Bobby Duffy, Peter Fisher, Noreena Hertz, Russ Hill, Mehmood Khan, Surya Kolluri, Richard Lloyd, Joseba Martinez, Jim Mellon, David Miles, Louise Newson, Robert Rowland Smith, Andrew Steele, Myra Strober and Tom Whipple.

Book writing may be solitary but my academic publishing has been a much more collaborative activity. I have been fortunate to work with a number of enormously talented individuals from whom I have learnt a lot. In various places this book draws on publications resulting from those collaborations. Heartfelt thanks are offered to Daron Acemoglu, Julian Ashwin, John Ataguba, David Bloom, Martin Ellison, Lynda Gratton, Nicolaj Mühlbach, Jonathan Old and David Sinclair.

I owe a special thanks to Dafina Grapci and Jim Mellon with whom I have run the Longevity Forum (www.thelongevityforum.com) these past few years. The Forum raises awareness and generates debate about the issues discussed in this book. From them both I have learnt many things but especially the importance of thinking broadly and in an open-minded way on all aspects of longevity. Their friendship, support and encouragement have played a major part in my digging deep into this field, and for that I am enormously grateful. If you are interested in the topics discussed in this book then do keep an eye on the Forum's website and especially the events and podcasts that form the annual Longevity Week.

Another co-conspirator I have to thank is Laura Carstensen whose New Map of Life project, run through her Stanford Center on Longevity, is an inspiration. Longevity as a separate intellectual topic is a nascent discipline, but discovering someone like Laura who has thought deeply on the topic and is prepared to share and debate in such an honest, open way has been a wonderful scholarly as well as personal experience. Those debates and her encouragement along with our various but too infrequent collaborations have been a joy and have made me to go deeper into the subject.

At Basic Books I thank Sarah Caro and Emily Taber. Sarah emboldened me from the start to write a book that outlined the importance of longevity as both a social trend and an individual imperative. I thank her for patiently waiting for the draft to appear and then providing invaluable editorial input as deadlines approached. Emily similarly provided crucial editorial guidance, pushing for logical clarity at key places and doing her best to convert my British English into American. For a book on ageing/aging, that is no mean task. Sincere thanks are also due to Tony Allen-Mills. I wish that sentence was written in a manner he would approve of but he read every line and offered great editorial advice and gave me an insight into the craft of a writer as well as a lifelong trauma of red highlighting. Thanks also to Martin Bryant for a final and diligent read through that further improved the flow with an impressive focus on detail.

More thanks than I can express are also due to Laura Brent Walker. Whether it is to do with my research, the Longevity Forum, my travel schedule or this book, Laura deals unflappably, brilliantly and with considerable charm and positivity with all that passes before her and is a constant source of support. I hope one day that Grace appreciates the book.

On a personal level, I have to thank my three children—Helena, Louis and Kit. Their very existence has prompted me to think hard about longevity and it has been enjoyable and an education to hear their views on the topic and their reactions to some of the issues discussed. I guess in the context of the book that can be filed as an example of intergenerational collaboration.

Most of all I have to thank my American family, my wife Diane and her parents Edward and Marie, for their support and kindness. I suspect at times Diane would have preferred if the book writing had been even more solitary so she wouldn't have to hear blow-by-blow accounts of how the work was proceeding or indeed not proceeding. But her unfailing strength, insight and encouragement on the book and so many other areas is amazing and the book wouldn't have happened without her. I can only hope that it really is a hundred-year life.

Notes

Chapter 1: A New Age

1. Human Mortality Database, https://www.mortality.org/ [Accessed May 25, 2023]
2. "World Population Prospects 2022," United Nations, Department of Economic and Social Affairs, https://population.un.org/wpp/ [Accessed May 25, 2023]
3. American Academy of Actuaries and Society of Actuaries, Actuaries Longevity Illustrator, https://www.longevityillustrator.org/ [Accessed April 14, 2023]
4. Human Mortality Database, https://www.mortality.org/ [Accessed May 25, 2023]
5. J. Oeppen and J. W. Vaupel, "Broken Limits to Life Expectancy," *Science*, vol. 296, no. 5570, 2002, 1029–31, https://www.science.org/doi/10.1126/science.1069675
6. UN DESA, "World Population Prospects 2022," https://population.un.org/wpp/ [Accessed April 14, 2023]
7. WHO Coronavirus Dashboard, https://covid19.who.int [Accessed April 14, 2023]
8. See, inter alia, "The Pandemic's True Death Toll," *The Economist*, October 25, 2022, https://www.economist.com/graphic-detail/coronavirus-excess-deaths-estimates
9. J. M. Arbuto, et al., "Quantifying Impacts of the Covid-19 Pandemic Through Life Expectancy Losses: A Population Level Study of 29 Countries," *International Journal of Epidemiology*, vol. 51, no. 1, 2022, 63–74, https://doi.org/10.1093/ije/dyab207
10. Ryan K. Masters, et al., "Changes in Life Expectancy Between 2019 and 2021 in the United States and 21 Peer Countries," medRxiv, June 1, 2022, https://doi.org/10.1101/2022.04.05.22273393

11. Human Mortality Database, https://www.mortality.org/ [Accessed May 25, 2023]

12. Julian Ashwin and Andrew Scott, "International Trends in Senescent Mortality: Implications for Life Expectancy, Lifespan and Lifespan Equality," London Business School, Mimeo 2023.

13. "Life Expectancy in the U.S. Dropped for the Second Year in a Row in 2021," National Center for Health Statistics, August 31, 2022, https://www.cdc.gov/nchs/pressroom/nchs_press_releases/2022/20220831.htm

14. World Bank Open Data, https://data.worldbank.org/indicator/SH.XPD.GHED.PC.CD?view=chart [Accessed May 25, 2023]

15. Raj Chetty, et al., "The Association Between Income and Life Expectancy in the United States, 2001–14," *Journal of the American Medical Association*, vol. 315, no. 6, 2016, 1750–66, https://www.ncbi.nlm.nih.gov/pmc/articles/PMC4866586/

16. Anne Case and Angus Deaton, *Deaths of Despair and the Future of Capitalism*, Princeton, N.J.: Princeton University Press, 2020.

17 Human Mortality Database, https://www.mortality.org/ [Accessed May 25, 2023]

18. Jesús-Adrián Alvarez, et al., "Regularities in Human Mortality after Age 105," *PLoS ONE*, vol. 16, no. 7, July 2021, e0253940, https://doi.org/10.1371/journal.pone.0253940

19. The World's Billionaires, https://en.wikipedia.org/wiki/The_World%27s_Billionaires#:~:text=In%20the%2037th%20annual%20Forbes,and%20%2424500%20billion%20from%202022

20. Robert D. Young, "Validated Living Worldwide Supercentenarians 113+, Living and Recently Deceased: February 2022," *Rejuvenation Research*, vol. 25, no. 1, 2022, https://doi.org/10.1089/rej.2022.0011

21. Alfred, Lord Tennyson, "Homeric Hymn to Aphrodite.," l. 218.

22. GBD 2019 Dementia Forecasting Collaborators, "Estimation of the Global Prevalence of Dementia in 2019 and Forecasted Prevalence in 2050," *Lancet Public Health*, vol. 7, no. 2, 2022, e105–125, https://www.thelancet.com/journals/lanpub/article/PIIS2468-2667(21)00249-8/fulltext

23. Frank J. Wolters, et al., "Twenty-Seven-Year Time Trends in Dementia Incidence in Europe and the United States: The Alzheimer Cohorts Consortium," *Neurology*, vol. 95, no. 5, August 2020, e519–31, https://n.neurology.org/content/95/5/e519

24. Ibid.

25. "Cancer Facts and Figures 2021," American Cancer Society, https://www.cancer.org/content/dam/cancer-org/research/

cancer-facts-and-statistics/annual-cancer-facts-and-figures/2021/
cancer-facts-and-figures-2021.pdf
26. "Obesity and Overweight," World Health Organization, https://
www.who.int/news-room/fact-sheets/detail/obesity-and-overweight
[Accessed May 25, 2023]
27. Andrew Scott, "The Long Good Life," *IMF Finance and
Development*, March 2020, https://www.imf.org/Publications/fandd/
issues/2020/03/the-future-of-aging-guide-for-policymakers-scott
28. D. E. Bloom, et al., "Valuing Productive Non-market Activities of
Older Adults in Europe and the US," *De Economist*, vol. 168, no. 2,
2020, 153–81.
29. David G. Blanchflower, "Is Happiness U-shaped Everywhere?
Age and Subjective Well-being in 145 Countries," *Journal of
Population Economics*, vol. 34, no. 2, April 2021, 575–624, https://doi.
org/10.1007/s00148-020-00797-z

Chapter 2: How We Age

1. "Ageing and Health," World Health Organization, https://www.
who.int/news-room/fact-sheets/detail/ageing-and-health [Accessed
May 25, 2023]
2. T. S. Eliot, "Whispers of Immortality," in *Collected Poems: 1909–1962*,
London: Faber & Faber, 2020.
3. Reuben Ng and Ting Yu Joanne Chow, "Aging Narratives over 210
Years (1810–2020)," *Journals of Gerontology* Series B, vol. 76, no. 9,
2021, 1799–1807, https://pubmed.ncbi.nlm.nih.gov/33300996/
4. Elizabeth Arias, et al., "United States Life Tables Eliminating
Certain Causes of Death, 1999–2001," *National Vital Statistics Report*,
vol. 61, no. 9, May 2013, https://www.cdc.gov/nchs/data/nvsr/
nvsr61/nvsr61_09.pdf
5. "Elon Musk Says Humans Trying to Live Longer Would Stop
Society from Advancing," *Independent*, March 27, 2022, https://www.
independent.co.uk/news/world/americas/human-life-expectancy-
elon-musk-b2044971.html
6. Michel de Montaigne, "On the Length of Life," in *The Complete
Essays* (trans. Michael Screech), Book 1, Chapter 57, Harmondsworth:
Penguin, 1991, p. 366; P. B. Medawar, *An Unsolved Problem in Biology*,
London: Lewis, 1951, p. 13.

7. J. F. Kennedy, "Special Message to the Congress on the Needs of the Nation's Senior Citizens," February 21, 1963, American Presidency Project, https://www.presidency.ucsb.edu/documents/special-message-the-congress-the-needs-the-nations-senior-citizens

8. Sky Ocean Flag Dollar Wife Machine Home Earth College Butter.

9. Robert S. Wilson, et al., "Cognitive Activity and Onset Age of Incident Alzheimer Disease Dementia," *Neurology*, vol. 97, no. 9, August 2021, e922–9, https://doi.org/10.1212/WNL.0000000000012388

10. Kenneth Rockwood and Arnold Mitnitski, "Frailty in Relation to the Accumulation of Deficits," *Journals of Gerontology*, Series A, vol. 62, no. 7, 2007, 722–7, https://doi.org/10.1093/gerona/62.7.722

11. Arnold Mitnitski, et al., "Relative Fitness and Frailty of Elderly Men and Women in Developed Countries and Their Relationship with Mortality," *Journal of the American Geriatrics Society*, vol. 53, no. 12, 2005, 2184–9, https://doi.org/10.1111/j.1532-5415.2005.00506.x

12. Ana Lucia Abeliansky and Holger Strulik, "How We Fall Apart: Similarities of Human Aging in 10 European Countries," *Demography*, vol. 55, no. 1, February 2018, 341–59, https://doi.org/10.1007/s13524-017-0641-8

13. For the United States see Morgan E. Levine and Eileen M. Crimmins, "Is 60 the New 50? Examining Changes in Biological Age over the Past Two Decades," *Demography*, vol. 55, no. 2, April 2018, 387–402, https://doi.org/10.1007/s13524-017-0644-5 and Ana Lucia Abeliansky and Holger Strulik, "How We Fall Apart: Similarities of Human Aging in 10 European Countries," *Demography*, vol. 55, no. 1, February 2018, 341–59, https://doi.org/10.1007/s13524-017-0641-8; and for England, Jonathan Old and Andrew Scott, "Healthy Ageing Trends in England between 2002 to 2018: Improving but Slowing and Unequal," *Journal of the Economics of Ageing*, vol. 26, no. 1, 2023, https://doi.org/10.1016/j.jeoa.2023.100470

14. David Boyd Haycock, *Mortal Coil: A Short History of Living Longer*, New Haven, C.T. and London: Yale University Press, 2008.

15. Jillian D'Onfro, "Why Elon Musk Doesn't Want to Live Forever," *Business Insider*, October 7, 2015, https://www.businessinsider.com/why-elon-musk-doesnt-want-to-live-forever-2015-10

16. Céline Ben Hassen, et al., "Association between Age at Onset of Multimorbidity and Incidence of Dementia: 30 Year Follow-up in Whitehall II Prospective Cohort Study," *BMJ*, February 2, 2022, e068005, https://doi.org/10.1136/bmj-2021-068005

17. Jonathan Old and Andrew Scott, "Healthy Ageing Trends in England Between 2002 to 2018: Improving but Slowing and Unequal," *Journal of the Economics of Ageing*, vol. 26, no. 1, 2023, https://doi.org/10.1016/j.jeoa.2023.100470

18. Saul Justin Newman, "Supercentenarian and Remarkable Age Records Exhibit Patterns Indicative of Clerical Errors and Pension Fraud," bioRxiv, May 3, 2020, https://doi.org/10.1101/704080

19. "Obesity Is a Common, Serious, and Costly Disease," Center for Disease Control and Prevention, July 20, 2022, https://www.cdc.gov/obesity/data/adult.html

20. C. M. McCay, et al., "The Effect of Retarded Growth upon the Length of Life Span and upon the Ultimate Body Size, 1935," *Nutrition*, vol. 5, no. 3, 1989, 155–71; discussion 172.

21. Fedor Galkin, et al., "Psychological Factors Substantially Contribute to Biological Aging: Evidence from the Aging Rate in Chinese Older Adults," *Aging*, vol. 14, no. 18, September 2022, 7206–22, https://doi.org/10.18632/aging.204264

22. Solja T. Nyberg, et al., "Association of Healthy Lifestyle with Years Lived without Major Chronic Diseases," *JAMA Internal Medicine*, vol. 180, no. 5, May 2020, 760, https://doi.org/10.1001/jamainternmed.2020.0618

Chapter 3: All's Well That Ages Well

1. "How Many Excess Deaths in England Are Associated with A&E Delays?," *The Economist*, January 11, 2023, https://www.economist.com/britain/2023/01/11/how-many-excess-deaths-in-england-are-associated-with-a-and-e-delays

2. Andrew J. Scott, M. Ellison, and D. A. Sinclair, "The Economic Value of Targeting Aging," *Nature Aging*, vol. 1, no. 7, July 2021, 616–23, https://doi.org/10.1038/s43587-021-00080-0

3. Simone de Beauvoir, *Old Age*, London: André Deutsch/New York: Weidenfeld & Nicolson, 1972.

4. J. Graham Ruby, et al., "Naked Mole-Rat Mortality Rates Defy Gompertzian Laws by Not Increasing with Age," *ELife*, vol. 7, January 2018, e31157, https://doi.org/10.7554/eLife.31157

5. Yael H. Edrey, et al., "Successful Aging and Sustained Good Health in the Naked Mole Rat: A Long-lived Mammalian Model for

Biogerontology and Biomedical Research," *ILAR Journal*, vol. 52, no. 1, 2011, 41–53, https://doi.org/10.1093/ilar.52.1.41

6. Lorna Hughes, "Mum Aged 98 Moves into Care Home to Look after Her 80-Year-Old Son," *Liverpool Echo*, October 29, 2017, http://www.liverpoolecho.co.uk/news/liverpool-news/mum-aged-98-moves-care-13825533

7. Ralf Schaible, et al., "Constant Mortality and Fertility over Age in *Hydra*," *Proceedings of the National Academy of Sciences*, vol. 112, no. 51, December 2015, 15701–6, https://doi.org/10.1073/pnas.1521002112

8. Neil Ferguson, et al., "Impact of Non-pharmaceutical Interventions (NPIs) to Reduce COVID-19 Mortality and Healthcare Demand," 2020, https://www.imperial.ac.uk/media/imperial-college/medicine/sph/ide/gida-fellowships/Imperial-College-COVID19-NPI-modelling-16-03-2020.pdf

9. Barthélémy Bonadio, et al., *Global Supply Chains in the Pandemic*, National Bureau of Economic Research, Working Paper 27224, May 2020, https://doi.org/10.3386/w27224

10. "Healthcare Expenditure, UK Health Accounts Provisional Estimates," Office for National Statistics, https://www.ons.gov.uk/peoplepopulationandcommunity/healthandsocialcare/healthcaresystem/bulletins/healthcareexpenditureukhealthaccountsprovisionalestimates/2021 [Accessed May 25, 2023]

11. John Appleby, et al., "NICE's Cost Effectiveness Threshold," *BMJ* Clinical Research Edition, vol. 335, no. 7616, 2007, 358–9, https://doi.org/10.1136/bmj.39308.560069.BE

12. Phoebe Weston, "NHS to Use World's Most Expensive Drug to Treat Spinal Muscular Atrophy," *Guardian*, March 8, 2021, https://www.theguardian.com/society/2021/mar/08/nhs-use-worlds-most-expensive-drug-treat-spinal-muscular-atrophy-zolgensma

13. W. Kip Viscusi, *Pricing Lives: Guideposts for a Safer Society*, Princeton, N.J.: Princeton University Press, 2018.

14. "U.S. Value of Statistical Life (VSL), 2013–22," United States Department of Agriculture.

15. Michael Greenstone and Visham Nigam, "Does Social Distancing Matter?," Becker Friedman Institute, University of Chicago, https://bfi.uchicago.edu/working-paper/2020-26/

16. Kevin M. Murphy and Robert H. Topel, "The Value of Health and Longevity," *Journal of Political Economy*, vol. 114, no. 5, October 2006, 871–904, https://doi.org/10.1086/508033

17. For US estimates see Andrew J. Scott, M. Ellison and D. A. Sinclair, "The Economic Value of Targeting Aging," *Nature Aging*, vol. 1, no. 7, July 2021, 616–23, https://doi.org/10.1038/s43587-021-00080-0 and for international calculations, Andrew J. Scott, et al., "International Gains to Achieving Healthy Longevity," *Cold Spring Harbor Perspectives in Medicine*, vol. 13, no. 2, February 2023, a041202, https://doi.org/10.1101/cshperspect.a041202

18. R. E. Hall and C. I. Jones, "The Value of Life and the Rise in Health Spending," *Quarterly Journal of Economics*, vol. 122, no. 1, February 2007, 39–72, https://doi.org/10.1162/qjec.122.1.39

Chapter 4: A Health Revolution

1. Donald A. Henderson, *Smallpox: The Death of a Disease: The inside Story of Eradicating a Worldwide Killer*, New York: Prometheus Books, 2009.

2. "Death Registration Summary Statistics England and Wales: 2022," Office for National Statistics, https://www.ons.gov.uk/peoplepopulationandcommunity/birthsdeathsandmarriages/deaths/articles/deathregistrationsummarystatisticsenglandandwales/2022 [Accessed May 25, 2023]

3. "What Do We Know about Spending Related to Public Health in the U.S. and Comparable Countries?," Peterson-KFF Health System Tracker, https://www.healthsystemtracker.org/chart-collection/what-do-we-know-about-spending-related-to-public-health-in-the-u-s-and-comparable-countries/

4. "Health Care Expenditures," Centers for Disease Control and Prevention, August 8, 2022, https://www.cdc.gov/nchs/hus/topics/health-care-expenditures.htm [Accessed May 25, 2023]

5. Carlyn M. Hood, et al., "County Health Rankings: Relationships Between Determinant Factors and Health Outcomes," *American Journal of Preventive Medicine*, vol. 50, no. 2, 2016, 129–35, https://doi.org/10.1016/j.amepre.2015.08.024

6. David U. Himmelstein and Steffie Woolhandler, "Public Health's Falling Share of US Health Spending," *American Journal of Public*

Health, vol. 106, no. 1, 2016, 56–7, https://doi.org/10.2105/
AJPH.2015.302908

7. Prabhat Jha, et al., "21st-Century Hazards of Smoking and
Benefits of Cessation in the United States," *New England Journal
of Medicine*, vol. 368, no. 4, 2013, 341–50, https://doi.org/10.1056/
NEJMsa1211128; H. Brønnum-Hansen and K. Juel, "Abstention
from Smoking Extends Life and Compresses Morbidity: A
Population Based Study of Health Expectancy Among Smokers and
Never Smokers in Denmark," *Tobacco Control*, vol. 10, no. 3, 2001,
273–8, https://doi.org/10.1136/tc.10.3.273

8. Prabhat Jha, "Avoidable Global Cancer Deaths and Total Deaths
from Smoking," *Nature Reviews Cancer*, vol. 9, no. 9, 2009, 655–64,
https://doi.org/10.1038/nrc2703

9. "Death Rate from Smoking, 1990 to 2019," Our World in Data, https://
ourworldindata.org/grapher/death-rate-smoking?country=FRA~CAF~USA

10. Hannah Ritchie and Max Roser, "Smoking," Our World in Data, May
2013, https://ourworldindata.org/smoking [Accessed May 25, 2023]

11. Jos Lelieveld, et al., "Loss of Life Expectancy from Air Pollution
Compared to Other Risk Factors: A Worldwide Perspective,"
Cardiovascular Research, vol. 116, no. 11, 2020, 1910–17, https://doi.
org/10.1093/cvr/cvaa025; "Air Pollution: Cognitive Decline and
Dementia," UK Health Security Agency, July 25, 2022, https://www.
gov.uk/government/publications/air-pollution-cognitive-decline-
and-dementia [Accessed May 25, 2023]

12. Noreena Hertz, *The Lonely Century: How Isolation Imperils Our Future*,
London: Sceptre, 2020.

13. Prospective Studies Collaboration, et al., "Body-mass Index and
Cause-specific Mortality in 900,000 Adults: Collaborative Analyses
of 57 Prospective Studies," *Lancet*, vol. 373, no. 9669, 2009, 1083–96,
https://doi.org/10.1016/S0140-6736(09)60318-4

14. "Submission to the Marmot Review: Overall Costs of Health
Inequalities," Frontier Economics, February 2010, https://www.
instituteofhealthequity.org/file-manager/FSHLrelateddocs/overall-
costs-fshl.pdf

15. Danny Sullivan, "Sir John Bell: 'No Health System in the
World is Currently Sustainable,'" Longevity.Technology,
November 2022, https://longevity.technology/news/
sir-john-bell-no-health-system-in-the-world-is-currently-sustainable/

16. "5 Things You Need to Know About the Battle of the Somme," Imperial War Museum, https://www.iwm.org.uk/history/5-things-you-need-to-know-about-the-battle-of-the-somme [Accessed October 25, 2023]

17. "Living Longer: Caring in Later Working Life," Office for National Statistics, March 15, 2019, https://www.ons.gov.uk/peoplepopulationandcommunity/birthsdeathsandmarriages/ageing/articles/livinglongerhowourpopulation ischangingandwhyitmatters/2019-03-15 [Accessed May 25, 2023]

18. *The Long Term Conditions Year of Care Commissioning Programme Implementation Handbook*, Department of Health, HMSO, 2017, https://www.england.nhs.uk/publication/the-long-term-conditions-year-of-care-commissioning-programme-implementation-handbook/

19. Apoorva Rama, "National Health Expenditures, 2020: Spending Accelerates Due to Spike in Federal Government Expenditures Related to the COVID-19 Pandemic," American Medical Association, 2022, https://www.ama-assn.org/system/files/prp-annual-spending-2020.pdf

20. "What Do We Know About Spending Related to Public Health in the U.S. and Comparable Countries?," Peterson-KFF Health System Tracker, https://www.healthsystemtracker.org/chart-collection/what-do-we-know-about-spending-related-to-public-health-in-the-u-s-and-comparable-countries/

21. Dr. Louise Newson, *Preparing for the Perimenopause and the Menopause*, London: Penguin Life, 2021.

22. Rossella E. Nappi, et al., "Menopause: A Cardiometabolic Transition," *Lancet, Diabetes & Endocrinology*, vol. 10, no. 6, 2022, 442–56, https://doi.org/10.1016/S2213-8587(22)00076-6

23. "Speech by Mr Ong Ye Kung, Minister for Health, at the Ministry of Health Committee of Supply Debate 2022," March 9, 2022, Ministry of Health, Singapore, https://www.moh.gov.sg/news-highlights/details/speech-by-mr-ong-ye-kung-minister-for-health-at-the-ministry-of-health-committee-of-supply-debate-2022

24. Carlos López-Otín, et al., "The Hallmarks of Aging," *Cell*, vol. 153, no. 6, 2013, 1194–217, https://doi.org/10.1016/j.cell.2013.05.039; a further three hallmarks were added in Carlos López-Otín, et al., "Hallmarks of Aging: An Expanding Universe," *Cell*, vol. 186, no. 2, January 2023, 243–78, https://doi.org/10.1016/j.cell.2022.11.001

25. See David A. Sinclair and Matthew D. LaPlante, *Lifespan: Why We Age and Why We Don't Have To*, New York: Atria Books, 2019;

Andrew Steele, *Ageless: The New Science of Getting Older Without Getting Old*, New York: Doubleday, 2020; and Nir Barzilai and Toni Robino, *Age Later: Health Span, Life Span, and the New Science of Longevity*, New York: St. Martin's Press, 2020.

26. Kazutoshi Takahashi and Shinya Yamanaka, "Induction of Pluripotent Stem Cells from Mouse Embryonic and Adult Fibroblast Cultures by Defined Factors," *Cell*, vol. 126, no. 4, 2006, 663–76, https://doi.org/10.1016/j.cell.2006.07.024

27. C. Kenyon, et al., "A *C. elegans* Mutant that Lives Twice as Long as Wild Type," *Nature*, vol. 366, no. 6454, 1993, 461–4, https://doi.org/10.1038/366461a0

28. Tad Friend, "Silicon Valley's Quest to Live Forever," *New Yorker*, March 27, 2017, https://www.newyorker.com/magazine/2017/04/03/silicon-valleys-quest-to-live-forever

29. David A. Sinclair and Matthew D. LaPlante, *Lifespan: Why We Age – and Why We Don't Have To*, New York: Atria Books 2019.

30. David Appell, "Methuselah Man," *MIT Technology Review*, April 9, 2004, https://www.technologyreview.com/2004/04/09/233020/methuselah-man/

31. Steve Horvath, "DNA Methylation Age of Human Tissues and Cell Types," *Genome Biology*, vol. 14, no. 10, 2013, R115, https://doi.org/10.1186/gb-2013-14-10-r115

32. Ingrid Torjesen, "Drug Development: The Journey of a Medicine from Lab to Shelf," *Pharmaceutical Journal*, May 12, 2015, https://pharmaceutical-journal.com/article/feature/drug-development-the-journey-of-a-medicine-from-lab-to-shelf

33. Oliver J. Wouters, et al., "Estimated Research and Development Investment Needed to Bring a New Medicine to Market, 2009–2018," *JAMA*, vol. 323, no. 9, 2020, 844–53, https://doi.org/10.1001/jama.2020.1166

34. Ameya S. Kulkarni, et al., "Benefits of Metformin in Attenuating the Hallmarks of Aging," *Cell Metabolism*, vol. 32, no. 1, 2020, 15–30, https://doi.org/10.1016/j.cmet.2020.04.001

35. Kiran Rabheru, et al., "How 'Old Age' Was Withdrawn as a Diagnosis from ICD-11," *Lancet, Healthy Longevity*, vol. 3, no. 7, 2022, e457–e459, https://doi.org/10.1016/S2666-7568(22)00102-7

36. Quoted in Sarah Sloat, "The Debate Over Whether Aging is a Disease Rages On," *MIT Technology Review*, October 19, 2022, https://www.technologyreview.com/2022/10/19/1061070/

is-old-age-a-disease/#:~:text=Sinclair%20is%20also%20
concerned%20about,in%20itself%2C"%20he%20says

37. Nir Barzilai, et al., "Metformin as a Tool to Target Aging," *Cell Metabolism*, vol. 23, no. 6, 2016, 1060–5, https://doi.org/10.1016/j.cmet.2016.05.011

38. Bruce A. Carnes and S. Jay Olshansky, *The Quest for Immortality: Science at the Frontiers of Aging*, New York: W. W. Norton, 2002, p. 13.

39. Jae-Hyun Yang, et al.,"Loss of Epigenetic Information as a Cause of Mammalian Aging," *Cell*, vol. 186, no. 2, 2023, 305–26.e27, https://doi.org/10.1016/j.cell.2022.12.027

40. Quoted in Marissa Taylor, "A 'Fountain of Youth' Pill? Sure, if You're a Mouse," KFF Health News, February 11, 2019, https://kffhealthnews.org/news/a-fountain-of-youth-pill-sure-if-youre-a-mouse/#:~:text="None%20of%20this%20is%20ready,Institute%20on%20Aging%20at%20NIH

41. Sam Shead, "Silicon Valley's Quest to Live Forever Could Benefit Humanity as a Whole—Here's Why," CNBC, September 21, 2021, https://www.cnbc.com/2021/09/21/silicon-valleys-quest-to-live-forever-could-benefit-the-rest-of-us.html

42. Nic Fleming, "Scientists Up Stakes in Bet on Whether Humans Will Live to 150," *Nature*, October 2016, www.nature.com, https://doi.org/10.1038/nature.2016.20818

Chapter 5: Seizing an Economic Dividend

1. "'I'm Going to Work Until I Die': The New Reality of Old Age in America," *Denver Post*, September 30, 2017, https://www.denverpost.com/2017/09/29/retirement-age-rising/

2. "Labor Force Statistics from the Current Population Survey," U.S. Bureau of Labor Statistics, https://www.bls.gov/cps/cpsaat03.htm [Accessed May 25, 2023]

3. "Pensions at a Glance 2021: OECD and G20 Indicators," OECD, 2021, https://www.oecd.org/publications/oecd-pensions-at-a-glance-19991363.htm

4. Gila Bronshtein, et al., "The Power of Working Longer," *Journal of Pension Economics and Finance*, vol. 18, no. 4, October 2019, 623–44, https://doi.org/10.1017/S1474747219000088

5. Samuel Beckett, *The Unnamable*, New York: Grove Press, 1978.

6. David E. Bloom, et al., "Valuing Productive Non-market Activities of Older Adults in Europe and the US," *De Economist*, vol. 168, no. 2, June 2020, 153–81, https://doi.org/10.1007/s10645-020-09362-1

7. "Working Later in Life Can Pay Off in More than Just Income," *Harvard Health*, June 1, 2018, https://www.health.harvard.edu/staying-healthy/working-later-in-life-can-pay-off-in-more-than-just-income

8. Lisa F. Berkman and Beth Truesdale (eds.), *Overtime: America's Aging Workforce and the Future of Working Longer*, New York: Oxford University Press, 2022.

9. Andrew Scott, "The Long Good Life," IMF Finance and Development, March 2020, https://www.imf.org/Publications/fandd/issues/2020/03 the-future-of-aging-guide-for-policymakers-scott

10. Marc Freedman, *How to Live Forever: The Enduring Power of Connecting the Generations*, New York: PublicAffairs, 2018.

11. Katalin Bodnár and Carolin Nerlich, *The Macroeconomic and Fiscal Impact of Population Ageing*, Frankfurt: European Central Bank, 2022.

12. Charles A. E. Goodhart and Manoj Pradhan, *The Great Demographic Reversal: Ageing Societies, Waning Inequality, and an Inflation Revival*, London: Palgrave Macmillan, 2020.

13. Adjusting for inflation refers to the fact these are real interest rates, which are defined as the actual interest rate less expected inflation. If interest rates are 5 percent and inflation is 1 percent then the real interest rate is 4 percent. The logic is that if you invest $100 in a year's time you will get back $105. If inflation is 1 percent what cost $100 a year ago now costs $101. So your real return is $4 or 4 percent. Compared to a year ago you can afford the item that used to cost $100 and still have $4 left over.

14. Andrew Bailey, "The Economic Landscape: Structural Change, Global R* and the Missing-Investment Puzzle," speech at the Official Monetary and Financial Institutions Forum, July 12, 2022 [Accessed May 25, 2023], https://www.bankofengland.co.uk/speech/2022/july/andrew-bailey-speech-at-omfif-the-economic-landscape

15. Richard Johnson, et al., "How Secure is Employment at Older Ages?," Urban Institute Research Report, 2018, https://www.urban.org/sites/default/files/publication/99570/how_secure_is_employment_at_older_ages_2.pdf

16. Lisa Berkman and Beth. C. Truesdale (eds.), *Overtime: America's Aging Workforce and the Future of Working Longer*, New York: Oxford University Press, 2022.

17. Andrew J. Scott and Lynda Gratton, *The New Long Life: A Framework for Flourishing in a Changing World*, London: Bloomsbury, 2021.

18. Dora L. Costa, *The Evolution of Retirement: An American Economic History, 1880–1990*, Chicago: University of Chicago Press, 1998.

19. Lynda Gratton and Andrew Scott, *The 100-Year Life: Living and Working in an Age of Longevity*, London: Bloomsbury Business, 2016.

20. David E. Bloom, et al., "Optimal Retirement with Increasing Longevity," *Scandinavian Journal of Economics*, vol. 116, no. 3, 2014, 838–58, http://www.jstor.org/stable/43673663 [Accessed May 25, 2023]

21. Michaël Boissonneault and Paola Rios, "Changes in Healthy and Unhealthy Working-Life Expectancy over the Period 2002–17: A Population-based Study in People Aged 51–65 Years in 14 OECD Countries," *Lancet, Healthy Longevity*, vol. 2, no. 10, 2021, e629–e638. https://doi.org/10.1016/S2666-7568(21)00202-6

22. "Chart Book: Social Security Disability Insurance," Center on Budget and Policy Priorities, https://www.cbpp.org/research/social-security/social-security-disability-insurance-0 [Accessed May 25, 2023]

23. It isn't quite that simple. Rising income increases the demand for leisure but also has an opposite effect (what economists call the substitution effect)—the more you get paid the more expensive it is to give up work. So rising income has two opposing effects on the demand for leisure. Only if the pure income effect is greater than the substitution effect does rising income mean more leisure overall.

24. This section draws heavily on Daron Acemoglu, Nicolaj Mühlbach, and Andrew J. Scott, "The Rise of Age-friendly Jobs," *Journal of the Economics of Ageing*, vol. 23, October 2022, 100416, https://doi.org/10.1016/j.jeoa.2022.100416

25. John Ameriks, et al., "Older Americans Would Work Longer if Jobs Were Flexible," *American Economic Journal: Macroeconomics*, vol. 12, no. 1, January 2020, 174–209, https://doi.org/10.1257/mac.20170403; Peter Hudomiet, et al., "The Effects of Job Characteristics on Retirement," RAND Corporation, 2019, https://doi.org/10.7249/WR1321; Nicole Maestas, et al., "The Value of Working Conditions in the United States and Implications for the Structure of Wages," National Bureau of Economic Research, October 2018, https://doi.org/10.3386/w25204

26. Nicole Maestas, et al., "The Value of Working Conditions in the United States and Implications for the Structure of Wages," National Bureau of Economic Research, October 2018, https://doi.org/10.3386/w25204

27. Daron Acemoglu, Nicolaj Mühlbach, and Andrew J. Scott, "The Rise of Age-friendly Jobs," *Journal of the Economics of Ageing*, vol. 23, October 2022, 100416, https://doi.org/10.1016/j.jeoa.2022.10146

28. Claudia Dale Goldin, *Career and Family: Women's Century-long Journey Toward Equity*, Princeton, N.J.: Princeton University Press, 2021.

29. Daron Acemoglu, Nicolaj Mühlbach, and Andrew J. Scott, "The Rise of Age-friendly Jobs," *Journal of the Economics of Ageing*, vol. 23, October 2022, 100416, https://doi.org/10.1016/j.jeoa.2022.10146

30. Daron Acemoglu and Pascual Restrepo, "Demographics and Automation," *Review of Economic Studies*, vol. 89, no. 1, January 2022, 1–44, https://doi.org/10.1093/restud/rdab031

31. Andrew J. Scott and Lynda Gratton, *The New Long Life: A Framework for Flourishing in a Changing World*, London: Bloomsbury, 2021.

32. Carlo Pizzinelli, et al., "Why Jobs are Plentiful While Workers are Scarce," International Monetary Fund, January 19, 2022, https://blogs.imf.org/2022/01/19/why-jobs-are-plentiful-while-workers-are-scarce/ [Accessed 25 May 2023]

33. S. G. Allen, "Demand for Older Workers: What Do We Know? What Do We Need to Learn?," *Journal of the Economics of Ageing*, vol. 24, February 2023, 100414, https://doi.org/10.1016/j.jeoa.2022.100414

34. Julian Birkinshaw, et al., "Older and Wiser? How Management Style Varies with Age," *MIT Sloan Management Review*, May 28, 2019, https://sloanreview.mit.edu/article/older-and-wiser-how-management-style-varies-with-age/

35. M. Packalen and J. Bhattacharya, "Age and the Trying Out of New Ideas," *Journal of Human Capital*, vol. 13, no. 2, Summer 2019, 341–73, https://doi.org/10.1086/703160

36. Charles I. Jones, "The Past and Future of Economic Growth: A Semi-endogenous Perspective," *Annual Review of Economics*, vol. 14, no. 1, August 2022, 125–52, https://doi.org/10.1146/annurev-economics-080521-012458

37. Benjamin F. Jones, "Age and Great Invention," *Review of Economics and Statistics*, vol. 92, no. 1, February 2010, 1–14, https://doi.org/10.1162/rest.2009.11724

38. Paul Millerd, "The Boomer Blockade: How One Generation Reshaped the Workforce and Left Everyone Behind," Boundless, https://think-boundless.com/the-boomer-blockade/#:~:text=So%20did%20the%20trend%20of%20younger%20company%20leaders%20continue%3F

39. Ben Lindbergh, "The Golden Age of the Aging Actor," *The Ringer*, June 27, 2022, https://www.theringer.com/movies/ 2022/6/27/23181232/old-actors-aging-tom-cruise-top-gun-maverick

Chapter 6: Money and Your Life

1. "Monthly Statistical Snapshot, April 2023," Social Security Administration, https://www.ssa.gov/policy/docs/quickfacts/stat_snapshot/ [Accessed May 25, 2023]
2. "Retirement and Investments" in "Economic Well-Being of U.S. Households in 2021," Board of Governors of the Federal Reserve System, https://www.federalreserve.gov/publications/2022-economic-well-being-of-us-households-in-2021-retirement.htm [Accessed May 25, 2023]
3. "Analysis of Future Pension Incomes," Department for Work and Pensions, March 3, 2023, https://www.gov.uk/government/statistics/analysis-of-future-pension-incomes/ [Accessed May 25, 2023]
4. "Solving the Global Pension Crisis," World Economic Forum, December 16, 2019, https://www.weforum.org/impact/solving-the-global-pension-crisis/
5. Luna Classic, https://www.coindesk.com/price/luna-classic/ [Accessed May 25, 2023]
6. Coinbase, https://www.coinbase.com/price/terra-luna#:~:text=The%20current%20price%20is%20%240.000084,circulating%20supply%20is%205%2C856%2C960%2C665%2C876.197%20LUNA [Accessed June 2, 2023]
7. From a 1987 class, as quoted in David L. Goodstein, "Richard P. Feynman, Teacher," *Physics Today*, vol. 42, no. 2, February 1989, pp. 70–5, p. 73, republished in Richard P. Feynman, *Six Easy Pieces*, New York: Basic Books, 1995.
8. "We'll Live to 100—How Can We Afford It?," World Economic Forum, May 26, 2017, https://www.weforum.org/whitepapers/we-ll-live-to-100-how-can-we-afford-it/
9. "Whole of Government Accounts, 2019–20," HM Treasury, https://www.gov.uk/government/publications/whole-of-government-accounts-2019-20 [Accessed May 25, 2023]

10. "CalPERS Announces Preliminary Net Investment Return of -6.1% for the 2021–22 Fiscal Year," CalPERS, https://www.calpers.ca.gov/page/newsroom/calpers-news/2022/calpers-preliminary-investment-return-2021-22 [Accessed May 25, 2023]

11. Anthony Randazzo, "Unfunded Liabilities for State Pension Plans in 2022," Equable, September 14, 2022, https://equable.org/unfunded-liabilities-for-state-pension-plans-2022/

12. "Social Protection for Older Women and Men: Pensions and Other Non-health Benefits," International Labour Organization, 2021, https://www.ilo.org/global/research/global-reports/world-social-security-report/2020-22/WCMS_821426/lang--en/index.htm [Accessed October 25, 2023]

13. "How to Fix the Gender Pension Gap," World Economic Forum, September 27, 2021, https://www.weforum.org/agenda/2021/09/how-to-fix-the-gender-pension-gap/

14. Travis Mitchell, "4. Retirement, Social Security and Long-term Care," Pew Research Center's Social & Demographic Trends Project, March 21, 2019, https://www.pewresearch.org/social-trends/2019/03/21/retirement-social-security-and-long-term-care/

15. "Occupational Outlook," U.S. Bureau of Labor Statistics, https://www.bls.gov/ooh/business-and-financial/personal-financial-advisors.htm [Accessed May 25, 2023]

16. "Global Pension Statistics," OECD, https://www.oecd.org/finance/private-pensions/globalpensionstatistics.htm [Accessed May 25, 2023]

17. Olivia S. Mitchell and Annamaria Lusardi, "Financial Literacy and Economic Outcomes: Evidence and Policy Implications," *Journal of Retirement*, vol. 3, no. 1, June 2015, 107–14, https://doi.org/10.3905/jor.2015.3.1.107

18. "Survey of Consumer Finances (SCF)," Board of Governors of the Federal Reserve System, https://www.federalreserve.gov/econres/scfindex.htm [Accessed May 25, 2023]

19. "Life Expectancy Comparison in 2021," SOA Research Institute, https://www.soa.org/globalassets/assets/files/resources/research-report/2019/life-expectancy.pdf [Accessed May 25, 2023]

20. "Financial Literacy, Longevity Literacy, and Retirement Readiness," TIAA Institute, January 12, 2023, https://www.tiaa.org/public/

institute/publication/2023/financial_literacy_longevity_literacy_
and_retirement_readiness

21. "Distribution of Household Wealth in the U.S. since 1989," Board of Governors of the Federal Reserve System, https://www.federalreserve. gov/releases/z1/dataviz/dfa/distribute/table/#quarter:131;series:Net%20 worth;demographic:generation;population:all;units:shares [Accessed May 25, 2023]

22. "Insurance Industry at a Glance," Insurance Information Institute, https://www.iii.org/publications/insurance-handbook/introduction/ insurance-industry-at-a-glance

23. "Actuaries Longevity Illustrator," http://www.longevityillustrator. org/ [Accessed May 25, 2023]

24. Atul Gawande, *Being Mortal: Illness, Medicine and What Matters in the End*, London: Profile, 2015.

25. Moshe Arye Milevsky, *King William's Tontine: Why the Retirement Annuity of the Future Should Resemble Its Past*, Cambridge: Cambridge University Press, 2015; Moshe Arye Milevsky, *Longevity Insurance for a Biological Age: Why Your Retirement Plan Shouldn't Be Based on the Number of Times You Circled the Sun*, privately published 2019; Kent McKeever, "A Short History of Tontines," *Fordham Corporate and Financial Law Review*, vol. 15, 2010, 491–521.

26. David R. Weir, "Tontines, Public Finance, and Revolution in France and England, 1688–1789," *Journal of Economic History*, vol. 49, no. 1, 1989, 95–124, http://www.jstor.org/stable/2121419

27. "US: Average Annual Costs of Long-term Care Services 2021," Statista, https://www.statista.com/statistics/310446/annual-median-rate-of-long-term-care-services-in-the-us/ [Accessed May 25, 2023]

28. "Global Longevity Economy Outlook," AARP, https://www.aarp. org/content/dam/aarp/research/surveys_statistics/econ/2022/ global-longevity-economy-report.doi.10.26419-2Fint.00052.001.pdf [Accessed May 25, 2023]

29. "Maximising the Longevity Dividend," International Longevity Centre UK, December 5, 2019, https://ilcuk.org.uk/maximising-the-longevity-dividend/

30. Chris Weller, "9 Signs Japan Has Become a 'Demographic Time Bomb,'" *Business Insider*, January 5, 2018, https://www. businessinsider.com/signs-japan-demographic-time-bomb-2017-3

Chapter 7: The Meaning of Life

1. "One in Seven Britons Expect to Live to Be 100 Years Old, Down by a Third Since 2019," IPSOS Mori, November 14, 2022, https://www.ipsos.com/en-uk/one-seven-britons-expect-live-be-100-years-old-down-third-2019

2. Jorge Luis Borges, "The Immortals," in *The Aleph and Other Stories* (trans. Andrew Hurley), London: Penguin Classics, 2000.

3. Simone de Beauvoir, *Old Age* (trans. Patrick O'Brian), London: André Deutsch, 1972, p. 541.

4. Becca R. Levy, et al., "Longevity Increased by Positive Self-perceptions of Aging," *Journal of Personality and Social Psychology*, vol. 83, no. 2, 2002, 261–70, https://doi.org/10.1037/0022-3514.83.2.261

5. Johann Peter Eckermann (ed.), *Conversations of Goethe*, New York: Da Capo Press, 1998.

6. Stephen Cave, *Immortality: The Quest to Live Forever and How it Drives Civilization*, New York: Crown, 2012.

7. Bertrand Russell, "How to Grow Old," in *Portraits from Memory and Other Essays*, Nottingham: Spokesman Books, 1995.

8. Philippe Ariès, *Centuries of Childhood: A Social History of Family Life*, London: Vintage, 1962.

9. Jeffrey Jensen Arnett, *Adolescence and Emerging Adulthood: A Cultural Approach*, 5th edition, Harlow, Essex: Pearson, 2013.

10. Patricia Cohen, *In Our Prime: The Invention of Middle Age*, New York: Scribner, 2012.

11. Barbara Lawrence, "The Myth of the Midlife Crisis," *Sloan Management Review*, vol. 21, no. 4, 1980, 35.

12. David Neumark, et al., "Is It Harder for Older Workers to Find Jobs? New and Improved Evidence from a Field Experiment," *Journal of Political Economy*, vol. 127, no. 2, April 2019, 922–70, https://doi.org/10.1086/701029

13. "Educational Attainment in the United States: 2021," US Census Bureau, https://www.census.gov/data/tables/2021/demo/educational-attainment/cps-detailed-tables.html [Accessed May 25, 2023]

14. "The Economic Impact of Age Discrimination," AARP, 2020, https://www.aarp.org/content/dam/aarp/research/surveys_statistics/econ/2020/impact-of-age-discrimination.doi.10.26419-2Fint.00042.003.pdf

15. "The Longevity Economy Outlook," AARP, 2019, https://www.aarp.org/content/dam/aarp/research/surveys_statistics/econ/2019/longevity-economy-outlook.doi.10.26419-2Fint.00042.001.pdf

16. Uwe Sunde, "Age, Longevity, and Preferences," *Journal of the Economics of Ageing*, vol. 24, February 2023, 100427, https://doi.org/10.1016/j.jeoa.2022.100427

17. Tom R. Tyler and Regina A. Schuller, "Aging and Attitude Change," *Journal of Personality and Social Psychology*, vol. 61, no. 5, 1991, 689–97, https://doi.org/10.1037/0022-3514.61.5.689

18. Osea Giuntella, et al., "The Midlife Crisis," *Economica*, vol. 90, no. 357, 2023, 65–110, https://doi.org/10.1111/ecca.12452

19. Laura L. Carstensen, et al., "Age Advantages in Emotional Experience Persist Even Under Threat from the COVID-19 Pandemic," *Psychological Science*, vol. 31, no. 11, November 2020, 1374–85, https://doi.org/10.1177/0956797620967261

20. Pat Thane (ed.), *The Long History of Old Age*, vol. 1, London: Thames & Hudson, 2005.

21. Corinna E. Löckenhoff, et al., "Perceptions of Aging Across 26 Cultures and Their Culture-level Associates," *Psychology and Aging*, vol. 24, no. 4, 2009, 941–54, https://doi.org/10.1037/a0016901

22. John W. Rowe and Robert L. Kahn, "Human Aging: Usual and Successful," *Science*, vol. 237, no. 4811, July 1987, 143–9, https://doi.org/10.1126/science.3299702

23. Human Mortality Database, https://www.mortality.org/ [Accessed May 25, 2023]

24. Warren C. Sanderson and Sergei Scherbov, *Prospective Longevity: A New Vision of Population Aging*, Cambridge, M.A.: Harvard University Press, 2019.

25. Steven Pinker, *The Language Instinct*, New York: Harper Perennial, 1995.

26. John Elster, *Reason and Rationality*, Princeton, N.J.: Princeton University Press, 2009.

27. David Edmonds, *Parfit: A Philosopher and His Mission to Save Morality*, Princeton, N.J.: Princeton University Press, 2023.

28. David Edmonds, "Reason and Romance: The World's Most Cerebral Marriage," *Prospect*, July 17, 2014, https://

www.prospectmagazine.co.uk/ideas/philosophy/46516/
reason-and-romance-the-worlds-most-cerebral-marriage

29. Derek Parfit, *Reasons and Persons*, Oxford: Oxford University Press, 1986, p. 281.

Chapter 8: The Generational Challenge

1. Karl Mannheim, "The Problem of Generations," 1922, https://marcuse.faculty.history.ucsb.edu/classes/201/articles/27MannheimGenerations.pdf
2. Corinna E. Löckenhoff, et al., "Perceptions of Aging Across 26 Cultures and Their Culture-level Associates," *Psychology and Aging*, vol. 24, no. 4, 2009, 941–54, https://doi.org/10.1037/a0016901
3. Life Expectancy Calculator, Office for National Statistics, https://www.ons.gov.uk/peoplepopulationandcommunity/healthandsocialcare/healthandlifeexpectancies/articles/lifeexpectancycalculator/2019-06-07 [Accessed May 26, 2023]
4. "Age and Voting Behaviour at the 2019 General Election," British Election Study, January 27, 2021, https://www.britishelectionstudy.com/bes-findings/age-and-voting-behaviour-at-the-2019-general-election/#.Y_3ZXC-l2Xo; Charles Franklin, "Age and Voter Turnout," Medium, February 25, 2018, https://medium.com/@PollsAndVotes/age-and-voter-turnout-52962b0884ef
5. "As Time Goes By: Shifting Incomes and Inequality Between and Within Generations," Resolution Foundation, February 13, 2017, https://www.resolutionfoundation.org/publications/as-time-goes-by-shifting-incomes-and-inequality-between-and-within-generations/
6. Laurence J. Kotlikoff and Scott Burns, *The Coming Generational Storm: What You Need to Know about America's Economic Future*, Cambridge, M.A.: MIT Press, 2005; Niall Ferguson and Eyck Freymann, "The Coming Generation War," *Atlantic*, May 6, 2019, https://www.theatlantic.com/ideas/archive/2019/05/coming-generation-war/588670/
7. Taylor Lorenz, "'OK Boomer' Marks the End of Friendly Generational Relations," *New York Times*, October 29, 2019, https://www.nytimes.com/2019/10/29/style/ok-boomer.html

8. George Orwell, "Review of *A Coat of Many Colours: Occasional Essays* by Herbert Read," *Poetry Quarterly*, Winter 1945.

9. Motoko Rich and Hikari Hida, "A Yale Professor Suggested Mass Suicide for Old People in Japan. What Did He Mean?," *New York Times*, February 12, 2023, https://www.nytimes.com/2023/02/12/world/asia/japan-elderly-mass-suicide.html

10. Jonathan Old and Andrew Scott, "Healthy Ageing Trends in England Between 2002 to 2018: Improving but Slowing and Unequal," *Journal of the Economics of Ageing*, vol. 26, no. 1, 2023, https://doi.org/10.1016/j.jeoa.2023.100470

11. "Prevalence of Overweight, Obesity, and Severe Obesity Among Adults Aged 20 and Over: United States, 1960–1962 Through 2017–2018," National Center for Health Statistics, https://www.cdc.gov/nchs/data/hestat/obesity-adult-17-18/overweight-obesity-adults-H.pdf [Accessed May 25, 2023]

12. "Prevalence of Overweight, Obesity, and Severe Obesity Among Children and Adolescents Aged 2–19 Years: United States, 1963–1965 Through 2017–2018," National Center for Health Statistics, https://www.cdc.gov/nchs/data/hestat/obesity-child-17-18/overweight-obesity-child-H.pdf [Accessed 25 May 2023]

13. Jon Haidt, "The Teen Mental Illness Epidemic Began Around 2012," After Babel Substack, February 8, 2023, https://jonathanhaidt.substack.com/p/the-teen-mental-illness-epidemic

14. Bridget F. Grant, et al., "Prevalence of 12-Month Alcohol Use, High-Risk Drinking, and DSM-IV Alcohol Use Disorder in the United States, 2001–2002 to 2012–2013," *JAMA Psychiatry*, vol. 74, no. 9, September 2017, 911–23, https://doi.org/10.1001/jamapsychiatry.2017.2161

15. Carol Graham, "Understanding the Role of Despair in America's Opioid Crisis," Brookings, October 15, 2019, https://www.brookings.edu/policy2020/votervital/how-can-policy-address-the-opioid-crisis-and-despair-in-america

16. Lindsay Judge and Jack Leslie, "Stakes and Ladders: The Costs and Benefits of Buying a First Home Over the Generations," Resolution Foundation, June 26, 2021, https://www.resolutionfoundation.org/publications/stakes-and-ladders/

17. Adam Corlett and Felicia Odamtten, "Hope to Buy: The Decline of Youth Home Ownership," Resolution Foundation, December 2, 2021, https://www.resolutionfoundation.org/publications/hope-to-buy/

18. Taylor Orth, "More Than Half of Americans Support a Maximum Age Limit for Elected Officials," YouGov, January 19, 2022, https://today.yougov.com/topics/politics/articles-reports/2022/01/19/elected-officials-maximum-age-limit-poll

19. Quoted in Mini Racker, "Nikki Haley Enters 2024 Race with Speech Implying Trump and Biden Are Too Old to Run," *Time*, February 15, 2023, https://time.com/6255878/nikki-haley-2024-announcement/

20. Bobby Duffy, *Generations: Does When You're Born Shape Who You Are?*, London: Atlantic 2021.

21. Ibid.

22. Alec Tyson, Brian Kenneddy, and Cary Funk, "Gen Z, Millennials Stand Out for Climate Change Activism, Social Media Engagement with Issue," Pew Research Center, May 26, 2021, https://www.pewresearch.org/science/2021/05/26/gen-z-millennials-stand-out-for-climate-change-activism-social-media-engagement-with-issue/

23. James Sefton, et al., "Wealth Booms and Debt Burdens," Resolution Foundation, November 14, 2022, https://www.resolutionfoundation.org/events/wealth-booms-and-debt-burdens/

24. Chris Giles, "OK Boomer, You're More Generous than We Thought," *Financial Times*, February 2, 2023, https://www.ft.com/content/5c482689-76a7-4a62-b042-acd4b4aaecf4

25. William MacAskill, "Age-Weighted Voting," Medium, July 12, 2019, https://medium.com/@william.macaskill/age-weighted-voting-8651b2a353cc

26. Rune J. Sørensen, "Does Aging Affect Preferences for Welfare Spending? A Study of People's Spending Preferences in 22 Countries, 1985–2006," *European Journal of Political Economy*, vol. 29, March 2013, 259–71, https://doi.org/10.1016/j.ejpoleco.2012.09.004

27. Congressional Budget Office, "The Budget and Economic Outlook 2022 to 2032," Congressional Budget Office, May 2022, https://www.cbo.gov/publication/57950; and "Historical Tables of the United States Government," Fiscal Year 2023, Office of Management and Budget, March 2022, https://www.whitehouse.gov/omb/budget/historical-tables/

28. Alan J. Auerbach, et al., "Generational Accounting: A Meaningful Way to Evaluate Fiscal Policy," *Journal of Economic Perspectives*, vol. 8, no. 1, 1994, 73–94, http://www.jstor.org/stable/2138152

Chapter 9: Pitfalls and Progress

1. All these statistics are from L. I. Dublin, A. J. Lotka, and M. Spiegelman, *Length of Life*, revised edition (New York: Ronald Press Company, 1949), pp. xxv and 379; *Journal of the Institute of Actuaries*, vol. 76, no. 1, June 1950, 76–9, https://doi.org/10.1017/S0020268100013299

2. "How Long a New Drug Takes to Go through Clinical Trials," Cancer Research UK, October 21, 2014, https://www.cancerresearchuk.org/about-cancer/find-a-clinical-trial/how-clinical-trials-are-planned-and-organised/how-long-it-takes-for-a-new-drug-to-go-through-clinical-trials

3. Gary Becker, et al., "The Value of Life Near its End and Terminal Care," National Bureau of Economic Research, August 2007, https://doi.org/10.3386/w13333

4. Eric Budish, et al., "Do Firms Underinvest in Long-term Research? Evidence from Cancer Clinical Trials," *American Economic Review*, vol. 105, no. 7, July 2015, 2044–85, https://doi.org/10.1257/aer.20131176; Johan Moen, a London Business School PhD student of mine, is also looking at this effect in his paper "No Time to Die: The Patent-Induced Bias Towards Acute Conditions in Pharmaceutical R&D."

5. Robert W. Fogel, "Catching Up with the Economy," *American Economic Review*, vol. 89, no. 1, March 1999, 1–21, https://doi.org/10.1257/aer.89.1.1

6. Tad Friend, "Silicon Valley's Quest to Live Forever," *New Yorker*, March 27, 2017, https://www.newyorker.com/magazine/2017/04/03/silicon-valleys-quest-to-live-forever

7. Jessica Hamzelou, "Inside the Billion-Dollar Meeting for the Mega-Rich Who Want to Live Forever," *MIT Technology Review*, November 16, 2022, https://www.technologyreview.com/2022/11/16/1063300/billion-dollar-mega-rich-live-forever/

8. Ashlee Vance, "How to Be 18 Years Old Again for Only $2 Million a Year," Bloomberg, January 25, 2023, https://www.bloomberg.com/news/features/2023-01-25/anti-aging-techniques-taken-to-extreme-by-bryan-johnson

9. Megan Molteni, "As Billionaires Race to Fund Anti-Aging Projects, a Much-Discussed Trial Goes Overlooked," STAT, August 9, 2022, https://www.statnews.com/2022/08/09/anti-aging-projects-funding-much-discussed-trial-overlooked/

10. "How Much Did the Apollo Program Cost?," Planetary Society, https://www.planetary.org/space-policy/cost-of-apollo

11. Hagai Levine, et al., "Temporal Trends in Sperm Count: A Systematic Review and Meta-regression Analysis of Samples Collected Globally in the 20th and 21st Centuries," *Human Reproduction Update*, vol. 29, no. 2, March 2023, 157–76, https://doi.org/10.1093/humupd/dmac035

12. David Miles, "Macroeconomic Impacts of Changes in Life Expectancy and Fertility," *Journal of the Economics of Ageing*, vol. 24, February 2023, 100425, https://doi.org/10.1016/j.jeoa.2022.100425

13. Michele Boldrin, et al., "Fertility and Social Security," *Journal of Demographic Economics*, vol. 81, no. 3, 2015, 261–99, https://www.jstor.org/stable/26417160

14. Seth Wynes and Kimberly A. Nicholas, "The Climate Mitigation Gap: Education and Government Recommendations Miss the Most Effective Individual Actions," *Environmental Research Letters*, vol. 12, no. 7, July 2017, 074024, https://doi.org/10.1088/1748-9326/aa7541

15. Joshua R. Goldstein and Wilhelm Schlag, "Longer Life and Population Growth," *Population and Development Review*, vol. 25, no. 4, 1999, 741–7, https://www.jstor.org/stable/172484

Epilogue: The Power of Love

1. Robert J. Waldinger and Marc S. Schulz, *The Good Life: Lessons from the World's Longest Scientific Study of Happiness*, New York: Simon & Schuster, 2023.

2. Chi Yan Leung, et al., "Association of Marital Status with Total and Cause-Specific Mortality in Asia," *JAMA Network Open*, vol. 5, no. 5, May 2022, e2214181, https://doi.org/10.1001/jamanetworkopen.2022.14181

3. J. Robin Moon, et al., "Short- and Long-term Associations Between Widowhood and Mortality in the United States: Longitudinal Analyses," *Journal of Public Health*, vol. 36, no. 3, 2014, 382–9, https://doi.org/10.1093/pubmed/fdt101

Index

money, managing (*cont.*)
  personal finances, 165–75
  retirement savings, 156–9
  silver economy, 185–9
Montaigne, Michel de, 45, 198
moonshot thinking, 265
Moore, G. E., 214, 272
mortality
  Dorian Gray scenario, 66–7
  intimations of, 40–5
  Peter Pan scenario, 68–71
  Struldbrugg scenario, 64–6
mortality rates, 23–6
motor neurone disease (ALS), 62
Mozart, Anna Maria, 69
Muller, Todd, 244–5
Musk, Elon, 44, 51–2, 70

NAD (nicotinamide adenine
  dinucleotide), 55
Narita, Yusuke, 237–8
National Health Service (NHS),
  63, 90–1, 95
National Institute for Health and
  Care Excellence (NICE), 74–5
National University of Singapore,
  116
naturalistic fallacy, 214
Nature, 104
New York Times, 51
New Yorker, 122
New Zealand, 16
Newman, Saul Justin, 56
NMN (nicotinamide
  mononucleotide), 55
Nobel Prize, 45, 105, 115, 140,
  152, 159, 195, 257, 259, 262
noncommunicable diseases, 26–31
Norway, 16

Ó hÉigeartaigh, Seán, 118
obesity, 30–1, 57–8, 94–5
Odyssey (Homer), 195
Oeppen, Jim, 16
"OK boomer" (phrase), 235
100-Year Life, The (Gratton and
  Scott), 135, 173, 231
Old (film), 50–1
old age
  contrasting views of, 212
  dying of, 44–5
  otherness of, 204
  redefining, 202, 214–16
  term, 111–12
old-age dependency ratio (OADR),
  31–3, 234
older workers, 151–3
Olshansky, Jay, 60–1, 114, 119
"On Old Age" (Cicero), 11, 212
OpenAI, 224
optimism, generational challenge,
  243–5
  Bank of Mum and Dad
    (BOMAD), 245–6
  politics, 246–51
Orwell, George, 236
Osler, Sir William, 134
Our Future Health, 98
overpopulation, 269–73
overpromising, 113–16

paradox of mortality, 198
Parfit, Derek, 217–21, 271
pensions, crisis involving, 159–65
period life expectancy, 19
person-focused approach, health
  systems, 99–100
personal finances, 167–8
  auto-enrollment, 165–6

retirement (*cont.*)
  trade-offs and, 169–72
risk, becoming more open to, 206–7
risks, 76, 92, 95, 97–8, 157–9, 166, 184, 204, 240, 273
"Road Not Taken, The" (Frost), 279–80
roadblocks, evergreen society, 254–5
  countering, 274–5
  fertility decline, 266–9
  incentives, 259–62
  luxury goods, 262–5
  overpopulation, 269–73
  revising expectations, 255–7
  urgency, 257–9
robo advisors, 168
rogai, term, 213
Ronaldo, Cristiano, 153
Roosevelt, Theodore, 224
Roth, Philip, 96
Rubber Soul, 9
Russell, Bertrand, 195, 199, 222

Sanderson, Warren, 215
Sassoon, Siegfried, 95–6
savings, stockpiling, 180
Scherbov, Sergei, 215
second longevity revolution, 13, 43, 79, 214, 257, 272
  health systems in, 89–120
  implications of, 13–14
Second World War, 18–19, 265
SECURE 2.0 Act, 166
Sefton, James, 245–6
Seligman, Martin, 53–4
senility, word, 111
sentimentalist, defining, 73–4

Shaw, Geroge Bernard, 140
shortgevity, 117, 255–6
Shyamalan, "M. Night," 50–1
Sierra, Felipe, 117
Silent Generation, 228
silver economy, 185–9
Silver Fleece Award for Anti-Aging Quackery, 114–15
silver tsunami, 247
Simpsons, The, 109
Sinclair, David, 77, 107, 112
Sinclair, Upton, 259–60
smoking, 57, 93–4
social isolation, 94
Social Security Amendment Act, 163
Social Security, US, 134, 156, 160–2
Society of Actuaries, 170–1, 179
socioemotional selectivity theory (SST), 208–10
Sorkin, Andrew Ross, 51
South Africa, 34–5
South Korea, total fertility rate in, 17
spinal muscular atrophy (SMA), 74–5, 264
Spitalfields Mathematical Society, 24
Stalin, Josef, 224
state pensions, 134–5
Steinach, Eugen, 114–15
Strong, Barrett, 156
Struldbrugg scenario, aging, 64–6, 77–8, 123, 132, 194, 257
  pensions crisis and, 165
  retirement and, 136–8
successful aging, 214
Sun Also Rises, The (Hemingway), 49
Sunak, Rishi, 250
supers, 166
survival of the fittest, 26
sustainability, 3–4

Credit: Mat Smith Photography

Andrew J. Scott is a professor of economics at London Business School, having previously taught at Oxford and Harvard University. He is cofounder of the Longevity Forum, a consulting scholar at the Stanford Center on Longevity, and coauthor of the global bestseller *The 100-Year Life*. He lives in London.